JUST HEALTH

JUST HEALTH

TREATING STRUCTURAL RACISM TO HEAL AMERICA

DAYNA BOWEN MATTHEW

NEW YORK UNIVERSITY PRESS

New York

To my parents, Marion Griffin and Vincent Edward Bowen, Jr.

Their love and extraordinary sacrifices made my life possible.

NEW YORK UNIVERSITY PRESS
New York
www.nyupress.org

© 2022 by New York University
Paperback edition published 2024
All rights reserved

References to internet websites (URLs) were accurate at the time of writing. Neither the author nor New York University Press is responsible for URLs that may have expired or changed since the manuscript was prepared.

Library of Congress Cataloging-in-Publication Data
Names: Matthew, Dayna Bowen, author.
Title: Just health : treating structural racism to heal America / Dayna Bowen Matthew.
Description: New York : New York University Press, [2022] | Includes bibliographical references and index.
Identifiers: LCCN 2021013294 | ISBN 9781479802661 (hardback) | ISBN 9781479831005 (paperback) | ISBN 9781479802692 (ebook) | ISBN 9781479802685 (ebook other)
Subjects: LCSH: Minorities—Medical care—United States. | Discrimination in medical care—United States. | Social medicine. | African Americans—Health and hygiene—Social aspects.
Classification: LCC RA563.M56 M28 2022 | DDC 362.1089—dc23
LC record available at https://lccn.loc.gov/2021013294

New York University Press books are printed on acid-free paper, and their binding materials are chosen for strength and durability. We strive to use environmentally responsible suppliers and materials to the greatest extent possible in publishing our books.

Manufactured in the United States of America

10 9 8 7 6 5 4 3 2

Also available as an ebook

CONTENTS

INTRODUCTION

> Well, if one really wishes to know how justice is administered
> in a country, one does not question the policemen, the law-
> yers, the judges, or the protected members of the middle class.
> One goes to the unprotected—those, precisely, who need the
> law's protection the most—and listens to their testimony.
> —James Baldwin, *No Name in the Street* (1972)

My father died at age forty-nine. He was an African American man, and therefore, his untimely death was not nearly as extraordinary as he was. I begin this book with his story to illustrate how structural inequality and, more specifically, structural racism work annually to kill tens of thousands of Black, Indigenous, and Latino people in our country well before their time. Vincent Edward Bowen Jr. was my intelligent, hard-working, and charming "Daddy." I had the benefit of his love, wisdom, protection, and counsel only for the first two decades of my life. He was an extrovert who lit up every room. He was my most trusted mentor. Yet I lost him before I completed my sophomore year of college, before I married, before I gave birth to his three grandchildren, and before I started my career. Most importantly for the purpose of this book, I lost my father before he could amass any property or wealth for me to inherit from his years of herculean labor born of his determination to achieve the American Dream.

His premature death cut short any chance for his family to realize the return on the considerable investments he made in going to college at night to become an entrepreneur and a residential real estate appraiser, or the years he toiled as a New York City subway motorman to finance his family's climb out of poverty. Although, thankfully, he did leave my mother enough to live on until her death—also premature—at age sixty-one, my family lost Vincent before my brother and I could avoid being counted among the ranks of families headed by a Black, single, low-wage-earning woman. To be absolutely clear: the facts of my family's story defy the myth that millions of other Black Americans share this all-too-familiar position because of a family breakdown or failure of personal responsibility.

My parents met in church and married young, before my brother and I were born. Both my parents also had two parents at home. Each of these individuals held multiple jobs so that they could pay taxes, pay bills, and provide the best housing that was available for their families in segregated neighborhoods from Brunswick, Georgia, to the South Bronx in New York City, where I grew up. Yet all except one of my parents and grandparents were dead before I turned thirty. Some might point to my father's overweight frame or his high blood pressure as the "comorbidities" that shortened his life. These factors certainly were not irrelevant. But the resounding message of this book is that structural inequality, not individual deficits, was the primary factor that contributed to my father's death. More precisely, I aim to show that structural racism, which is the structural inequality that results from racial discrimination, was the primary cause of my father's early demise. But my father wasn't the only casualty of structural racism; the same racism caused the early deaths of most of my father's relatives and all my father's friends that I knew growing up. Some researchers estimate that up to 25 percent of deaths annually are directly attributable to income inequality. The best estimate is that structural inequality accounts for more American deaths each year than does diabetes or the flu; in 2000, an estimated 119,000 Americans lives were lost because of income inequality.[1]

Afflictions of Structural Inequality: Poverty, Prejudice, and Poor Health

In the pages that follow, I will disabuse the fallacious notion that my father's genetics—indeed that any individual's *biological* comorbidities—are the most important contributors to the disproportionately high morbidity and mortality that poor and minority populations suffer in America. I will recount the evidence showing that instead, the systemically inequitable *social* comorbidities that our nation tolerates are the primary drivers of these disparities. Epidemiologists define *comorbidity* as the different conditions present that adversely affect a population's health outcomes.[2] In this book, I explain the most dangerous and deadly comorbidity of all—structural inequality—and how it damages the lives of all Americans. By *structural inequality,* I mean the deliberately and unintentionally constructed disruptions that a society uses to systematically displace humans from standing on equal footing in life. This inequality is structural because it operates through enduring societal institutions to relegate some groups to an inferior status and elevate other groups to superiority solely because of their group membership and without regard to their individuality or shared humanity.

Structural inequality organizes preferential treatment on such a large scale and powerful scope that it operates as a virtually inexorable guarantee of predictably stratified social outcomes that reflect predetermined hierarchies, often for generations. In America, structural inequality sorts people by numerous metrics; this book is concerned with structural inequality based on socioeconomic status and race. Not only did this structural inequality contribute to my father's poor health and kill him before his time, but it is also killing the American Dream for us all. Structural inequality works in at least two ways. Let's examine them.

First, it perpetuates prejudice. It separates and isolates Americans from one another, physically grouping us by caste, concentrating enmity and poverty among us. In other words, place matters. The geographic location where, and near where, people reside significantly influences how they think and feel about themselves and whom they perceive as different from themselves. For example, living in a place that provides exposure to people from different economic groups in a way that could lead to positive, interpersonal contacts is likely to increase tolerance and empathy among groups while reducing negative assumptions about others. Social psychologists call this *group contact theory*, which posits that "bringing members of opposing groups together under conditions involving cooperation, equal status, and personal acquaintance can improve attitudes . . . and facilitate intergroup harmony."[3] Intergroup contact can improve relationships across differences in socioeconomic status, gender, sexuality, religion, and even differences in race and national origin. Since 1947, an overwhelming number of social science studies have shown that increased intergroup interaction reduces racial prejudice among individuals and among groups.[4]

The strongest evidence that racial integration reduces racial prejudice comes from data related to housing. Researchers have repeatedly found that when Black and White neighbors live near one another in integrated public housing, they hold one another in higher esteem and more often support policies that help others than when they live in racially isolated settings.[5] At the same time, when residential settings are economically or racially isolated, people have no experiences to contradict their worst assumptions and narratives about people they do not know or understand. Not only do the social conditions in each isolated community produce vastly different life experiences, but segregation also complicates the politics of solving social problems. Instead of a country that sees its identity as one nation, in which all are "created equal . . . endowed by the Creator with certain unalienable rights," we built a country in which notions of individualism and even hierarchical attitudes regarding people's relative worth emerge and often prevail.

These views of differences have real life-and-death consequences. One group of researchers identified "Eight Americas" to estimate how our comparative differences are revealed in life-expectancy disparities.[6] The researchers surveyed more than two thousand residential counties in the United States and divided them into eight distinctive subgroups: (1) Asian American, (2) below-median-income White people living in the "Northland," (3) middle America, (4) poor White people living in Appalachia and the Mississippi Valley, (5) Indigenous people living on reservations in the West, (6) Black "middle America," (7) poor

Black people living in the rural South, and (8) Black people living in high-risk urban environments. The study then examined differences in health and the risk of violence among the various communities.

The health consequences of these geographic and demographic differences were "enormous." For example, the gap that separated the life expectancy of Black men, like my father, who lived in "America 8," from Asian American women who live in "America 1" was more than 20 years. Within genders, the differences remained; White and Asian American men lived up to 15.4 years longer than did men like my father. And the study even revealed wide differences within White populations. Low-income White people in the South—"America 4," according to the researchers—had average income levels similar to those of "America 2," northern rural White people, but lived only as long as people in Mexico and Panama did. "In other words," the researchers said, "millions of Americans, distinctly identified by their socio-demographic characteristics and place of residence, have life expectancies that are similar to some low-income developing countries." When my father died in 1979, though he was born and had lived his entire life in New York City, his life expectancy matched men in the developing nations of Djibouti, Zambia, Mauritania, and the Republic of Congo. Structural income inequality is foundational to the deadly differences among the Eight Americas that cut his life short.

Second, structural economic inequality perpetuates poverty. It constrains a large segment of the population to low-wage work while rewarding a relatively small segment of the population with extremely high incomes. A recent report showed that 44 percent of Americans earn wages of only $10.22 per hour. That means 53 million people in this country work jobs that do not pay enough for them to escape poverty. At the same time, the wealthiest Americans have seen their incomes increase from 33 percent of total earnings in 1978 to half of all income earned in 2014.

Several problems result from this huge disparity. My father's life illustrates the human cost these differences impose. Daddy worked three or four jobs for as long as I could remember. He shouldered this load because, together, his multiple jobs never combined to pay him a living wage. The last time I helped him complete my parents' 1040 income tax form—an exercise he used to teach me money management—I recall that our family of four had an annual income of $29,000, including my mother's salary as a teacher's aide in a public school. This would have been before I left for college in 1977; my best guess is that by his death, my father made approximately $36,000 per year. To make this sum, my father drove a subway train for New York City's Metropolitan Transit Authority by night.[7] "Motorman Bowen" drove the Number 4 to Wood-lawn during the graveyard shift until 7:00 a.m. He then rushed home to change and head out to work as a real estate appraiser at the Bowery Savings Bank each weekday morning. One of my favorite memories was watching my dad stride proudly through our segregated South Bronx neighborhood—the only man I can remember who wore a suit to work. He would catch the same subway line he had driven the night before, but he was now a passenger on the way to his day job in Grand Central Station each morning by 9:00 a.m.

For my father, structural inequality meant that he, like 44 percent of Americans who work low-wage jobs today, could not earn enough to keep his family out of poverty without working multiple jobs, to the detriment of his physical and mental health.[8] While he worked sixteen of every twenty-four hours daily to feed, clothe, and house his family of four, he seldom slept more than four hours each night. For him, a lack of sleep and exercise was not an individual health choice he made; it was made for him by his economic circumstances. The same was true for my father's parents—Vincent Sr. and Rachel, who never earned above-poverty wages—and it was also true for my great-grandparents, who worked as sharecroppers or tobacco farmhands during Reconstruction. My family's work history illustrates that, despite the well-known relationship between socioeconomic status, unhealthy behaviors, and even poor medical history, health disparities and premature death are not driven primarily by individual choice or biology. Increased tobacco use, physical inactivity, and poor nutrition concentrated among similarly situated groups of people are often thought of as classically poor choices made by poor people. Instead, they are better explained as indicators of structural problems, not as personal defects. Indeed, these problems are exacerbated dramatically by the persistently inequitable lack of financial and physical resources that minority families experience in America for generations, and the stress that accompanies their living in a disadvantaged social position.[9] Much more to the point, low wages were a primary cause of my father's poor health and early death. The same disadvantages apply to White miners in Appalachia, Indigenous laborers in western states, and Latino farmworkers in California.[10] Income inequality is bad for your health, no matter the color of your skin or how your ancestors came to live in this country.[11]

The inequality separating the top 1 percent of American earners from the 40 million Americans living in poverty is not the only cause of these adverse health outcomes. A much larger group creates a much larger divide that harms health at all income levels. Structural income inequality exists because the top 20 percent—the upper middle class of Americans—has separated from the rest of American earners at warp speed. Political theorist Richard Reeves calls our society a "ruthlessly efficient class reproductive machine."[12] The machine is ruthless for many reasons, but this book will focus on the disproportionate sickness and premature death that it confers on low-income populations throughout America. This is the third result of structural inequality: it ensures widely disparate and generally inferior health outcomes.

Generally, inequitable societies are the least healthy in the world. The United States, however, takes the direct correlation between greater inequality, worse health, and early death to new and extreme levels. Hundreds of research articles confirm that income inequality in America, when compared with other nations, causes more of our babies to die early, more adults to suffer homicides, a higher prevalence of HIV, lower life expectancy, and a greater incidence of obesity and mental illness.[13] These terrible outcomes are not limited to the underclass, but all Americans are less healthy because of economic inequality. Some of the most distressing evidence points to how severely the detrimental effects of inequality in the United States outpace those impacts in other developed countries.

Researchers Kate Pickett and Richard Wilkinson constructed an index that combines data on life expectancy, mental illness, obesity, infant mortality, teen pregnancy, homicides, educational attainment, incarceration rates, and social mobility. They found that large income differences between the rich and poor damage a nation's health (figure 1.1).

In this graph, income inequality is measured along the horizontal axis as the difference between income among the top and the bottom 20 percent of the population in each country. The combined index of health and social outcomes, shown on the vertical axis, is closely related to income inequality. The upwardly sloping line shows that as income inequality increases, health and other population outcomes worsen. As the figure shows, Japan, located on the lowest left-hand corner, has the smallest gap between what wealthy and poor people earn. Consequently, the people in that nation enjoy healthier and safer living than do those in all other countries shown. In contrast, the United States, located in the top, rightmost corner of the graph, is an outlier at the other end of the spectrum. Here, the gap between rich and poor Americans is wider than in all other nations pictured. As a consequence, our society overall is the least healthy and most violent of all our industrialized peers. These data show, remarkably, that the declining quality of health and social outcomes has less to do with absolute wealth or poverty in a society than with the inequality which has a greater bearing on these outcomes. Deteriorating outcomes occur across all income levels of society. Researchers have found that even middle-income households that annually earn between $50,000 and $75,000 suffer greater risk of death and poor health than do wealthier households when inequality prevails.[14]

The same relationship seen here between income inequality and poor health outcomes among different countries is also found among different regions in the United States. American states and cities with great disparities in income have greater numbers of excess deaths than do

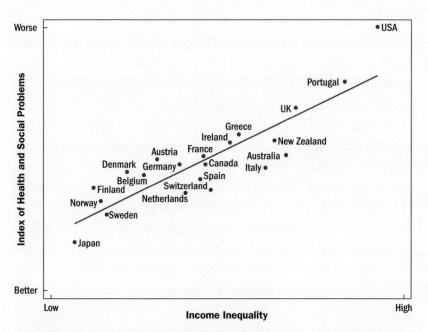

FIGURE I.1: Index of Health and Social Problems Related to Income Inequality in Wealthy Nations. Source: Adapted from Kate Pickett and Richard Wilkinson, "Income Inequality and Health: A Causal Review," *Social Science & Medicine* 12 (2015): 316–326.

states and cities with less income inequality. Arguably, this relationship explains why US health outcomes lag so far behind those of all other rich nations. Not all outcomes included in the index are similarly associated with income inequality, however. Prostate and breast cancer appear less sensitive to inequality, while heart disease and diabetes are more prevalent in societies more economically inequitable.

These data are consistent with my father's narrative. His early death was a complication of heart disease and a family history of diabetes. The main point of figure I.1, however, is to show that my father's death was not just a function of his *individual* health history. Instead, his death was part of the structural relationship between adverse population health outcomes in his demographic community and nationwide income inequality, which affects all Americans.

Besides stratifying society by class, income, and health, the fourth affliction that accompanies structural inequality is the unfair distribution of the resources all humans need to live. Put another way, structural inequality blocks equal access to the social determinants of health. Since the health of populations is determined primarily by social resources such as clean, decent, safe housing; adequate education; nutritious food; and access to recreational spaces, structural inequality consigns people who lack these social determinants of health to disproportionate illness and early death. Here is where place truly matters. These social determinants of health are geographically fixed to the neighborhoods where people reside. As structural inequality sorts and segregates people into neighborhoods largely by income level, it also sorts and segregates access to the social determinants of health. Wealthy neighborhoods have a wealth of life's basic resources, and less wealthy neighborhoods have inferior access to these resources.

My family was sorted and segregated to live among other low-income, predominately Black and Puerto Rican families in the South Bronx; we lived in one of the five poorest congressional districts in the United States.[15] Living in the South Bronx, as compared to a wealthier area, subtracted years from my father's life in numerous ways. First, the South Bronx limited his children's educational opportunities. Second, it exposed us to increased risks of health hazards such as violence and pollution that characterize many working-class neighborhoods but few middle- and upper-class ones. Considering these two situations in turn will make clear how residential segregation forms the bedrock of structural inequality.

Segregated housing meant, above all, that my father's children were assigned to attend some of the worst public schools in the city. Schools in the South Bronx were under-resourced, underperforming, and dangerous. My experience in public school was typical for the neighborhood. I began elementary school at PS 93. To get there daily, I walked past a garbage-strewn empty lot on the corner of Ward Avenue and Bruckner Boulevard, wound past a couple of low-budget convenience stores, and then crossed an overpass at the intersection of three interstate highways. After school, I ate the junk food fare nearby stores offered, enjoyed concrete-conducive recreation like Ringolevio or "sewer-to-sewer" touch football, and, by fourth grade, regularly got into fights with other kids walking to and from school on the overpass.

Had I stayed in PS 93, on graduation from sixth grade I would have been assigned to attend PS 123 for middle school. That school closed, for reasons made clear in reviews still available online today, and that echo the school's reputation when I was a child:

> 123 is an awful school. The principal, staff and security are not responsive to the kids. There is a problem with girls in the bathrooms, constant fighting, teachers cursing and the kids are rude. No discipline or structure. . . . I heard the school is worse than last year. Please don't send your kid to this school.

My father saw where this was going and went to work to get me out of the South Bronx public school system. Residential segregation made moving to a better neighborhood with better free public schools impossible. And so structurally, the only option left was for my father's job count to go from two low-paying jobs to three so that I would never have to attend PS 123. The plan worked. Daddy got both my brother and me out of the pipeline leading to PS 123 and, thankfully, into affirmative action outreach programs at the Fieldston School. Fieldston, a private, college-preparatory school located in the Riverdale section of the Bronx, continues to educate at-risk kids like me. It does so out of a commitment to help build an ethical society. By public transportation, my trip from the South Bronx, where I lived, to Fieldston in the North Bronx, took only an hour and a half. But the school might as well have been on the other side of the world.

In Riverdale, specialty grocers replaced convenience stores. Grassy, tree-studded parks replaced asphalt basketball courts and concrete handball walls. Gracious homes sprawled across manicured lawns and replaced the line of shotgun row houses and apartment buildings on my block, proudly guarded by elaborate, scrolling iron bars. The contrasts often (though not always) delighted me as a kid but also seemed an omnipresent reminder that our South Bronx lives were only worthy of inferior quality homes, food, employment, education, air to breathe and water to drink. Notably, PS 123 has since reopened as a magnet school, which is a welcome structural change that may save parents from having to work to the deadly detriment of their health in order to get a decent education for their children.

I look back today on memories I found puzzling as a teen but understand much better today as evidence of the stress of structural inequality. My family's access to education in Riverdale certainly provided great benefits. But it also introduced the stress of trying to reconcile the dichotomies presented by this obvious inequality.

For example, I recall my father's frenzied and desperate attempts to insert family vacations at budget hotels or a Long Island trailer park as substitutes for trips he could not pay for us to make when invited by our Fieldston classmates. I remember his fiercely angry reminders not to forget where I came from whenever I imitated my Fieldston friends' unfamiliar manners such as calling adults by their given names. Perhaps most tragically, I remember that my father tried for a time to find us a house in Riverdale. We made futile Sunday afternoon trips with real estate agents to examine what our money could buy. Finding even the humblest abodes out of reach, my father devised a plan to save up the money we lacked by selling our South Bronx home, moving into an apartment building, and then moving again to Riverdale when we had enough saved. My mother, who had grown up in public housing projects, put her foot down. She was deathly afraid of going backward and so refused to move from a house—even a humble one—to return to a segregated apartment building.

Around this time, my father took on his fourth job. But it was not enough. Structurally depressed wages for men like him meant that he never earned enough to move his family to Riverdale. The strife of that failure came between my parents and never left. My dad's health began to decline, and his dissatisfaction with his life chances increased. These were hard times in the Bowen household. But I do remember some things fondly. My academic success and my brother's and my ability to navigate a strange new world of opportunity pleased my dad enormously. He saw me admitted to Harvard College and once told me that as soon as I graduated, I would be able to leave poverty behind forever. He met and blessed my marriage to the classmate who later became and remains my husband. And although he did not live to see the fruits of his labor, I know with a certainty that getting my brother and me out of the segregated South Bronx schools saved our lives. I also know with certainty that it cost my father his.

I am forever grateful to him because in finding a way to educate his children, my dad beat structural inequality. I do not know of a single success story from among all the kids from my old neighborhood who stayed and attended PS 123. In fact, to a person, I cannot name one friend from my neighborhood who remained who is alive today, drug-free, without a criminal record, and earning a salary above the bottom quintile of Americans.

Still, in just about every other way, structural inequality beat my dad. Adopting the World Health Organization's definition of political violence, I assert that the housing, income, educational, and other social deprivations that constitute the structural inequality that characterized Daddy's life were a virulent use of state power. This power worked to achieve the racial and economic hierarchies that inevitably led to physical violence and the deterioration of our South Bronx neighborhood and neighbors.[16]

Self-Medicating Inequality: Cost-Benefit of Crime

Structural inequality got the best of my dad when it turned our segregated neighborhood into a gang-infested war zone. This transformation happened in a blink; it was like the onset of puberty. For my early childhood years, we lived in a poor but quiet Black and Latino neighborhood. And then seemingly overnight—when my age cohort hit the teen years—we spilled out of elementary school and onto the streets, finding more to capture the imagination there than in failing schools like PS 123.

Nobel laureate economist Gary Becker laid the theoretical foundation to explain this transformation. He described the relationship between inequality and crime that took a toll on my father's health and life. In his famous 1968 article, "Crime and Punishment: An Economic Approach," Dr. Becker explained that that all crime is economic. Criminals are rational actors who commit crimes as long as their marginal costs are less than the marginal gain of criminal activity.[17] Therefore, in places with wider differences between rich and poor, criminals forgo fewer opportunity costs by avoiding criminal behavior and reap greater marginal gains by engaging in crime that will pay more than any noncriminal activity available to them. For example, the opportunity cost of not getting an education at PS 123 or getting the jobs, wages, homes, and future most likely to follow graduation from South Bronx schools were quite low. The result is that crime actually could pay more than playing by systemically inequitable rules. Thus, inequitable societies suffer more crime than societies where income is more equally distributed.

In 2000, Morgan Kelly extended Becker's theory using data from all metropolitan counties in the United States. He similarly found that inequality has a large impact on increasing violent crime, but he took this observation further by testing three theories to explain this relationship. Some theorists claim that inequality leads to more crime because of instability in family structure, racially mixed neighborhoods, and residential mobility. These explanations find no support whatsoever in my lived experience and virtually no support in the data. Others posit that inequality leads to crime because criminals are rational actors who see better returns for themselves available in crime than in the alternative labor market. This explanation, together with Dr. Kelly's findings that inequality leads to crime when individuals face pressure because of their inability to attain the success they see in those around them, resonates both empirically and experientially.[18]

Two years after Kelly's groundbreaking paper, researchers replicated the positive correlation between crime and inequality using homicide and robbery data from thirty-nine nations worldwide. They concluded that the correlation "reflects causation from inequality to crime rates even after controlling for other crime determinants."[19] And in 2020, the *Economist* published the results of Gallup's Law and Order Index—a composite score that reflects people's reported feelings of personal safety from crime. Again, the level of safety felt was inversely related to the level of income inequality in the respondents' communities. In short, researchers have repeatedly and irrefutably found that as income inequality rises, the incidence of violent crime increases as well. This well-established structural relationship between inequality and crime in the South Bronx was a large part of my father's poor health narrative. Structural inequality notwithstanding, our family unit remained unchanged until he died, but many families in our neighborhood were not so lucky. Although we were the same two-parent, two-child household until my father's death, other families that could find no escape were overcome as crime rates rose. A few kids went into the military. A few more landed in jail and today are living with the aftermath of that indelible legacy. But for my father's cohort, the price was even higher.

My father was a living example of the limited returns to be had in the legal labor market for Black male heads of households. The physical and mental strain of the John Henryism efforts produced frustration that led some to crime.[20] In fact, I can think of two fathers of stable two-parent households in our family's close social network—one a physician and the other a laborer—who buckled under the pressure of inequality and turned to crime when the contrast between their lives and the American Dream became more than they could bear. While my father did not choose this path, we remained close friends with those who did because we all understood that the weight of inequality could, eventually, make a person lose all hope. We knew that the unfairness of it could make a rational actor see street crime as an acceptable alternative to the random inequities that surrounded their lives. One was shot dead, with his son, under circumstances I never got clear even on the night we all huddled in the family's recently acquired suburban home to mourn. The other received a presidential pardon and lived in relative poverty until he died. I maintain that structural inequality played a leading role in these men's premature deaths just as it did in my father's.

As the political violence of structural inequality took over the streets around us, my father's answer was to work harder still. He and my mother were determined not to allow us to remain in the South Bronx during the summers as our neighborhood began to fill with drugs and violence. This seasonal variation in safety was never a concern for my classmates in Riverdale. And so, our family's safety added another burden that drove my father to work so much harder than other Fieldston dads. When he could get scholarships for us, my brother and I spent the summer—the entire summer—in New England at sleepaway camps that offered outreach programs for city kids like us. My dad wrote us long letters every week while we were away. In one, Daddy lamented that he could not get scholarships for our two cousins to join us at camp, though he had tried everything he could think of to get them out of the city. Both those cousins died before age forty; one from drugs and the other took his life. In other letters, my father provided occasional reports of one or another of my friends from the block ending up in jail or on drugs or pregnant (these stories, I suspect, were embellished) to underscore how hard life was for kids back home. At all costs, we could not stay home, he declared. When he could not get scholarships, my mother volunteered as a helper at Camp Minisink—a New York Mission Camp for low-income kids—and this camp allowed us to go at least as far away from the South Bronx as New Jersey. Some summers we got shipped off to our aunt's house in rural North Carolina. This was how I learned that segregation in the South was not that different than segregation in the North, though my social networks extended farther in New York than they did down South.

When his many jobs did not provide enough money for any of these options, my father frequently stopped at my grandparents' house in the projects to borrow cash as we left the city to drive north to camp or south to North Carolina. One of my grandfathers ran numbers—a lottery game deemed illegal, especially once the state began to sponsor its own lottery games. My other grandfather ran a shoe repair shop and secondhand clothing store. Both my grandfathers, therefore, always had cash and shared it generously. They were proof that sometimes what is called a crime is simply a logical parallel market solution when seen as part of the economics and politics of structural inequality. And therefore, again, my life experience taught me that structural inequality can lead some to conclude that crime does pay, especially when other employers do not.

Over time, crime was not the only thing that got worse in my neighborhood. The local branch of a national supermarket chain closed, and we began driving distances those without cars could not travel either to Harlem or across Bruckner Boulevard to shop for groceries. By the time I reached high school, White Castle was the closest food outlet to my home; we ate there whenever we drove to the closest supermarket where overnight hours allowed families who worked swing shift like my dad to shop up until midnight. When the city of New York stopped maintaining the playgrounds, Little League baseball games ceased and the nearby ballpark became strewn with glass and drug paraphernalia. Moreover, the youth basketball league and cheering squad my parents ran through our church fell victim to my dad's need to trade recreation for additional work. Soon the inequality behaved like an infectious disease that spread throughout the whole neighborhood.

Thus, structural inequality eliminated healthy food and exercise opportunities and provides a much better explanation for how my father became overweight and developed hypertension than "personal choice" theory.[21] It also explains his shortness of breath. Though we did not know it then, my old neighborhood is now called Asthma Alley, mainly because of the three interstate highways—the Major Deegan Expressway (I-87), the Cross Bronx Expressway (I-95), and Bruckner Expressway (I-278)—that carry truck and automobile traffic right past my house, beneath the overpass I walked each day to school. My zip code remains one of New York City's most polluted, with high levels of $PM_{2.5}$ (particulate matter smaller than 2.5 micrometers—small enough to be inhaled) air pollution.[22] Unsurprisingly, my old neighborhood also suffers among the shortest life expectancies and highest infant mortality rates. As our neighborhood's community health outcomes got worse, so did my father's individual physical health. But it was the burden on my father's mental health that structural inequality imposed that was most crushing.

Racialized Structural Inequality

Thus far, I have spoken of structural inequality in race-neutral terms. However, structural inequality is not race neutral. In its most virulent and vicious form, it is operationalized by discrimination against racial and ethnic minorities specifically. This discrimination in the United States systematically and relentlessly hurts members of Black, Latino, and Indigenous populations, whether or not they are poor, because structural inequality based on race and national origin is still rampant in America. This form of structural inequality is called *structural racism*. According to Dr. Camara Jones, structural racism is a social, economic, and political system that allocates opportunity and assigns intrinsic personal value and worth according to a hierarchy based on a social, not biological, construct called "race."[23] Structural racism uses the way that people look to unfairly advantage some people and communities that are therefore valued highly, at the expense of unfairly disadvantaging other communities that are not valued. It solidifies these disadvantages economically, politically, and socially. My father's life illustrates the pernicious effects of the special case of structural inequality called structural racism.

The structural inequality of low wages, substandard education, residential segregation, neighborhood violence, environmental toxins, and life in a food desert all shortened my father's life. But racism permeated every one of these social comorbidities, allocating resources and assigning my father an inferior societal status specifically because he was a Black man. Structural racism affected him in many ways I may never fully appreciate. I do know that my dad often made fun of the White men who got promoted over him at the bank's real estate department where he worked by day, even though they could not speak clear English or read a balance sheet. My father also confronted overt racism regularly on his weekend business that he had built. Daddy had hired himself out to manage apartment buildings. He was what we call a *super* in New York; he was the superintendent in charge of collecting rent, doing repairs, and maintaining rental properties in Brooklyn.[24] One of my most loathsome memories was how my father did business over the phone for this job, changing his voice inflection to pose as a White man to get fairer treatment. That this was the way to get his job done exemplified structural racism. For example, when he had to buy paint or nails, or plumbing hardware, he would call stores from our kitchen phone and feign a Jewish accent as he placed his phone order. He would end the call by saying he was going to "send his boy"—that would be him—to pick up the purchase. That way, he could enter forbidden spaces without being questioned. My dad's enormous booming laughter and hearty voice disappeared and became small in the presence of White people, as he shushed himself to usher my brother and me out into a world where he himself could not comfortably go.

I remember a terrible argument between him and my mother whenever she expressed fear or discomfort about attending a school function at the predominantly White Fieldston. She felt she lacked the right clothes, elocution, or connections. My dad shouted angrily at her at home but also seemed to grow quiet and subservient whenever he entered the White schools or camps where he sent us.

Two examples stand out. He once drove hours to attend visiting hours at my summer camp in Vermont. But instead of touring cabins and the waterfront docks, he sat in the car most of the day because he felt unsafe when he realized White girls would be darting about in swimsuits. He explained (in graphic detail) how history taught him that things could go fatally wrong for a Black man in such circumstances. In another instance, I remember him literally dropping whatever he was doing to run down a boat dock to tie lines for White families he did not know, as if his generosity would earn him a place in the club. If it did, I never saw it.

Navigating this kind of well-founded fear is what living with structural racism looked like for my father almost every day. My parents were brave for venturing out of their assigned strata for work and for play. But it cost them dearly. They were relentless in their pursuit of opportunity for their children. But their perseverance eventually wore them down. The stress of everyday discrimination eroded their mental health—I watched as their efforts to straddle two worlds caused them to internalize the effects of the racism they experienced.[25] Moreover, the toxic stress of individually mediated racial discrimination aimed at my parents personally was compounded by the terrible racism that enveloped them and the nation during the turbulent times in which they lived. My father, born in 1930 in the shadow of America's lynching era, lived as a Black man through the racialized terror of the Jim Crow era, the violent attempts to suppress the civil rights movement, and the hate-filled degradation of the White world's massive resistance to racial equality.[26]

Social scientists have empirically documented the destructive spillover effects that such pervasive racial violence has on the mental health of Black Americans. Empirical evidence has shown that massive violence against Black Americans anywhere in the country can damage the mental health of Black Americans everywhere, even those not directly victimized. For example, one study documented that police killings of Black people are associated with worse mental health among other Black Americans in the general population.[27] In another study, researchers showed that the life expectancy for Black men aged forty-five fell in response to the 1972 disclosure that for the forty years between 1932 to 1972—most of my father's life—the US Public Health Service had withheld highly effective and inexpensive medical care to Black men with syphilis, under the guise of a study to monitor the natural course of the disease.[28]

My father died in 1973, one year after the unethical and deadly US Public Health Service Study at Tuskegee was revealed. In my last conversation with him, my father lay in the hospital, preparing for neurosurgery to remove a cerebral aneurism. I stepped into the preoperative holding area to let him know I would be looking forward to seeing him right after his surgery. He shunned my optimism, and instead, mirroring the well-documented and well-founded mistrust that Black men justifiably have of the American medical system, he gave me a list of his final dos and don'ts.

Even today, I still regard that final conversation between us as my father's blessing and charge for my life: "Marry a Southern man—they are respectful. That boy you like, Thomas, is not Southern, but he is a good choice." Check. I did marry Thomas in 1981. "Finish Harvard. You'll be fine if you just do that." Check. I also did that in 1981. "Take care of your mother and brother." Check. Though Mommy is in heaven with him now, my brother and I are still taking care of one another. "And I love you." His last words to me were "I love you." Daddy suffered a massive ruptured aneurism and never regained consciousness. He died in the hospital where I was born, before his fiftieth birthday. But his love sustains me to this day.

The lessons I take from my father's life are legion. This book will explore three. First, my father's high blood pressure, heart disease, and obesity were not the primary risk factors that killed him; systemic inequality was. This book challenges the mistaken view that would point solely to his underlying biological comorbidities or personal behavior to explain my father's early death and premature morbidity. In fact, the lack of adequate employment to earn a decent living, quality public schools to educate his children, or safe housing in a desegregated and therefore well-resourced neighborhood had far more to do with robbing my children and grandchildren of their patriarch than did anything else. Moreover, these same disparate social and economic conditions are highly correlated with the risky health behaviors that some would insist were within his control to help himself live longer. This is also erroneous thinking. Poor health behaviors are a predictable and indeed unavoidable outcome for a low-wage earner who sleeps only during the four hours between dinnertime and midnight to report to his second eight-hour shift each day and to earn a lifetime maximum income of $29,000 per year. That man will eat more than he sleeps and sleep more than he exercises, not by choice, but because of the structures that have ordered his financial life.

Second, the structural inequality that my father experienced was the direct result of structural racism. My father's narrative is unremarkable in this regard. All Black, Indigenous, and Latino people in the United States contend with structural racism. And all are suffering the health effects thereof. Structural racism dictates that most African American and Latino men, like my father, will live in neighborhoods more like the South Bronx than Riverdale, have their children attend schools more like PS 123 than Fieldston, and re-create in places more like the asphalt and concrete playgrounds in the Soundview section of New York City than the leafy, open spaces of Van Cortland Park or the Wave Hill Public Garden. Structural racism is responsible for the fact that African American, Indigenous, and Latino people are the groups most likely to be disproportionately denied equal access to the social determinants of health because of overt and covert discrimination. Structural racism means that the probability of finding men who share my father's narrative is distressingly high among Black men and artificially low for White men. Indeed, the disproportionate prevalence of chronic illnesses in minoritized communities—not just poor ones but middle-class communities as well—merely reveals the power and pervasiveness of structural racism. Racism is empirically associated with poor mental health, hypertension, heart disease, pain, and respiratory illness, among other health conditions.[29] My father's life has inspired me to compile in this book the empirically documented evidence that structural racism has a serious impact on, and operates as a social determinant of, racial minority and immigrant health in America.[30] I use this evidence to explain why African American men are the least healthy population in the United States.[31]

The third lesson is that law plays a central role in erecting structural inequality and racism and therefore is the requisite tool for dismantling them. Specifically, I aim to correct misunderstandings that have led to underenforcement of the constitutional provision that prohibits discrimination based on race and national origin. Although the United States professes to value equal justice for all, the health of our people suggests that nothing could be further from the truth.

The next chapter introduces the three core legal messages concerning structural racism; these messages constitute the overarching thesis of this book. First, *legally enabled* inequality is the reason the health of the entire American population is the worst of all industrialized nations in the world.[32] In fact, the United States is the most unequal society of all thirty-seven nations of the Organisation for Economic Co-operation and Development (OECD). Inequality in a nation is most commonly measured by the *Gini index*, a widely accepted measure of income and wealth inequality. On this index, zero represents complete equality, where every individual in a country has exactly equal incomes, and 100 represents total inequality, where one individual has all the nation's income and all others have none. The Gini index was introduced by an Italian economist in 1912. The formula has changed, and the Gini index is not without its critics.[33] But the United States is the nation whose Gini index is closest to 100 percent, which is correlated with the embarrassingly poor health status of Americans compared with our OECD peers. I further demonstrate that the structural inequality that threatens the health of our entire population, not just the underclass or poor communities, could not exist apart from the legal institutions that sustain it. The ability of structural inequality to seriously damage the social and economic stability of the entire society and the health of everyone—across all racial and ethnic groups—is due to the laws that facilitate economic and therefore social stratification.

Second, the well-known fact that Black Americans have the poorest health of all groups in the nation, followed by Indigenous and Latino populations, is due not to individual factors but to structural inequality. In fact, racial and ethnic discrimination against these groups lies at the root of these inequities and indeed fuels the widest gaps in them nationwide. Importantly, the discrimination that most decisively threatens health in America is not only the individualized instances of prejudice directed at people by bigots or racist individuals. The most pernicious discrimination is the systemic discrimination that has relentlessly asserted itself in institutions and organizational structures from the moment the United States was formed, throughout our nation's history to the present. This systemic discrimination effectively erects structures and institutions that allocate the benefits of living in an organized society to White populations and systematically withhold such benefits from Black, Latino, and Indigenous populations across the country. Disparate health outcomes are the result.

Throughout this book, I will correct the misimpression that health disparities are evidence of individual-level differences. The tale that health disparities arise out of differences in health behaviors such as diet and exercise or from biological differences such as susceptibility to co-morbid conditions ignores the compelling evidence that the driving factors of health inequity are structural. While smoking, diet, and exercise are not irrelevant and can contribute to individual health outcomes, the massive population differences that we see across the American health landscape are caused by centuries of unjust subordination. Throughout this book, we will see how the history of discrimination and racial inequality has permeated our social structures to produce the poorest health outcomes in the entire industrialized world. Moreover, we will see that these poor health outcomes are consistently distributed to those who also bear the burden of centuries of targeted injustice in a nation that was organized on the premise that "all men are created equal." Clearly, racially disparate health outcomes are the evidence that our society is organized to institutionalize systems of inequality so that the vast majority of our resources, power, and opportunity are sequestered for the benefit of almost-exclusively White members of society. What is left is also divided along racial lines, leaving most of our nation's racial minority groups to attempt healthy living under the worst conditions.

The third legal lesson is that in the United States, from its inception to today, structural racism has been constructed, maintained, and sustained by federal, state, and local law. We must clearly understand this third lesson if we want to do anything more than just talk about structural racism and bemoan its consequences. By recognizing that US law is the primary mechanism by which structural racism prevails, we equip and justify the aggressive use of legal reforms to dismantle it. In fact, reforming and enforcing the laws of this nation are the most important corrective measures available to reduce the disproportionately high death rate of minority populations in America. Simply put, if it weren't for structural racism, my father might be alive today. And not just my father. My entire family could have looked different today since thus far, all the men in my immediate and extended family—all African American—died before age seventy-five. Had they been born White, they would have enjoyed the privilege of living without the effects of structural racism.

* * *

Ask any Mexican, any Puerto Rican, any black man, any poor person— ask the wretched how they fare in the halls of justice, and then you will know, not whether or not the country is just, but whether or not it has any love for justice, or any concept of it. It is certain, in any case, that ignorance, allied with power, is the most ferocious enemy justice can have. —James Baldwin, *No Name in the Street* (1972)

In this chapter, I have used my father's life as an exemplar of the injustice of structural inequality and racism; these uniquely American forms of state-sponsored political violence are the subject of this book. My father's short life vividly illustrates the impacts of structural inequality and racism. But his life is not the only instance of these impacts. Quite the opposite. Indeed, Vincent Edward Bowen Jr.'s life experiences are useful narratives of structural inequality precisely because of how utterly unremarkable they are. The ubiquity of my father's life experiences in African American and other marginalized communities in fact confirms the *structural* nature of inequality and racism in America. I will continue to share lessons from my parents' lives to personalize the alarm and call to action that I sound in the chapters that follow. And to the extent that I succeed in moving some readers to action, my father and mother will not have lived briefly or died prematurely in vain.

1

STRUCTURAL RACISM

Health is the by-product of justice. . . . In a just society, health inequalities will be minimized and population health status will be improved—in short, social justice is good for our health.

—Norman Daniels, Bruce Kennedy, and Ichiro Kawachi, 2000

Structural racism is the form of structural inequality that is caused by racial and ethnic discrimination. It is distinguished from individual prejudice, bigotry, or bias by its scope. Structural racism does not merely affect individual interactions and relationships. Instead, it exerts its effects through the *systemic*, hierarchical organization within institutions at all levels of society.[1] It thereby bases differential access to all societal resources, privileges, and opportunities on race. Structural racism is built on the premise that people of all socially constructed racial groups are not equally valuable and that, therefore, their race best determines the extent of their entitlement to societal goods and services. Put another way, structural racism in America is informed by the ideological belief that White people are a superior form of humanity to non-White people and that their racial superiority entitles them to greater resources, more power, and preferential treatment.

Despite the recent rise in White supremacist rhetoric and influences, largely since 1954 fewer and fewer private and public institutions overtly espouse White supremacist beliefs to justify the preferential outcomes that White people enjoy over most other racial groups. Yet racial differentials in household income, educational attainment, occupational status, and home ownership, for example, consistently reveal racial biases that allocate the benefits of America's major societal institutions according to race.[2] Moreover, this racial hegemony is not accidental and does not reflect naturally occurring differences. Instead, the results follow from the intentional and unintentional operation of stereotypes, prejudices, and biases that generally favor European descendants over non-Europeans. In short, structural racism institutionalizes the false ideology of White supremacy. The ideology becomes especially effective when it finds expression through legal enactments and actors who give the false dogma a cloak of legal legitimacy at local, state, and federal levels. Examples include all the Jim Crow laws of the first half of the twentieth century and discriminatory bans on natural hairstyles enforced by state and local governments against Black schoolchildren today.

Structural racism is unjust because it foments inequality based on race and thereby violates the essential equality of all humankind. It is unethical because it disparately visits severely harmful and avoidable consequences on groups of people according to race—people who are similar in all other respects to the groups of people it disparately advantages. Structural racism is also inefficient because it makes all people less free. This chapter shows that structural racism operates through laws to produce racial and ethnic health disparities that harm the health of minority populations and destroy the self-evident truth on which this nation and our democracy was formed: "That all men are created equal, that they are endowed by their Creator with certain unalienable Rights, that among these are Life, Liberty and the pursuit of Happiness."[3]

My Father's Fight against Structural Racism

Structural racism fixes the probability of lifetime success on race so that race, rather than one's effort, talent, ambition, or humanity, predicts one's life chances.

In 1930, for example, when my father was born, structural racism was shaping vastly different life chances for Black and White Americans. His life expectancy at birth as a Black male was 47.3 years, 12.4 years shorter than a White male born the same year, and 16.2 years shorter than a White woman his age.[4] Importantly, these disparities did not reflect significant biological differences between the races; indeed, as the sequencing of the human genome has shown, the White and Black babies born in the United States—whether in 1930 or today—all are genetically more alike than different.[5] Nevertheless, the life-expectancy tables accurately predicted that my father would die well ahead of the White people born in the same year, because the *quality* of life that my father had access to as a Black man differed greatly from that generally available to White people in this country. For example, during my father's peak earning years from 1939 to 1960, he could earn an income equal to only between 41.4 and 59.9 percent of the incomes that White men in his age group could earn.[6] Worse yet, during the Great Depression, he would have been among the approximately 50 percent of African American men in New York City who were unemployed. In those days, White workers called for Black workers to be fired from any jobs that were available, as long as White people were out of work and could hold those jobs. My father's answer to this systemic racism was to exit the job market completely during the Depression, returning only after he married, in 1952.

He and my grandfather instead opened a secondhand shoe and thrift shop on Fifth Avenue and 133rd Street in Harlem. My grandfather taught him to make and repair shoes. In this way, they removed themselves from the structural economy that placed White workers ahead of them for jobs and wages merely because they were White. Instead, my father's income rested principally on his ability to purchase and refurbish a pair of old children's shoes for less than the $0.25 price that I remember collecting for each pair sold when I worked on Saturdays at Grandpa's shop.

Later my father joined the military. After he completed his military service in a segregated US Army unit, he was honorably discharged just in time to join the wave of integration that opened Transit Authority jobs for Black people in New York City. My dad was a beneficiary of the integration efforts that resulted after city councilman Adam Clayton

Powell Jr. led a boycott to challenge racial discrimination that had excluded Black workers from joining transportation unions.

And so, my father's journey demonstrates just how tenacious structural racism can be. He escaped the systemic employment discrimination first by becoming a merchant helping other low-income Black
families survive the Depression and then by joining the army. Daddy
also used his right to vote for, and boycott transportation discrimination with, Powell, who by then was running for—and won—a seat in
Congress. Powell was an often-sung hero in my household when I was
a child. Both civic engagement and civil disobedience were required
to overcome some of the powerful political structures that supported
structural racism's hold on low-wage job markets.

And finally, for as long as I can remember, my father had our entire
family spend every Sunday (and many Saturdays), from sunup to sun-
down, in the Walker Memorial Baptist Church on West 116th Street in
Harlem. As I became old enough to voice my objections to this practice,
my father explained that being in church was a way for him and many
others in our community to reclaim their humanity after waging psychological warfare against the onslaught of White supremacy that Black
people confronted daily during the week. My father was a member of the
deacon board and a prominent member of the church board of trust-
ees. That meant that although he may have collected discarded scraps of
clothing and old shoes to make a living during the week, on Sundays he
was a respected leader with a title, decisional responsibility, and a reason to dress in a suit. My father pointed out that even though men who
cleaned floors and women who cared for others' children might have to
answer to "Hey girl" or "Hey boy" during the week, on Sundays, they
were recognized as "Deacon Bowen," "Pastor Jones," or "Sister Brown."
In this way, church membership became another weapon of choice to
fight the impacts of structural racism for my father and my family. However, all these techniques are more properly understood as coping mechanisms that provided partial protection for the individual exposed to a
world infected by structural racism. In the end, structural racism took

years off my father's life, though his ingenuity and perseverance made sure that every year of his life counted toward the goal of ensuring that his children would live longer and stronger than he had, to carry on the fight against structural racism.

Structural Racism: A Public Health Crisis

Dr. Rochelle P. Walensky, director of the Centers for Disease Control and Prevention, recently declared that racism is a serious public health threat. Along these lines, Professor Ibram X. Kendi likens racism to a metastatic cancer that has invaded the American body politic.[7] I contend that US law is the primary vector by which racial prejudices are embedded in structural policies and practices, thereby making American society a comfortable, welcoming host for the disease of racism to take up long-term residence. The disease has been festering in our country since its inception; efforts to treat the disease have yet to succeed. Therefore, the premise of this chapter and book is that structural racism in the United States is a public health crisis. My objective is to outline the manifestations of, and treatment for, this disease.

In her seminal work, "A Gardener's Tale," Dr. Camara Jones compares the pervasively corrosive impact of structural racism to nutrient-deficient soil that is detrimental to planted seeds.[8] She further explains the genesis of structural racism: "the initial historical insult of separating the seed into the two different types of soil; the contemporary structural factors of the flower boxes which keep the soils separate; and the acts of omission in not addressing the differences between the soils over the years." Slave laws and, later, Jim Crow laws served the separating function. Lending, zoning, and property laws that erected residential segregation introduced contemporary structures that keep populations separate to this day. And despite the copious antidiscrimination laws passed during the Civil Rights era, lax enforcement left discriminatory acts unaddressed for years. Over time, structural racism persists and aggregates inequalities by race and national origin chronologically through generations, while geographically concentrating inequities in locations where disfavored populations live, work, and play. As structural racism operates cumulatively according to historical and cultural presumptions of racial hierarchy, it perpetuates discriminatory beliefs and values that persist in contemporary social institutions.[9] Researchers have theorized that structural racism is the cumulative totality of laws that control societal institutions to reinforce racial discrimination and disproportionately constrain access to resources.[10] The ultimate proof of its effectiveness is the correlation between structural racism and disproportionately poor health outcomes in marginalized populations.

Structural racism has been described as a fundamental cause of all health and social disparities.[11] Such a root source will reproduce bad outcomes until it is permanently eradicated. According to sociologists, a fundamental cause satisfies at least three characteristics: First, it affects multiple pathways and a wide range of circumstances to generate superior or inferior outcomes among social groups. This book focuses on population health outcomes as the measurable, inferior outcomes produced by structural racism. It explores the many pathways that discrimination travels to produce poor health. Discrimination operates in America's education, housing, employment, and legal settings, creating advantages for White groups and disadvantages for Black and other minoritized groups in many social determinants of health.[12] Moreover, in a wide range of health-care settings, minority patients have poorer access to, and lower quality of, medical care than do White patients. This observation also qualifies as the first characteristic of a fundamental cause.

Second, a fundamental cause can be replicated not only through multiple pathways but also across a wide variety of health outcomes. For example, health-care disparities unsupported by clinical differences are well documented in the treatment for heart disease, pain, lung cancer, renal transplantation, pneumonia, immunizations, and mammograms.[13]

A third characteristic of a fundamental cause speaks to the ineffectiveness of partial solutions. Interventions that aim to change the poor health outcomes caused by structural racism but not to change the cause itself will have only modest effects on the problem. Because a fundamental solution concerns the distribution of resources needed for good health, even effective solutions will allocate these resources unfairly if no one is focusing on structural inequities. The American experience during the 2020 COVID-19 crisis is a tragically compelling example of how structural racism satisfies this predictive quality of all three characteristics of a fundamental cause.

The COVID-19 Pandemic: A Case Study in Structural Racism

In 2020, we experienced a global outbreak of coronavirus disease that infected more than 81 million people. The United States, arguably the world's most medically advanced nation, has recorded the highest number of coronavirus cases and deaths in the world. By July 10, 2021, more than 33 million COVID-19 cases had been confirmed in the United States, and of these, more than 606,600 had died from the illness.[14] According to the available, though incomplete, data compiled to date, at the height of the pandemic, the hospitalization rate from COVID-19 for American Indian or Alaska Natives was 5.3 times the rate for the White population and 4.6 times higher for Latino populations. Black, Indigenous, and Latino people had a COVID-19 death rate more than 2.7 times greater than that for White Americans, who had the lowest age-adjusted death rates.[15] Through targeted health-equity efforts, these gaps have narrowed somewhat. Examining how this pandemic disproportionately has killed Indigenous, Black, and Latino Americans will help us understand what structural racism is and how it harms health. Moreover, it will illustrate why eradicating racism is not merely a political ideal or part of a policy agenda from a single political perspective. Indeed, liberals and conservatives, Democrats and Republicans, people of all racial and ethnic backgrounds, have reason to end structural racism as an act of self-preservation. The data from the US experience with the coronavirus pandemic convincingly show that structural racism is literally killing us all.

In late December 2019, officials in Wuhan, a city in China's central Hubei province, reported dozens of cases of a mysterious pneumonia from an unknown cause. On January 7, 2020, Chinese officials identified the outbreak as new or novel coronavirus, SARS-CoV-2, which causes a respiratory disease that spreads from person to person, even among asymptomatic carriers. Within two weeks, the first index case was reported in the United States, on January 21, 2020. Within three weeks of the Chinese outbreak, nations around the world, including France, Singapore, Japan, and South Korea, had reported their first cases, prompting the World Health Organization, on January 30, 2020, to declare the outbreak a Public Health Emergency of International Concern.

The American response to the global pandemic was to successively close its borders, first to non-European nations and, much later, to European ones. On January 31, the United States banned travel from China.[16] This ban followed after fewer than 14 cases of coronavirus disease were diagnosed in the United States, 12 of which involved travelers arriving from China. On February 29, after the Islamic Republic of Iran reported 583 coronavirus cases and 43 deaths, the US president issued a proclamation suspending entry into the United States from Iran.[17] On March 11, the World Health Organization declared the COVID-19 a global pandemic. That same day, when the number of European cases had reached 17,442, with 711 deaths, the White House finally made a third proclamation, banning travel from twenty-six European states known as the "Schengen Area."[18] Two days later, on March 13, the US government declared a national emergency.[19]

The progression of US border closures was more favorable to European than to non-European nations. America's border was not closed to Europe until cases from that region exceeded 17,000, whereas bans were imposed on Chinese and Iranian travel after only 14 and 593 cases were confirmed, respectively. Professor Khiara Bridges rightly concludes, "Race and racism disallowed the U.S. from recognizing Europe as a threat."[20] The result, according to molecular epidemiologists, was that the European strand of coronavirus that we did not defend against vigorously is the one that killed us.[21] A Mount Sinai Health System study showed that the source of the COVID-19 epidemic in New York City was untracked European SARS-CoV-2 cases, with little direct introduction from China.[22] We could reasonably argue that our preferential treatment of Europeans over Asians and Muslims proved deadly.

The COVID-19 pandemic revealed structural racism beyond the nation's global responses. States responded individually, closing public schools, then businesses, and issuing various types of stay-at-home orders. But by March 26, the United States reported 163,539 cases, by then the highest number of confirmed COVID-19 cases of any nation in the world. In densely populated cities especially, racial and ethnic minority groups were disproportionately affected by the COVID-19 outbreak. For example, in Chicago and in the state of Louisiana, African Americans accounted for 70 percent of COVID-29 deaths, though they represented fewer than one-third of the population. By the summer of 2020, nearly one-third of all COVID-19 cases in the United States occurred in New York, where Latino and Black New Yorkers died at rates far exceeding their percentage of the population. Yet in early June, while the virus was still hitting hardest in urban centers, only 65 percent of Americans said they were regularly wearing masks, according to a Pew Research Center survey.[23]

The novel coronavirus certainly proved more deadly for those with such underlying medical conditions as diabetes, heart disease, and hypertension. However, any analysis that stops short of recognizing that the disproportionate prevalence of these comorbid diseases among people of color is primarily due to the social and environmental risks that these populations disproportionately face misses the full story. In fact, structural racism was a primary contributor to the disproportionately high numbers of people from racial and ethnic minority groups with medical conditions that made them more susceptible to serious complications from the coronavirus infection. Therefore, at bottom, structural racism contributed to the "causes of the cause" of excessive morbidity and mortality among Indigenous, Latino, and Black communities during the pandemic.

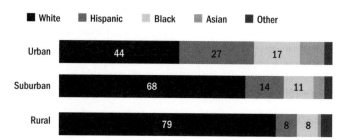

FIGURE 1.1: Residential Patterns by Race in the United States, by Percentage of Population. Source: Shan Li, "New York City's Coronavirus Deaths Match Demographics in Other Hot Spots," *Wall Street Journal,* April 18, 2020.

The excessive morbidity and mortality had several causes. Structural racism in the United States produced the prevalent racialized residential patterns that helped the virus reach Indigenous, African American, and Latino groups first during this pandemic. The virus spread rapidly through densely populated cities designated *urban* areas, where higher concentrations of Black and Latino people live, work, and play (figure 1.1). It ravaged Indigenous and poor White communities living on reservations characterized as *rural*, with limited access to adequate medical care, testing, and even epidemiological surveillance. The larger proportion of White people living in suburban communities, however, have been relatively insulated from the virus's deadliest attacks.

Figure 1.2 compares COVID-19 cases and deaths by region and by racial makeup. The places listed in the figure include urban centers like Detroit, Chicago, New Orleans, and New York City, areas that proved to be the first hot spots for viral transmission. People in these densely populated cities live close to one another, for example, residing in apartment buildings, ascending to work in elevators, traveling in crowds on public transportation, and closely encountering one another in public places much more frequently than do people in suburban or rural settings. This proximity proved deadly for a virus that spread primarily through airborne droplets from breathing, coughing, or sneezing even while the carrier was otherwise asymptomatic. Today's map recording the spread of coronavirus disease, however, tells a very different story. The Centers for Disease Control and Prevention regularly publishes maps showing COVID-19 hot spots all across the nation, proving that rural states, Midwestern states, and states in the Deep South have ignored the threat of the virus that was originally concentrated in large cities, to their peril.

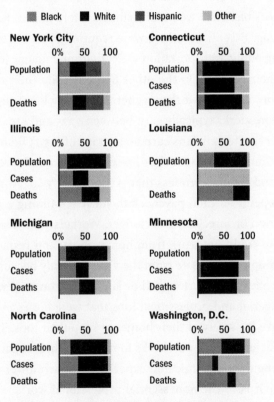

FIGURE 1.2: Structural Residential Patterns and COVID-19 Morbidity and Mortality. Source: Shan Li, "New York City's Coronavirus Deaths Match Demographics in Other Hot Spots," *Wall Street Journal,* April 18, 2020.

Second, the racially stratified American labor market proved another indispensable vehicle for structural racism to expose minority populations to greater-than-average risk of coronavirus disease during the early stages of the pandemic. Nationwide, 30 percent of all bus drivers and nearly 20 percent of all food service workers, store stockers, and custodians are Black.[24] The majority of farmworkers—68 percent— were born in Mexico. These numbers show that Black and Latino workers were disproportionately represented in the low-wage fields deemed essential. On the one hand, *essential* meant that these workers were indispensable to the rest of us because they made the basic necessities of our lives possible. Their essential status therefore meant they could not stop working. Essential workers were required to report to their jobs, often riding public transportation to get there and unable to quarantine safely in their homes. On the other hand, despite their centrality to the economy, essential workers generally occupy low-wage positions. Grocery store clerks typically earn between $7.25 and $10.00 per hour; hospital service technicians earn an average of $15.13 hourly; certified nurse assistants make $16.05 per hour. Amazon employees who handle cargo and freight earn less than $35,000 per year. At these wages, workers depend on each paycheck to survive. Missing a check could mean eviction or foreclosure or hunger. Workers who were nonessential but who could not work from home—hotel and restaurant workers, for example—were safe from the virus but only because they were sent home after being furloughed or laid off. In contrast, workers who held managerial and professional jobs that were *not* essential did not have to leave the safety of their homes to keep their jobs. These people earned sufficiently large paychecks to maintain their usual standard of living during the pandemic and experienced much lower exposure to the coronavirus.[25] The nonessential professional workers in this category are overwhelmingly White (79.4 percent). The essential and other low-wage workers are not.[26]

The highly racialized feature of the built environment is a third example of how structural racism has affected COVID-19 disparities.

When researchers analyze the susceptibility of minority populations to comorbid medical conditions, the studies often place much focus on risk factors related to individual health behaviors such as smoking, physical inactivity, and poor diet. These behaviors, while certainly relevant, must also be seen as related to the racial characteristics of various neighborhoods. To the extent that health behaviors differ by race, ethnicity, and socioeconomic status, the differences are partly influenced by deficiencies in the built environment. For example, some neighborhoods have limited access to recreational spaces; high concentration of liquor stores, fast food restaurants, and tobacco retail outlets; and a proliferation of billboards that invite poor health behavior.[27] Both urban neighborhoods and poor rural areas also lack high-quality preventive medical care and healthy food sources.[28] Moreover, unhealthy behavior choices are associated with poverty and discrimination. For example, social scientists have shown that both the financial stress of poverty and racial discrimination are linked to depression, anxiety, and anger, all of which are risk factors for heart disease and high blood pressure and are associated with poor health habits.[29] Unsurprisingly, people who are stressed and depressed do not exercise regularly.

A fourth avenue through which structural racism operated during the pandemic is Black and Latino communities' higher-than-average exposure to environmental pollution such as lead, asbestos, carbon dioxide, and industrial waste. Studies have shown that air pollution contributed to racially disparate vulnerability to COVID-19 disease. For example, a Harvard University study showed that people living in regions with high levels of $PM_{2.5}$ air pollution are more likely to die from COVID-19 than those in less polluted areas.[30] Even after accounting for behavioral differences such as obesity and smoking, researchers found that small increases in air pollution increase the likelihood of death from COVID-19. Environmental justice expert Vernice Miller-Travis insightfully points to "systemic race-based local land use policies and practices [that] give rise to the phenomenon of Environmental Racism" to explain health disparities generally and COVID-19 specifically.[31]

The systemic racism that characterized the COVID-19 pandemic is not new. Though the virus strain was deemed novel, the history of America's systemic discrimination laid bare during this national emergency is not. This is a fifth characteristic of structural racism: it is enduring. Structural racism replicates itself in different eras and circumstances. COVID-19 is but one example of a national emergency exacerbated by this kind of racism.

Of course, another tragic example occurred during Hurricane Katrina in August 2005. The death caused by that storm was devastating everywhere and for everyone, but structural racism compounded the tragedy disproportionately. In New Orleans, 62 percent of those who died were Black, and 42 percent of the bodies found in Orleans and St. Bernard Parishes were recovered in places where the poverty rate was greater than 30 percent.[32] Overall, more than thirteen hundred people were killed in the Category 5 storm; approximately half were from racial and ethnic minority groups. These people lived in the segregated Lower Ninth Ward, a low-lying neighborhood located below sea level and surrounded by poorly maintained levees. Transportation was unavailable in this neighborhood, which had no evacuation plan in place despite prior warning.

As I have said, the story of structural racism's impact on the built environment is not new. In the 1928 great flood of Lake Okeechobee, a Florida hurricane killed an estimated twenty-five hundred people, 75 percent of whom were Black migrant workers. As in New Orleans, the victims lived in segregated neighborhoods with flimsily constructed homes, inadequate access to transportation, and no evacuation planning despite ample forewarning of the tragedy.[33] Today, nearly a century later and more than fifteen years after Hurricane Katrina, reports (including one by the National Academies of Sciences, Engineering, and Medicine) found that minority and low-income communities remain most vulnerable to urban flooding. In Houston, Chicago, and Louisiana, Black and low-income residents still occupy the lowest-lying lands, receive less flood protection, and have sewer systems in poorer condition than do their White, wealthy neighbors. This is how structural racism kills.[34]

Sixth, structural racism increases minority morbidity and mortality though the systemically discriminatory policies of powerful state actors. This tradition of state-sponsored structural racism and its disproportionate cost of minority lives in this country is more than a hundred years old. In his brilliant study, *Contagious Divides: Epidemics and Race in San Francisco's Chinatown*, Professor Nayan Shah recounts the pivotal role public health authorities played during the nineteenth century to erect the scaffolding of structural racism that harmed thousands of Chinese Americans. Quoting the San Francisco Board of Health, he writes, "Health authorities readily conflated the physical condition of Chinatown with the characteristics of Chinese people. They depicted Chinese immigrants as a filthy and diseased 'race' who incubated such incurable afflictions as smallpox, syphilis, and bubonic plague and infected White Americans."[35] Dr. Shah then demonstrates that after the concept of race was married to disease, public health officials exercised their governmental authority to ensure that Chinese communities faced dilapidated living conditions. Unsurprisingly, these conditions were structurally unhealthy.

Perhaps Dr. Shah's most important contribution is to show how structural racism can be reversed. He proposes that public health law and authority can dismantle the structural racism this same authority previously built. During the twentieth century, public health officials redoubled their efforts to test, trace, and treat disease in the Chinese community and created strong advocacy and health promotion campaigns: "But the authorities did more than demonize the Chinese; they also marshaled civic resources that promoted sewer construction, vaccination programs, and public health management."[36] The result, Dr. Shah explains, was a transformation from a society of exclusion to one of inclusion in which Chinese citizens could become full political participants in the liberal democracy of the nation.

The idea of the citizen emphasizes the equality of the independent individual in political participation and in access to privilege and resources, while the subject is constituted in disciplinary practices in places such as schools, prisons, factories, hospitals, and clinics that inculcate the individual self with the norms of the population. The modern process of public health reform emerged within a web of social, political, and cultural linkages that produced a new conception of the human subject in the nineteenth and early twentieth centuries.[37]

The powerful lesson here as Americans and officials across the globe seek to emerge from the COVID-19 crisis is that the racial policies of a government's public health authority have broad impacts on structural racism throughout all institutions of our society. These policies can either help deconstruct racism to advance justice, equality, and democracy or wreak disastrous destruction of the same.

An Equal-Opportunity Killer

Structural racism, like all structural inequality, makes America a less healthy society for everyone. It does not discriminate whose life it takes; it increases morbidity and mortality of all races. Recent innovative studies confirm this conclusion. Several researchers have designed metrics to measure the extent of this racism in a given geographic location. These metrics allow researchers to compare the level of structural racism in different US counties, states, or regions and to analyze the link between it and the poor health of various populations. Unsurprisingly, the data confirm that as structural racism increases, the health of minority populations declines. Consider the following three studies.

David Chae measured area racism by counting the number of times people searched for racial epithets on the internet.[38] Dr. Chae used the frequency of queries containing the N-word as a proxy for the sociodemographic characteristics of the population in a given area. His study analyzed the relationship between these internet queries and African American mortality rates due to heart disease, cancer, stroke, and diabetes—four of the leading causes of death in the United States. Theorizing that racial discrimination causes stress, anxiety, anger, and depression, Chae sought to evaluate whether negative cognitive experiences could increase the risk of chronic disease because of the physical impact of what public health researcher Dr. Arline Geronimus has brilliantly identified as "weathering"—that is, mobilizing physiological resources to meet the demands of structural racism.[39] Weathering could include compensating for physical risk factors such as excess pollution and violence, or it could point to the risk of maladaptive health behaviors to relieve personal stress due to racism. Dr. Chae's team found that racism does indeed have a psychophysiological impact on the body. "Area racism, as indexed by the proportion of Google searches containing the 'N-word,' is significantly associated with not only the all-cause Black mortality rate, but also Black-White disparities in mortality" even after controlling for education, poverty, and White mortality.[40] Using the same methodology in another study to estimate area racism, Chae and his colleagues also found that racism contributes to poor birth outcomes among Black people.[41]

In another study, Alicia Lukachko and her coauthors showed that African Americans living in states with high structural racism have a greater probability of suffering a heart attack than do African Americans living in states whose structural racism measures are low. Dr. Lukachko's team found no similar impact of racism on the health of White people.[42] This study analyzed data from a sample of 32,752 Black and White participants who completed face-to-face interviews related to physical and mental health.

The team measured structural racism at the state level by aggregating ratios of Black-White disparities using data in four domains: political participation, employment and job status, educational attainment, and judicial treatment. The researchers compared two variables: the composite numeric index compiled from these ratios and the incidence of myocardial infarction within the past twelve months among the respondents. High levels of structural racism in political participation, employment, and judicial treatment were associated with increased odds of myocardial infarction.

Numerous other studies confirm that racial prejudice harms the health of the marginalized populations that are targeted. For example, using US county-level data from a million participants who took the Implicit Association test between 2002 and 2012, Dr. Jacob Orchard and Dr. Joseph Price found that the Black-White gap in infant mortality was 14 percent higher in counties with high implicit racial prejudice than in counties with low prejudice. Moreover, the racial gap in preterm births was 29 percent higher in high-prejudice counties. And the racial disparities between Black and White babies' health outcomes were sadly larger still when the extent of racism in each county was measured by explicit rather than implicit racial prejudice data.[43]

Without question, these findings are disturbing. Moreover, surprisingly, several studies document not only that structural racism has a strong, negative effect on minority health but also that White people as well as Black people have poorer health outcomes because of racism. The next three studies are examples of research that confirms this important finding.

Yeonjin Lee and her research staff analyzed survey data from 10,950 White and Black respondents across the United States to compare their survival rates with the level of negative racial attitudes toward Black people in their neighborhoods. This study analyzed data from respondents' answers to five questions posed during the annual General Social Survey. The survey measures racial prejudice in one hundred metropolitan and rural US counties. The questions ask for views on African Americans' intelligence, work ethic, and eligibility to marry White people. Next, the researchers summarized the survey data to estimate community-level prejudice in each location. They then compared the aggregated views to age-adjusted death rates in the relevant communities between 1993 and 2002. Remarkably, this study found that the odds of dying for both Black and White residents were higher when they lived in communities with more racist attitudes. The researchers estimated that "living in a community with higher levels of anti-Black prejudice increased participants' odds of death by 31%." In short, Dr. Lee and her team showed that "living in a highly prejudiced community was harmful for both Blacks and Whites."[44]

In another study showing that all populations suffer because of racism, Jordan Leitner and his colleagues found that Black and White death rates are positively related to explicit racial bias.[45] Dr. Leitner's group analyzed evidence of explicit racial bias data from approximately 1.4 million White respondents collected by Project Implicit from 2003 to 2013.[46] The study participants were volunteers and therefore self-selected to answer questions about their feelings toward White and Black Americans on a scale of 0 (not warm) to 10 (warmest). Using the internet protocol addresses of each respondent's computer, the researchers set the general geographic location for each response and used those data to measure the number of responses in 1,835 counties around the country. Dr. Leitner and his team then compared the evidence of racial prejudice in each county with the number of people diagnosed with circulatory problems such as heart attack, angina, or coronary heart disease. The data on circulatory problems were obtained from the 2012 Behavioral Risk Factor Surveillance System survey. The researchers accounted for several confounding factors such as age and geographic density. They also created a geographic mobility index to account for healthier people's freedom to choose to live in less biased counties. In this way, the researchers sought to ensure that their results were related to racial bias and were not influenced by social selection.

The findings were stunning. "In counties where White respondents harbored more explicit racial bias," the researchers concluded, "the rate of death from circulatory disease was increased for both Whites and Blacks" albeit more strongly for Black people than for White.[47] Moreover, Dr. Leitner and his coauthors noted two explanations for these results: White people's explicit bias, which has historically exerted strong effects on structural factors such as the regulation of environmental pollution, and overtly negative personal interactions that adversely affect health outcomes.

Dr. Bruce Kennedy and Dr. Ichiro Kawachi led another study of data collected from thirty-nine states.[48] They and their team compared collective community disrespect for Black people with age-adjusted mortality rates for Black and White populations across the United States. The researchers based their measure of collective disrespect toward Black people on responses to a national survey collected from White respondents. The survey asked participants to select what they believed was the correct explanation for the assertion "On average Blacks have worse jobs, income, and housing than White people." Two of the possible explanations that the survey offered for this and other statements describing real disparities identified discrimination as the reason. However, an additional two explanations were more nefarious. For each US state, the researchers calculated the percentage of respondents who chose one of these two discriminatory explanations: "Because most Blacks have less in-born ability to learn" or "Because most Blacks just don't have the motivation or will power to pull themselves up out of poverty." These latter two answers were coded as disrespectful of Black people.

The study found a strong correlation between the measures of collective disrespect and higher mortality rates for both Black and White people. In fact, for each 1 percent increase in the prevalence of those who believed that Black people lacked innate ability, Kennedy and Kawachi's team observed an associated increase in age-adjusted Black mortality rates of 359.8 deaths per 100,000 (95 percent confidence index) and an increase in age-adjusted White mortality of at least 187.5 deaths per 100,000. The researchers conclude, "These data suggest that racism, measured as an ecologic characteristic is associated with higher mortality in both blacks and whites."

An important study published in 2017 clarified that the association between racism and poor health is not merely caused by self-selection.[49] Sarah McKetta and her colleagues refuted the notion that racism is associated with poor health because Black people with good health move away from racism and leave behind only those in poor health. Before beginning their study, Dr. McKetta and her team recognized that the correlation between racism and poor health could have two explanations: (1) exposure to racism causes poor health or (2) Black people with good health have the resources to move away from racist environments.

To find out which explanation was the most likely, the researchers measured state-level racism as a percentage of Google searches for racially charged terms in each state. They then identified Black people who reported poor health and those who reported good health. Next, they compared these outcomes with the people's moving patterns from state to state. Among those who moved out of state, African Americans who self-reported good health were more likely to move to a state with less racial animus than were those who self-reported poor health. This finding, of course, supports the conclusion that Black people with better health leave racist environments. However, McKetta and her colleagues also found that among African Americans who moved to another state, more than 80 percent moved to a state within the same quartile of racial animus, and fewer than 5 percent resided in states with the lowest levels of racial animus.

Their analysis showed that even among Black people who could select what states they moved to, the overwhelming majority found themselves in equally racist environments, whether they were healthy or unhealthy. The study's authors concluded, "While selection is occurring, it only contributes to a small part of the observed racial differences in self-reported health." Therefore, the conclusion that racism causes poor health is a much more likely explanation for the association seen repeatedly in these studies than is the suggestion that self-directed mobility (or the lack thereof) creates the connection. Put simply, the best explanation for why people in racist regions have poor health is that racism causes poor health.

To be sure, structural racism has a particularly pernicious impact on minority health. Despite progress in some health outcomes, structural racism accounts for the fact that African Americans remain among the least healthy populations in America. In many key areas, the racial divide in health is tragically widening. For example, the gap in the infant mortality rates between Black and White babies born in the United States is larger today than it was in 1850, fifteen years before slavery ended.[50] Although overall differences in US life expectancy for Black and White populations are shrinking, the trends vary widely among the nation's fifty states and among locations within states.[51] For example, in segregated cities, the differential life expectancy can be as large as twenty years.[52] The disturbing racial differences persist, even after controlling for income and education. But make no mistake about it, structural racism is a danger to the health of people of all races. Indeed, the COVID-19 pandemic showed that structural racism threatens to destroy not only our health but also the future of our economy and democracy.

During the COVID-19 pandemic, more than 334,000 people of all races and ethnicities died tragically, defying the notion that disease could be limited to the poor or marginalized segments of our population. The entire American population was affected as all in-person work, study, and communication ceased. The economy came to a virtual halt; catastrophically, US unemployment rose to 14.7 percent, the worst since the Great Depression.[53] People in low-wage, essential positions delivered groceries, health care, and take-out meals to people who sheltered in the safety of their homes. Arguably, Americans from majority or privileged population groups took the virus less seriously while it affected predominately older and minority communities. Eventually, however, coronavirus's explosive growth was driven in no small part by structural racism but affected us all. We all were locked down at home; restricted in our movement and choice; robbed of the freedom to work, the liberty to worship, or the autonomy to walk where we chose. In this way, the COVID-19 pandemic demonstrates how structural racism makes all of society less free. Not only does structural racism unfairly advantage the life chances of some communities and unfairly disadvantage opportunities for other communities because of race, but it also wastes precious human resources of the entire society.[54]

Connecting the Dots

Taken together, the studies linking structural racism to increased death and disease, and the pandemic's highlighting of disproportionately poor health in marginalized communities, teach three critical lessons. These lessons underlie a comprehensive theoretical framework for understanding the relationship between structural racism and population health.

Lesson number one is that the structural inequality revealed in the COVID-19 crisis is structural *racism* because it is the direct result of raced-based discriminatory allocation of resources and opportunity to people. Lesson number two is twofold: not only does this form of racism contradict the very goals that the US Constitution and laws are designed to serve, but each pathway through which structural racism disproportionately caused COVID-19 deaths was constructed or enabled by laws. The urbanization pathway revealed a physically crowded landscape only made possible by a relentless network of race-motivated laws such as segregation ordinances, restrictive covenants, zoning ordinances, and mortgage lending regulations. That this landscape was then resource-starved by inadequate access to transportation, breathable air, safe recreational spaces, and healthy food sources is also enabled by law. Uneven application of zoning, business, and land use laws as well as indifferent enforcement of antidiscrimination enactments and building code regulations created the inadequate housing, food, and transportation in these urban landscapes. These forces also increased people's exposure to pollution and violence. From the use of property and vagrancy laws during the colonial period to the inequitable application of labor and civil rights laws today, the concentration of low-wage, vulnerable jobs in Black, Latino, and Indigenous communities is the work of structural racism.

In summary, all these features contributed mightily to the disproportionately high morbidity and mortality of the Black population during the COVID-19 pandemic. The point not to be missed for the purpose of this analysis is this: the SARS-CoV-2 virus disproportionately killed minority populations because of structural racism resulting from government and private actors' use and misuse of their legally conferred authority.

Lesson number three is that structural racism shortens lives and compromises the quality of life for all of us, regardless of race, ethnicity, gender, income, or wealth. We are all worse off because of structural racism. The interpersonal prejudice that fuels structural racism is a taxing, toxic, health-harming stressor on the body for both perpetrator and victim of the racist's ideology. No individual escapes the adverse health impacts of racism entirely. Moreover, we are all worse off because structural racism damages every structure it touches. Like SARS-CoV-2 itself, the disease this virus causes may strike some people more seriously than it does others, but everyone it touches gets sick. Structural racism sickens every social, economic, and governmental institution it touches. All are connected, and all are susceptible.

A Theory of Structural Racism and Population Health

The final lesson to be drawn from the COVID-19 pandemic is to understand how structural racism affects health. Figure 1.3 illustrates the three theoretical assertions that underlie this book. First, structural racism is the aggregative systemization of *interpersonal prejudice* that collectively operates as a fundamental cause of unjust health in America. As long as it is allowed to flourish, this form of racism will shape-shift to relentlessly manifest itself throughout societal institutions, including the US health-care system. Structural racism will produce wildly disparate living, working, and health conditions between Black and White populations unless and until it is directly targeted and addressed. That is, no matter what interventions are conceived to address interpersonal prejudice at the individual level, or even to improve intermediate factors that contribute to health disparities and the social determinants of communities' health, structural racism will doggedly adjust to ensure that racial gaps in health and social outcomes persist and grow.

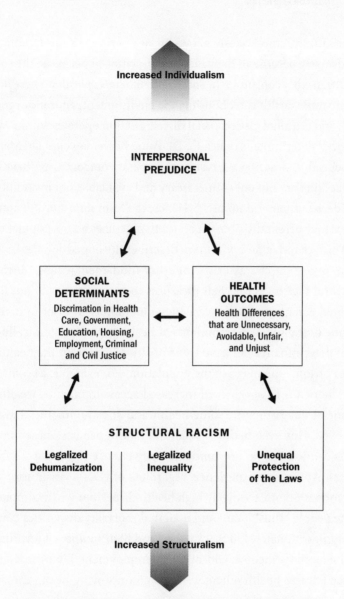

Increased Individualism

INTERPERSONAL PREJUDICE

SOCIAL DETERMINANTS

Discrimation in Health Care, Government, Education, Housing, Employment, Criminal and Civil Justice

HEALTH OUTCOMES

Health Differences that are Unnecessary, Avoidable, Unfair, and Unjust

STRUCTURAL RACISM

Legalized Dehumanization

Legalized Inequality

Unequal Protection of the Laws

Increased Structuralism

FIGURE 1.3: Structural Racism and Population Health: A Conceptual Framework.

Second, structural racism allows racial discrimination—treating people adversely because of their race or ethnicity—to permeate the societal institutions that constitute the *social determinants of health*. These institutions include health care, housing, the environment, education, government, and criminal justice: racial discrimination operates within each of the social determinants of health. Dr. Paula Braveman cites Dr. Margaret Whitehead to describe the resultant disparate outcomes as "health differences that are not only unnecessary and avoidable, but in addition are considered unfair and unjust."[55] Hence, the term *unjust health* aptly describes the current distribution of health outcomes across populations in the America today, and *just health* describes the hoped-for ideal.

An important characteristic of every fundamental cause, including structural racism, is that half measures to correct them do not help—they make matters worse. Reducing vulnerability to discrimination in any one of the social determinants of health but not systemically in all social determinants can have some positive impact on the health outcomes of some members of the population. For example, as some African Americans have achieved increased access to income, wealth, and the social determinants, some health and social outcomes have also improved. However, because structural racism persists, these improvements cannot and do not fundamentally change the exposure that all African Americans experience, regardless of class to institutionalized discrimination or excessively high health disparities when compared to White people. Thus, infant and maternal mortality disparities continue to disproportionately kill Black babies and their mothers, notwithstanding the mother's income, education, or employment. Likewise, efforts to reduce adverse health outcomes through improving health care, clinical research, or workforce diversity will only marginally narrow racial gaps in health outcomes but will not significantly reduce and can never eradicate health disparities overall until the foundational influences of structural racism are addressed.

Finally, our founders, legislatures, and courts are the primary mechanisms that construct and empower *structural racism*. At the base of the diagram in figure 1.3, I identify the three legal components of structural racism: legalized dehumanization of disfavored populations, legalized inequality, and unequal protection of the laws. These legal mechanisms erect the indispensable platform on which structural racism stands and are the subject of chapters 2 and 3.

How Law Institutionalizes Prejudice

Before delving deeply into the legal origins of structural racism, we need to understand how laws institutionalize racism. They multiply the scope and influence that individual-level prejudices have throughout society, effectively erecting the structures of racism that are embedded in a society's culture and government. For example, law plays a leading role in organizing the structural separation of the races through segregated housing. Thus, law makes the association between poor minority health and inferior, segregated housing possible. For example, during the period from 1900 to 1920, cities and towns throughout the South enacted laws decreeing that Black and White inhabitants could not live in the same neighborhoods or houses. As recently as the late 1960s, courts across the country also enforced restrictive racial covenants to ensure that American neighborhoods remained racially segregated. And separate-but-equal discriminatory laws controlled federally financed lending institutions, hospital development and construction, and GI home ownership programs for veterans. All these laws directly constructed a rock-solid edifice of national residential segregation because of structural racism.

Similarly, other laws gave structure to disseminate racial prejudice through various societal institutions. For instance, school financing laws relegate minority children in low-income communities to inferior public schools. Moreover, zoning ordinances permit environmentally hazardous highways, power plants, landfills, and marijuana dispensaries to proliferate near elementary, middle, and high schools in minority communities. And today, police presence is permitted to militarize our children's educational environments. All these laws, which indirectly ensure poor educational attainment, will plague the health of African Americans throughout the course of their lives, because of structural racism. The core assertion of this book, therefore, is that to eradicate health inequity, we need to change the laws that support structural racism.

Figure 1.3 shows the dynamic and destructive nature of the interaction between the law, structural racism, and health. The five bidirectional arrows in the figure are important. Ultimately, they all connect structural racism with interpersonal prejudice to illustrate the reciprocal, chicken-and-egg nature of the law as the mechanism that both reflects and shapes the social norms of cross-racial relationships. The law may operate as an expression of citizens' or officials' individually held, bigoted social norms. But it may also create social norms by segregating populations from one another and then lending its authoritative imprimatur to validate that separation. Laws can both cause discrimination (e.g., the separate-but-equal doctrine the US Supreme Court announced in *Plessy v. Ferguson*) and be caused by discrimination (e.g., anti-miscegenation laws). In summary, figure 1.3 displays the scope of influence that racism has as it becomes increasingly structural moving from the top, where racism infects individual, interpersonal relationships, to the bottom, where racism shapes the overall structure of where people live, work, and play.

The bidirectional arrows also show the damage from both explicit and implicit interpersonal prejudice. When permitted to flourish, prejudice fuels racial discrimination and limits access to the institutions that control essential resources for good health. For example, racial discrimination in school admissions limits African Americans' opportunities to have the high-quality education that White students enjoy. Racial discrimination also generates great disparities in White and non-White students' access to such resources as experienced teachers, small classes, advanced curricula, and enriching extracurricular programs. The resulting differences in educational attainment are thus no surprise. Neither are the disparate earnings that disfavored groups will have because of inferior employment, income, wealth accumulation, housing, neighborhoods, and more. Compounding the problem, when marginalized populations experience or exhibit poor social and health outcomes, their vulnerability to discrimination increases. The multidirectional arrows also illustrate that racism in interpersonal interactions directly hurts mental and physical health outcomes, while the disproportionately poor health outcomes that minority groups experience can negatively inform the attitudes and stereotypes individuals form about people who do not look like them.

In closing, we can apply the theoretical framework illustrated in figure 1.3 to better understand that the racially unbalanced impact of the COVID-19 pandemic derives from structural racism. No one would argue that individual prejudice was the sole or even the direct cause of the disproportionate morbidity and mortality that African Americans suffered during the pandemic. Yet figure 1.3 reflects the empirical evidence that the disproportionate prevalence of medical comorbidities among minority populations is evidence of the biologization of individual, interpersonal prejudices that aggregate to form structural racism. Furthermore, the same types of interpersonal prejudices informed public and private decision-makers at various levels—city councils, real estate agents, residents, and judges—to use law to segregate minority communities in densely populated, unhealthy neighborhoods. Cumulatively, these decisions institutionalized racial discrimination in all the social determinants, ensuring disproportionate representation of minority populations in low-wage or "essential" jobs, crowded cities, or isolated Indigenous reservations. Interpersonal prejudice was also institutionalized in the health-care system, diminishing the quantity and quality of preventive health care that minority populations received before and during the pandemic and will receive after it. The structural nature of housing segregation confined vulnerable minority populations in densely populated cities, with inferior access to healthy foods and recreational spaces as well as discretionary time to enjoy them. These social disparities contributed significantly to the underlying biological comorbidities such as diabetes and heart disease that predisposed minority populations to higher death and disease from the virus.

My father, if he were alive and reading this book today, may have lost interest in the details of the ecosocial theory of racism and health that I have presented in this chapter.[56] But I am sure he would have appreciated and agreed with its conclusion: that structural racism does grievous harm to the health of American people of all races, injures the American economy, and makes a travesty of the promise for a just and equitable future that our national creed purports to guarantee for our children.

2

LEGALIZED DEHUMANIZATION

By the laws of the country from whence I came, I was deprived of myself—of my own body, soul, and spirit, and I am free only because I succeeded in escaping the clutches of the man who claimed me as his property.
—Frederick Douglass, 1845

All of our humanity is dependent upon recognizing the humanity in others.
—Archbishop Desmond Tutu

In many ways, this chapter—describing the dehumanization of African Americans as a foundation of structural racism—is the darkest and most disturbing of this entire book. Therefore, now is a good time to introduce my mother—Marion ("Mae") Griffin Bowen, to introduce a bright ray of hope. She, like my father, died before her time and would have lived longer if she had enjoyed equal access to the opportunities available to White women during her lifetime. Still, she lived to laugh and bring joy to every life she touched, even under the worst of circumstances. Her story will help illustrate the legalized racial dehumanization described in this chapter. Of note, although I was advised to stop calling my mother "Mommy" once I became an adult, I never did. Therefore, as I describe my mother's contribution to overcoming the systemic dehumanization of Black people in this country, readers also will know her as Mommy.

Dehumanization is the term social psychologists use to describe the process of denying the human status of a person or group of people by discounting their capacity for conscious experience, rational thought, or emotional feeling.[1] Dehumanization can operate at many levels, from individual to community-wide. It can be blatant and explicit, or it can be subtle and covert. Dehumanization may cause the outright commission of cruel violations against another, or it may influence a callous omission. At bottom, the process allows a person or group of people to treat another group of people inhumanely, simply by denying their humanity. Throughout history, dehumanization has paved the way for humans to justify to themselves that they may commit unspeakable atrocities against other humans by convincing themselves that their victims are less than human. This chapter describes the history of the dehumanization of Black people—a history that is both reflected in and advanced by the American legal system. It also examines how legalized dehumanization of Black populations persists today. I will draw out the clear connections between legalized dehumanization and poor health, both in the past and in the present. Legalized dehumanization is an indispensable cause of excessive Black morbidity and mortality in this country, because it is a key component of structural racism. Indeed, dehumanization is what makes structural racism morally possible.

The work of dehumanization is to substantially and sufficiently distinguish oneself from another group of people, so that treatment that plainly would violate human decency if directed toward you becomes permissible, justified, or even desirable in light of the rationalization that the other group is nothing like you. If the other group is not human, then there is no need to treat its members as human. In the case of *blatant dehumanization*, this rationalization is accomplished by associating others with animals or objects to reduce their status and worth below that of other humans. Examples include associations of Black Americans with apes, or Muslims with camels, and Arabs with dogs or other animals.[2] This degrading association allows a group of people to assert that Black Americans, Muslims, or Arabs have nothing in common with themselves or other human beings but instead share characteristics and therefore deserve the same regard as much lesser beings.

Alternatively, dehumanization can affect individuals on a subtle or unconscious level. Subtle or implicit dehumanization similarly affects attitudes and behavior toward others, but instead of outright nonhuman associations, subtle dehumanization assumes that others lack certain uniquely human tendencies. This subtle dehumanization, also called *infrahumanization*, works more indirectly.[3] It denies the similarity between oneself and others, by robbing another of the feelings or attributes that define you as human. Subtle dehumanization, for example, underlies beliefs that Black people experience pain differently than White people do, have lesser cognitive ability than White people have, or do not share the same basic physical needs that other humans have.[4] Subtle dehumanization can influence people to deny medical treatment, support excessively cruel laws and policies, or withhold necessary resources from those considered less valued or with whom they have little in common. Presumptions informed by both blatant and subtle dehumanization of Black people pervasively animated American colonial law. Moreover, these presumptions have continued to inform American law today. The deeply damaging result of dehumanization is American law's devastating impact on Black American health historically and today. Figure 2.1 describes the relationship between legalized dehumanization and health outcomes.

The health outcomes of dehumanization as shown in figure 2.1 also ultimately had an effect on my mother's health. She died an avoidable death at age sixty-one; the cause of her death was meningitis. Bacterial meningitis is commonly treated with antibiotics except when, as was the case for my mother, patients live in underserved urban (or rural) medical communities. She complained of an earache when we spoke on New Year's Day, and she was hospitalized a day later. She died on January 3 in a small hospital that did not see fit, until it was too late, to treat the sepsis that had developed from an ear infection. But though my mother's death was premature, throughout her life, she triumphed over dehumanization against all odds. Her story follows chronologically.

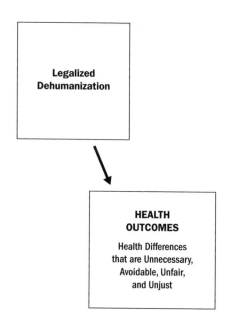

FIGURE 2.1: Legalized Dehumanization and Unjust American Health.

Blatant Dehumanization: Colonial Law

Even before slavery became institutionalized, colonial laws dehumanized Black inhabitants by elevating the status of White servants above
Black servants as early as the 1630s. New England colonies enacted provincial laws that provided, for example, that White servants could never
be sold for life, while Black indentured servants were eligible for this
interminable fate.[5] Moreover, in colonies that prohibited slavery, the law
evinced the difference with which White people and those of African
descent were regarded as humans. Rhode Island, for example, enacted
in 1652 an antislavery law that was one of the most stringent prohibitions
against enslaving Black people. Yet even the language of the statute distinguished "blacke mankind" from "English men" and "servants." Rhode
Island's law provided:

> Whereas, there is a common course practiced amongst English men to
> buy negers, to that end they may have them for service or slaves forever;

for the preventing of such practices among us, let it be ordered that no blacke mankind or white being forced by covenant bond, or otherwise, to serve any man or his assighnes longer than ten years, or until they come to bee twentie four years of age, if they bee taken in under fourteen, from the time of their cominge within the liberties of this collonie. And at the end of terme of ten years to sett them free, as the manner is with the English servants. And that man that will not let them goe free, or shall sell them away elsewhere, to that end that they may bee enslaved to others for a long time hee or they shall forfeit to the Collonie forty pounds.[6]

Thus, colonial slavers prospered in Rhode Island, where the antislavery law provided a break-even price that made trading in black bodies profitable for those not inclined to set black people free after a term of service "as the manner is with the English servants." This law reveals that "blacke mankind" is essentially different from a "white being forced by covenant or bond" to serve for ten years, in that the White person must go free, whereas the "blacke" could be owned as property for life. The statute allowed colonists not only to trade in "blacke" humans as property but also to pass ownership of their bodies, as though the people were animals, simply by paying a fee of forty pounds. Figure 2.2, an 1834 engraving, showing colonists determining the purchase price of a woman as one would purchase a raw meat. The engraving was published in a book by an abolitionist named George Bourne, who compiled pictures of slavery in the United States to expose what he called "demoniac slavery's turpitude."

The law of slavery legalized dehumanization. For example, in a seminal treatise, Thomas Reade Cobb, reporter for the Georgia Supreme Court in the mid-1800s, explained that slaves had a "double character" under the law. They were both persons and property. Slaves were persons under the criminal law and held accountable for their criminal behavior. But they were also property for purposes of contracts of sale or hire. As property, if they were shown to be physically or morally "defective" for contractual purposes, slaveholders could sue for breach of

FIGURE 2.2: "Selling Females by the Pound." Source: Library of Congress
Z62-30823.

warranty just as if they were livestock or a piece of farm equipment. Slaveholders had the right to sue other parties for damage to their property, such as when an overseer too zealously beat or neglected the enslaved people's bodies, making them less productive machines for profit. The law then stripped Black people of their humanity and instead constructed a "double identity as human subjects and the objects of property relations at *one and the same time.*"[7]

The blatant dehumanization that underlay these laws did not necessarily grow out of hostility. It could also emanate from apathy or ambivalence toward Black people. Thomas Jefferson displayed such apathy when he likened Black people to animals in describing the difference between Black and White people in his 1787 book, *Notes on the State of Virginia*:

And is this difference of no importance? Is it not the foundation of a greater or less share of beauty in the two races? Are not the fine mixtures of red and white, the expressions of every passion by greater or less suffusions of color in the one, preferable to that eternal monotony, which reigns in the countenances, that immoveable veil of black which covers all the emotions of the other race? Add to these, flowing hair, a more elegant symmetry of form, their own judgment in favor of the whites, declared by their preference of them, as uniformly as is the preference of the orangutan for the black women over those of his own species. The circumstance of superior beauty, is thought worthy attention in the propagation of our horses, dogs, and other domestic animals; why not in that of man?[8]

In another stunning example of the law's embrace of blatant dehumanization, the captain of the slave ship *Zong* successfully sued in court to recover insurance payment for the loss of his slave cargo at sea in 1781. Captain Luke Collingwood murdered 132 Black human beings by throwing them overboard into the ocean, some shackled, others jumping before they were bound, but all while they were alive. Captain Collingwood and his crew engaged in this mass murder when the ship had run dangerously short of water, suffered an outbreak of dysentery, and by-passed its destination. To save the remaining people aboard, he ordered the crew to carry out the murders on three successive days. Collingwood won insurance payments for the people he had killed; his argument appealed to the doctrine of "public necessity." The White jurors found that the "Cap" had done what was right to save the remaining crew members, since the enslaved people were no more than animals. In summarizing the case after the jury found for the slavers, William Murphy (the Earl of Mansfield), who was the lord chief justice of the king's bench, explained,

> The Matter left to the Jury was, whether [the mass murder arose] . . . from necessity[,] for they had no doubt (tho' it shocks one very much) the Case of Slaves was the same as if Horses had been thrown over board. . . . The Question was, whether there was not an Absolute Necessity for throwing them over board to save the rest, [and] the Jury were of opinion there was.[9]

One historian aptly summed up this horrific dehumanization, saying that when Chief Justice Lord Mansfield likened the enslaved humans to animals, "he kills the victims of the *Zong* a second time. The slave-traders had physically destroyed them in the massacre; Mansfield refused them a posthumous human existence under the law."[10]

An engraving titled *Negrier Poursuivi, Jetant ses Negres à la Mer* (Slave ship being pursued, throwing its blacks into the sea), from the educational website Slavery Images: A Visual Record of the African Slave Trade and Slave Life in the Early African Diaspora, does not depict the *Zong* massacre.[11] But it is an artist's rendering of another one of innumerable reported incidents of the barbarous, indeed murderous, disposal of Black human beings who still lived and breathed but who, for whatever reason, had lost their usefulness as property. Thomas Jefferson, Chief Judge Lord Mansfield, Captain Collingwood, and even the *Zong's* insurers had no reason to fear the publicity of a lawsuit to deny an insurance claim on murdered Black bodies. Each circumstance involving these men offers examples of what psychologists call extreme blatant dehumanization. The attitudes the White men held reveal the worst kind of prejudice and exemplify the social norms that permitted White people from all walks of life and every societal institution to enjoy legal protection while excluding Black people entirely from full humanity.

In his seminal book titled *The Nature of Prejudice*, Gordon Allport explained how these dehumanizing attitudes held by individuals can escalate to structural racism, institutionalized violence against people and property, and, ultimately, violent hatred and aggression leading to genocide.[12] One of Allport's most important contributions has been to explain the clear relationship between horridly objectionable individualized bigotry and collectively racist violence—both political and physical—against human beings. Jefferson's assessment of the differences between White and Black people, therefore, represents the blatant dehumanization that prevailed among *individual* European colonists. But in the aggregate, his and others' views supplied the virulent fuel that drove governments to codify the exercise of White dominance and authoritarianism over enslaved African American human beings.

American slavery is but one example of the viciousness made possible by blatant dehumanization. Social scientists cite countless examples from wars and genocides, where one group of people acts with extreme cruelty and violence toward another group because of a collective perception of blatant dehumanization.[13] During the Holocaust, for example, Nazis dehumanized the Jews they slaughtered by referring to them as subhuman "rats," "parasites," and "vermin."[14] Racism, at the core of the Nazi ideology, drove the violent movement toward its goal of achieving an imagined new strain of Nordic human perfection. In 1994, Rwandan militias intent on genocide dehumanized the Tutsi people, calling them "inyenzi," which means cockroaches, as they brutally executed a million Tutsi and Hutu people in murderous pursuit of their goal of ethnic cleansing.[15] During the Vietnam War, American troops carried out unspeakable atrocities such as the Mỹ Lai massacre against people they dehumanized by calling them "dinks, gooks, slopes, slants."[16] This dehumanization cloaked the moral travesty of bombings in peasant villages, search-and-destroy missions, and campaigns to deny food to defenseless rural populations. Plainly, the first impact of legalized dehumanization is that it supplies justification for untold cruelty. A second by-product of dehumanization is subtler.

Colonial America and Subtle Legal Approaches

Clearly, dehumanization need not grow from explicit hostility but can also implicitly deny that another group of people shares such uniquely human traits as warmth, affection, and pain.[17] In this way, subtle dehumanization provides a basis for indifference to human suffering. This subtle attitude also allows people to profess their commitment to equality, justice, and freedom while ignoring the presence of manifest inequality, pervasive injustice, and human bondage. Jefferson's writings again provide a pristine example of how subtle dehumanization of Black people in colonial America could dull the collective senses to slavery's horror. On the one hand, historians at Jefferson's Monticello laud Jefferson's moral stance on slavery:

> Throughout his entire life, Thomas Jefferson was publicly a consistent opponent of slavery. Calling it a "moral depravity" and a "hideous blot," he believed that slavery presented the greatest threat to the survival of the new American Nation. Jefferson also thought that slavery was contrary to the laws of nature, which decreed that everyone had a right to personal liberty.[18]

Yet Jefferson himself participated in this hideousness and depravity to the tune of claiming ownership of six hundred African American human beings, apparently valuing the wealth and political advantages the peculiar institution afforded him and his new nation above the rights that he declared belonged to all men. How could this be? Dehumanization theory provides an answer: Jefferson's subtle dehumanization of Black people allowed him to regard them as less than human and thereby relieved his moral conscience. Again, in *Notes on the State of Virginia*, he compared Black sensibilities to White ones:

They are more ardent after their female: but love seems with them to be more an eager desire, than a tender delicate mixture of sentiment and sensation. Their griefs are transient. Those numberless afflictions, which render it doubtful whether heaven has given life to us in mercy or in wrath, are less felt, and sooner forgotten with them. In general, their existence appears to participate more of sensation than reflection.[19]

Dehumanization in this instance is cloaked in pseudoscientific-sounding observations that offer a false assessment of differences that in turn justify inhumane treatment. The belief that "their griefs are transient" and "less felt" by Black people made the untenable tolerable to Jefferson and to the nation. Dehumanization served as a powerful national narcotic to numb the sensibilities to the horror of selling people. When courts were faced with settling ownership disputes among slaveholders, the law could callously frame the issue at bar by likening Black human beings to animals:

The same question might arise upon the sale of a gang of negroes, one of which, unknown or know to the plaintiff, had been exposed to small-pox; or to the sale of a plantation of horses, stock, negroes and dogs . . . so as to cause great loss, would the vendor in such a case, be liable for all the consequential damages? . . . Nor is the plaintiff in this instance responsible for the remote consequences which the instructions assumed.[20]

Subtle or implicit dehumanization, unlike blatant dehumanization, is less likely to be associated with the attitudes and behaviors that lead directly to large-scale atrocities such as mass killings. Instead, this subtle denial of humanity creates a third by-product in addition to the indifference toward, and tolerance of, tragic outcomes and even absolution from any responsibility for these outcomes. Furthermore, the subtle attitude inspires aggressive control over those who have been denied their humanity, perhaps as a form of self-preservation, allowing the deniers to escape not only retribution but also any guilt for the pain and suffering that dehumanization allows.[21] For example, according to one recent study of a large, representative group of White Americans, the researchers found that White people who dehumanized Black people were more likely to support punitive policies such as three-strikes criminal justice legislation that had disproportionately affected Black citizens. These results held, even after the researchers controlled for political party affiliation, conservatism, racial resentment, and stereotyping.[22] Subtle dehumanization enables a dominant group of people to void themselves of compassion or even acceptance of those who are different while giving them license to rationalize aggression and minimize responsibility for their own misdeeds.[23] In another recent study of Americans' attitudes toward Muslims and Mexican immigrants, Dr. Nour Kteily and Dr. Emile Bruneau showed that Americans blatantly dehumanize these groups of people and that the subtle dehumanizing views are associated with support for aggressive policies in the name of antiterrorism.[24] Thus, colonial America and modern America have depended on both blatant and subtle dehumanization to establish a hierarchical social order in which African Americans and other people of color are thoroughly and unequivocally subjugated to White dominance. All forms of dehumanization continue to supply the requisite underlying amoral code on which the hegemonic laws firmly rest, just as they did in the days of chattel slavery.

Legal Dehumanization

According to historian Jonathan Alpert, "American slavery was above all else a product of the law," promulgated by legislatures and enforced by courts.[25] A brief survey of colonial law not only proves Alpert's point but also reveals how extensively the dehumanizing view of Black people was codified into law. In Article 91 of a Massachusetts law titled Body of Liberties, the legislature referenced the Holy Bible to support subtle dehumanization that distinguished White Christians from the subhuman Black population:

> There shall never be any bond slaverie, villinage or captivitie amongs us unless it be lawfull captives taken in just warres, and such strangers as willingly selle themselves or are sold to us. And these shall have all the liberties and Christian usages which the law of God established in Israell concerning such persons doeth morally require. This exempts none from servitude who shall be Judged thereto by Authoritie.

The legal distinction in this Massachusetts code provision, of course, was that by referring to Black people and Indigenous people as either prisoners of war or "strangers," the law distinguished them from Christian brethren, who, according to Old Testament laws, were Israel's descendants and thus prohibited from being held as slaves. In this way, Black and Indigenous people were deemed legally different from White Christians and therefore biblically eligible to become White people's possessions.[26] By putting distance between themselves (White Christians who identified with the chosen Israelite nation) and enslaved people (Black and other "strangers"), the Massachusetts lawmakers could ignore the immorality of trading humans as property by subtly denying that the Black inhabitants were human at all. Notably, the states of Maryland and Virginia enacted provisions to confirm that just because a Negro slave might convert to Christianity, spiritual salvation could not make a Black person free as other humans were under the law.

This Maryland law, enacted in 1671, provides an example of the contorted reasoning needed to construct racist structures based on a fundamentally false notion of dehumanization. In the first instance, the legislature expressed pity and grief for the enslaved people in the province, saluting the practice of baptizing African Americans:

> Whereas Severall of the good people of this Province have been discouraged to import into or purchase within this Province any Negroes or other

Slaves and such as have Imported or purchased any such Negroes or Slaves have to the great displeasure of Almighty God and the prejudice of the Soules of those poore people Neglected to instruct them in the Christian faith or to Endure or permit them to Receive the holy Sacrament of Babtisme for the remission of their Sinns.

But quickly, the statute takes a sinister turn to disabuse "good people" who were White from any crisis of conscience. The law corrected any

mistake and ungrounded apprehension that by becoming Christians they and the Issues of their bodies are actually manuited and made free and discharged from their Servitude and bondage be itt declared and Enacted . . . That where any Negro or Negroes Slave or Slaves being in Servitude of bondage is are or shall become Christian or Christians and . . . Receive the Holy Sacrament of Babtizme before or after his her or their Importation in to this Province the same is not shall or ought the same be . . . taken to be or amount unto a manumission or freeing Inlarging or discharging any such . . . Negroes Slave or Slaves . . . or their Issue . . . from their Servitude . . . any opinion or other matter or thing to the Contrary in any wise Notwithstanding.[27]

These examples of provincial law from the American colonies demonstrate that subtle and blatant forms of dehumanization can operate together, informing legal treatment of a group of people, with or without out a conscious choice to be harmful or degrading.[28] In fact, as the Maryland provision demonstrates, neither blatant nor subtle dehumanization need arise from dislike of another group. In that case, the legal pronouncement that declared Black people were to remain unalterably the property of White people was cloaked in tender expressions of concern for "the prejudice of the Soules of those poore people," showing that dehumanizing assumptions are more functional than emotional. Both subtle and blatant dehumanization separate and sort people into groups.

When dehumanization operates to attribute fewer human traits to another group of people, the dehumanized group is known as the "out-group," which compares unfavorably to the humanity possessed by their own people, known as the "in-group."[29] The relationship between blatant and subtle dehumanization is still a matter of investigation among social scientists. However, there is abundant evidence that colonial lawmakers embraced both.

In Maryland, for example, the 1665 law that provided that Black people would be relegated to slavery for life reduced children of a White-Black union to the same lowly status as their enslaved fathers if a White woman stooped so low as to marry a Negro.

> Bee it Enacted by the Right Honorable the Lord Proprietary by the advice and Consent of the upper and lower house of this present General Assembly That al Negroes or other slaves already within the Province And all Negroes and other slaves to bee hereafter imported into the Province shall serve Durante Vita (for life) And all Children born of any Negro or other slave shall be Slaves as their ffathers were for the terme of their lives.[30]

In this same enactment, the Maryland legislature expressed its disdain for interracial marriages and their offspring, providing further that White women who married slaves became slaves themselves:

> And forasmuch as divers freeborne English women forgettful of their free Condition and to the disgrace of our Nation doe intermarry with Negro Slaves by which also divers suites may arise touching the Issue of such woemen and a great damage doth befall the Masters of such Negros for prevention whereof for deterring such freeborne women from such shamefull Matches Bee it further enacted by the Authority advice and Consent aforesaid That whatsoever free borne woman shall inter marry with any slave from and after the Last day of this present Assembly shall serve the master of such slave during the life of her husband

And that all the Issue of such freeborne woemen soe marryed shall be slaves as their fathers were.

Preposterously, the law did not, however, visit the same fate on men who had sexual relations with enslaved Black women. For example, to allow White men to sexually dominate enslaved women but to ensure their offspring would remain property, Virginia's General Assembly enacted this slave code provision in 1662:

> Whereas some doubts have arisen whether children got by any English- man upon a Negro woman should be slave or free be it therefore enacted and declared by this present Grand Assembly, that all children born in this country shall be held bond or free only according to the condition of the mother.[31]

Whether White people married Negro women or men, the law made clear that the practice was a disgrace. Later, in 1678, Maryland law codified dehumanization by requiring that all births, marriages, and deaths in each county were to be recorded by the department of health. However, the law excluded some whose lives were not worthy of record:

> Bee itt Enacted by the Right Honble the Lord Proprietary by& with the advice and Consent of this present Generall Assembly and the Authority of the same that the names Surnames and places of abode of all man- ner of persons within this Province Except Negroes Indians & Molottos that shall from and after the Publicacon of this Act be borne married or buryed within this Province.[32]

Legalized dehumanization may also take the form of ascribing superhuman—monstrous powers—to a group of people who are to be feared and exterminated for the threat they present.[33] For example, Vir- ginia passed a law in October 1669 to legally absolve White citizens from all responsibility of violence against Black people even if the violence resulted in their death. Written into the *law* was the dehumanizing justification that Black people could not be controlled by any other means except by the use of deadly force or other violence:

> Whereas the only law in force for the punishment of refractory servants resisting their master, mistress, or overseer cannot be inflicted upon Negroes, nor the obstinacy of many of them be suppressed by other than violent means be it enacted and declared by this Grand Assembly if any slave resists his master (or other by his master's order correcting him) and by the extremity of the correction should chance to die, that his death shall not be accounted a felony, but the master (or that other person appointed by the master to punish him) be acquitted from molestation, since it cannot be presumed that premeditated malice (which alone makes murder a felony) should induce any man to destroy his own estate.[34]

Virginia's law was not unique; many states had such laws, and courts regularly enforced White owners' legal rights to punish and kill their slaves while simultaneously protecting the valuable human property from destruction because of excessively severe punishment.[35] In 1690, Connecticut's General Court, observing that Black servants were running away, passed a law to require that all "negroe or negroes shall be required to have a pass in order to travel outside the boundaries of their towns, and anyone, slave or free could stop a Negroe and have them brought before a magistrate if they were found without a pass." Then, in 1717, Connecticut became the first colony to legally forbid black residents in Connecticut from owning land.[36] Massachusetts laws managed the movement of Black people and Indians by enacting a legal curfew.

The same legalized dehumanization that prevailed in the American colonies seeped into the founding documents of the new nation. However, these historical accounts of legalized dehumanization must not be read as bygone history. Instead, America has steadily built on the foundation laid under colonial and early American law to construct an edifice of dehumanizing law that persists today.

Legalized Dehumanization in the Twentieth Century

As the United States entered the twentieth century, Black Americans were subjected to what one historian calls "an epidemic of lynching that replaced the 'disciplining effect of slavery.'" The prevalence of this violence was evidence that White dominance was fragile in the United States. As a response to this potential loss of dominance, the law was charged with the unenviable task of maintaining a "rigid caste division between racial groups that were inextricably involved in the same culture, society, economy, and legal system." The crucial hegemonic work of legalized dehumanization was to maintain an uneasy and fraudulent social order. Expressly racist laws gave support to the psychological ruse of blatant dehumanization and expressly assigned different races dominant and inferior statuses. Laws that allowed White society to ignore the egregious effect of racial hierarchies enshrined subtle dehumanization in legitimacy. The legal system helped White people validate and rationalize their dehumanizing practices and absolve themselves of any guilt or reticence to treat Black and other marginalized communities in ways they themselves would not want to be treated.

The laws that constructed residential segregation were one of the most important examples of legalized blatant and subtle dehumanization. Segregated neighborhoods were created by municipal laws that expressly forbade one race from living next door to another race. When overt segregation ordinances became illegal, the law was used to enforce blatantly dehumanizing restrictive racial covenants in property deeds, so that one race could not sell or buy a house from another race. Subtle dehumanization was codified later as laws were used to restrict the process by which Black people might find equal housing, rather than their direct, legal entitlement to equal housing. Blatant legal prohibitions based on race were replaced with subtle obstacles that had the same segregationist effect. Lending laws, for example, ensured that mortgage funding was allocated according to redlined maps to maintain racial segregation. And when these laws were deemed unconstitutional, they were replaced by discriminatory zoning ordinances, mortgage lending laws, and land use laws designed to keep the races physically separated. Though racially neutral on their face, these laws preserved and protected residential segregation so effectively that today, the United States is barely less segregated by race than it was before the Civil Rights era.

Chapter 4 discusses the story and impact of segregation on health in further detail. But residential segregation laws are mentioned here to point out their role in systematizing dehumanization. Once populations were segregated, dehumanizing laws and policies could be precisely aimed at selected geographic locations to target groups by race. When Black and White groups were physically isolated from one another, the unfair distribution of resources and power by race was made simple. In this way, both expressly blatant dehumanization worked through laws to separate Black and White groups spatially, while subtly dehumanizing laws maintained subhuman conditions within geographic spaces accessible to Black people. Though structurally successful, legalized dehumanization was not always effective on the targeted psyche. My mother is a case in point.

My Mother's Fight (and Triumph) against Legalized Dehumanization

Mommy's weapon of choice against legalized dehumanization was to live in a way that discredited its abhorrent attitudes even while operating within the structures erected by the dehumanizing lies. As far as I can tell, she found so much pleasure in her own community, and so little to confirm the messages sent her way from outsiders, that the degradation was simply lost on her. And this observation is not to say that the dehumanizing messages were always subtle.

My mother was born and raised in a very small segregated town in eastern North Carolina. The laws that placed her family on one side of town and White families on another were blatant. Her parents picked peanuts and tobacco for subsistence wages. Seasonally, they made extra money by packing in boarders and selling meals to migrants who came to work in the fields. Even now, I can recall that when I went back "down South" to visit as a child, plenty about their work and their housing conditions was dehumanizing. But the legal infrastructure that set wages, permitted unsafe working conditions, or winked at dilapidated homes was the product of subtle dehumanization. Still, I recall seeing my mother revel in the warmth of extended family, her raucous laughter at church or during card games, and the pride she felt in sharing her amazing cooking. I saw this pleasure when my mother was at our home in New York City and whenever we traveled "down home" to our little Southern town; my mother found a way to be at home in her skin, regardless of her geographical limitations.

As a teen, Mommy moved north during the Great Migration, when my grandmother found work in New York City cleaning train cars on the Pennsylvania Railroad. Again, the work was backbreaking and dehumanizing, I am sure, but my mother never ever spoke ill of it. My grandmother supplemented this income as a day worker. This meant she stood with other "domestics" on an appointed street corner on weekends until women would drive by and select her to clean their houses for the day. Laws that permitted employers like the railroad to pay subsistence wages so employees must also hire themselves out like farm equipment are both blatantly and subtly dehumanizing.

My mother lived on the ground floor of a small tenement apartment building on 124th Street in Harlem. Though I never saw the building, I know it could not have been fancy, because the highest wages either of her parents ever earned came from the food service jobs they eventually got, cooking, cleaning, and driving for New York City public school kitchens. When my grandparents got these "good jobs," they moved downtown to East Harlem to live in the projects owned and developed by the New York City Housing Authority exclusively for more prosperous Black laborers. Theirs was Apartment 10G, and although I loved to visit there as a child, I look back and wonder where my mother found any privacy living with her parents there in the one-bedroom flat. As tiny as it was, a forest of green potted plants lined the back wall of the living room (which also served as the dining room, a second bedroom, and a guest room). I have albums dotted with photographs of my mother and her friends posing among those plants—dressed to the nines before an evening out on the town—looking for all the world as though they were part of a photoshoot in the Kew Royal Botanic Gardens of London.

My mother attended Washington Irving High School—known also as Girls Technical High School—where she majored in fashion design and sewing. Nothing about her education was intended to make her an educated woman or give her the choice to go to college with her White counterparts. Instead, she was educated by the public school system to go to work in a sweatshop. But substandard housing and education notwithstanding, dehumanizing work was not in my mother's vocabulary. Instead, she took her technical high school diploma and sashayed (so I am told) to Midtown Manhattan and got a job as a seamstress in the very tony B. Altman department store. There she chose to finish her training and become a true fashion icon and shopper extraordinaire. My mother was the best-dressed woman I have ever known. Ever. She made sure everyone around her was the best dressed they could possibly be. She made fashion shopping high art, buying for everyone she knew. I secretly believe she plotted to lure my then boyfriend (now husband) by buying him jackets and a winter coat when we came home from college during winter breaks! It worked.

The dehumanizing contrasts between her living conditions uptown in Harlem or the South Bronx and those of the people she saw daily in Midtown Manhattan seemed to do nothing but fuel my mother's penchant for advocacy and innovation. She transplanted what she could from the White world that had excluded her and put it to work enhancing the Black world that she loved. For example, she formed a committee of women, lobbied the church trustee board for funds, and built a first-rate nursery program at our Harlem church. In addition to the curriculum she developed, she found ways to decorate cribs, stock craft tables, and deck the walls in each room. As I recall, they looked like something from the pages of a Pottery Barn or FAO Schwarz catalog.

My mother sewed uniforms for the cheerleading squad of young girls to deck them out for the church league's Saturday basketball games. Though she only graduated from high school herself, she founded the church College Club to teach parents how to save for their kids' college education. And my personal favorite, because of the swanky outfits she wore, was the Blue Sect Celebrity Club that Mommy founded. The club aimed to help young married women save funds for vacation travel and fancy dress balls. Whenever she traveled, I remember that my mother and her friends stayed up all night to make matching hats, gloves, coats, dresses, *and* purses to go with dyed shoes for airplane trips. I could never understand what was so exciting about going to all the American Baptist Women's Conventions or other segregated venues she attended. But then she made it sound as if she had been to Bali when she returned home laden with trinkets from afar.

What was my mother's secret defense against dehumanization? I never asked her directly, but here is what I observed: She loved being an African American woman. She loved her African American family, friends, culture, history, food, church, and neighborhood. And most of all, she seemed to simply love Black *people* so much that she lived in a way that immunized her against the psychological scourge of dehumanization.

This is my surmise because of the beauty she always showed me in Blackness. Sometimes I caught her staring admiringly at me and my brother—and then she would just tell us we hung the moon. She found poetry celebrating Black culture by Langston Hughes, James Weldon Johnson, and others, and she taught me to memorize, dramatize, and recite the poems with pride at evening church programs. She bought toys and artwork that depicted Black faces. And looking back, I now note that when we started to attend Fieldston, she neither shunned nor sought out company or approval from White families. Sadly, I saw some Black families at Fieldston who lost themselves that way because they were awestruck by other cultures they deemed superior, and critical of their own. This is the intended consequence of dehumanization—a subtle but self-serving emphasis on the superiority of Whiteness or wealth. But instead, Mommy and Daddy made it abundantly—even *painfully*—clear that they had absolutely no patience for any hint that I preferred my private-school friends or lifestyle over my neighborhood friends and culture once I started traveling to Riverdale. Disrespecting what my parents loved about our Black culture was truly a capital offense in my household. Dehumanization did not stand a chance.

Mommy was not oblivious to dehumanizing injustices. She found them appalling. She was an outspoken advocate against them, in fact— many times to my naive embarrassment. I remember her once publicly shouting to lecture a crowd of Black and Latino shoppers she felt were being mistreated by a bargain basement store. She loudly admonished the crowd of perfect strangers to take their money elsewhere if the store could not give respectful service. She told them that they and their money had value. I, on the other hand, hid beneath a clothing rack, hoping not to be seen as she quite literally cleared the place out. We never returned.

But most often, my mother's advocacy was on behalf of individuals. She sat and talked for hours, encouraging young people to stay in school, stay married, or go out and change the world. When my mother died, I was astounded at her funeral service by the number of young people who rose to speak about how she had guided them. They spoke of how she had talked them into continuing their Harvard educations despite the loneliness and isolation they felt. I was amazed to hear about the numbers of people she had found jobs for at B. Altman, at Head Start, or in the New York City public school system. And I felt warmed by the many people who had to laugh out loud through their tears because of some absurd antics my mother had pulled.

Mommy's life as an extroverted socialite revolved around the neighbors she had in Harlem, the friends she made in public school, and the church community she shaped into a social and political juggernaut. The key, I have determined, to my mother's success in overcoming dehumanization was that she loved her own humanity—and nobody outside her community could disabuse her of that conviction. I will admit that I saw she was vulnerable to dehumanization from within her community—but that is a story for another book. Here, my mother's story of triumph over the psychology of dehumanization as an individual serves most importantly to underscore the overwhelming structural power that legalized dehumanization ultimately had over her as a member of a marginalized population group.

In the end, like my father, my mother had her life cut short when the structures of racism failed to place the high and equal value on her life that she deserved and that would have been afforded her if she had been White. As is often the case, the ambulance that was called to her segregated neighborhood took more than an hour to arrive. Despite being near death, she was taken to a nearby, now shuttered St. Mary's Hospital. St. Mary's had a reputation for providing inferior care to the predominately Black and Latino patients it then served. My mother's New York apartment was in the Crown Heights section of Brooklyn, which, at the time of her death, had been declared a "primary poverty area," with high unemployment, high crime rates, low family income, and a population that was 70 percent Black. By the time it closed, St. Mary's was reported to serve primarily poor and uninsured patients, principally through emergency room visits, which tripled the number of overnight stays.

St. Mary's was typical of many hospitals that deliver care in low-income and minority communities. It was poorly equipped, poorly funded, and poorly staffed to care for in-patient needs, even relatively straightforward ones like my mother's.[37] All she needed to live was a timely course of antibiotics. Yet, when her Harvard-educated children called to speak to physicians, the lack of enthusiasm (or perhaps capacity) for aggressively caring for this sixty-one-year-old Black church lady was palpable.

And so, dehumanization won that day and took my mother's life before she had lived it completely. She became one of an estimated nearly eighty-four thousand victims of structural racism—people who die preventable deaths each year because their race relegates them to inferior access to, and quality of, medical care in America.[38] Without question, the legalized dehumanization that undergirds structural racism had a tragic effect on my mother's life. The laws that concentrated poverty among the mostly Black population in Crown Heights ignored the failure of market forces to distribute equal or even adequate access to health care for that community. The system required no accountability for the substandard care that flourished there—all the forces were a part of the legalized dehumanization conspired to shorten my mother's life.

And yet, I take a hopeful, even inspiring lesson from the way she lived. Every day of my mother's life, with every single fiber of her being, she triumphed over the cards dealt her by structural racism. Marion Griffin Bowen lived so that every day before her untimely death counted for good, not just for herself but also for the good of others. And as a consequence, she made certain that she equipped her two children and the innumerable others she influenced to continue her fight for racial equality in America.

Legalized Dehumanization Today

The contemporary effects of legalized dehumanization remain evident in the systemic use of law to restrict or entirely withhold access to the basic necessities of human life and health from Black Americans. These obvious present-day aspects of legalized dehumanization clearly challenge the myth that it was a relic of slavery or even of the Jim Crow era. This dangerous myth cloaks the desperate need for legal and social reform today. Disparate access to clean drinking water is the best modern-day example of legalized dehumanization.

In recognition that access to water and sanitation are basic human rights, the United Nations has identified the assurance of these rights as the sixth sustainable development goal for nations.[39] This goal reflects the simple scientific truth that humans cannot live without water.[40] Moreover, humans cannot remain healthy without adequate sanitation.[41] In light of these two facts about humanity, a review of the laws that have excluded Black communities from access to water and sanitation affords powerful proof of persistent, legalized dehumanization. The modern US legal record is replete with such examples of African American communities struggling to gain access to clean drinking water and adequate sanitation required to live as healthy humans.

The ongoing Flint, Michigan, crisis around lead contamination of the water supply is, of course, the most infamous.[42] In January 2016, Michigan's governor declared a public health emergency in Flint. There was evidence that the citizens—especially young children—had dangerously elevated blood lead levels because of toxic lead pollution in the city's drinking water. This human-made environmental disaster exemplifies both legalized dehumanization by commission and by omission. Michigan law represented dehumanization by commission, where it enabled government officials to treat Michigan residents inhumanely. For example, under Michigan's Local Financial Stability and Choice Act, the city's emergency manager had unfettered decision-making power to disregard basic human health needs in favor of saving money.[43] In April 2014, Michigan's legislature appointed an emergency manager to replace the democratically elected mayor because the city was in receivership. The city manager then switched Flint's drinking water supply to the visibly filthy, polluted Flint River to save money.

In addition, underenforcement of environmental protection and civil rights laws in Flint represented numerous acts of legalized dehumanization by omission. First, the government switched Flint's water source without following the federal Safe Drinking Water Act's lead and copper regulations that limit lead allowed in drinking water. Second was the "management weakness" of the Michigan Department of Environmental Quality (MDEQ), which similarly failed to exercise regulatory oversight to compel compliance. Third, the city disregarded the complaints and entreaties of the city's residents—53.7 percent of whom are African American, and 40.4 percent of whom are poor—either continuing to ignore complaints or issuing inhumane stopgap measures such as boil-water advisories. Fourth, other government authorities ignored complaints of skin rashes, hair loss, gastrointestinal disease, and deaths from Legionnaires' disease, treating the people of Flint as irrelevant or simply actors that served their managerial goals.[44] Finally, and importantly for this analysis, the equal protection laws that could have held these officials accountable for discrimination were not enforced.[45] Until August 2015, Flint residents suffered from this underenforcement of the Equal Protection Clause, which prohibits the MDEQ's pattern and practice of discrimination against them.

Researchers at Virginia Tech then intervened to publicly report that lead was leaching into Flint's water supply. At about the same time in 2015, pediatrician Dr. Mona Hanna-Attisha released an alarming report informing city officials that the lead in Flint children's blood had nearly doubled since the water supply switch. Still, not until the end of the year did the mayor of Detroit declare a state of emergency, and in January 2016, the state's governor followed. Only then did the US Environmental Protection Agency begin sampling and testing water in this predominately Black and poor neighborhood. By then, the public health damage that would last for generations had been done. Lead poisoning is irreversible, and no level of contamination is safe. The children in Flint have been exposed to the risk of anemia, kidney damage, colic, muscle weakness, and permanent brain and nervous system damage. These children display developmental delays, cognitive deficits, and behavioral disabilities for life. Adults are also susceptible to health harms from the polluted water; the risks include exposure to *Legionella*, a bacterium associated with Legionnaires' disease, which can cause lung disease and death. The pipes in Flint have since been replaced, but the damage to public health continues.

The legal failures that triggered the Flint water crisis are numerous. Causes include the perverse incentives embedded in laws that influenced the city manager's decision-making, the rate-setting laws that imposed onerous taxes on Flint's residents for the purchase of poisoned water, and the failure of legal protections that governed the EPA. The law has failed and continues to fail the people of Flint, Michigan, on many counts. A plethora of lawsuits have been filed. Criminal and civil suits seek to hold government officials accountable for severe, permanent health and economic losses. However, the scale of health devastation caused by legalized dehumanization throughout the nation goes far beyond the city of Flint. In a 2016 study, Reuters found 2,606 census tracts and 278 zip codes with lead poising levels at least twice that of Flint, Michigan. These cities, unsurprisingly, are home to large Black populations. Baltimore (62.5 percent), Cleveland (53.3 percent), Philadelphia (42.3 percent), and Milwaukee (38.8 percent) are among the thousands of cities and rural areas that are largely Black, poor, or both and that lack access to clean, safe drinking water in twenty-first-century America.[46]

Figure 2.3 shows Black residents of Michigan marching for the right to clean drinking water. The tragedy that medical providers must march today to demand such a basic human right is eclipsed only by the immorality by which this basic right has been withheld from some groups in the United States.

Residential segregation is the structural mechanism that concentrates the deprivation of clean water and sanitation in Black communities. Segregation in all aspects of life—whether in public parks, golf courses, railways, restaurants, or theaters—is demeaning. Segregation laws overtly communicated that one group of people was not fit to live their lives in the same spaces occupied by another group. Legalized segregation was tantamount to legalized dehumanization; it denied the human dignity of African Americans wherever it was allowed to manifest itself. However, residential segregation did the logistical work to make dehumanization efficient.

Beginning in the Jim Crow era and continuing well beyond the Civil Rights era, examples of disparate distribution of basic necessities like water and sanitation are all too common. For instance, governments allocated access to clean drinking water by laying abundant water mains in city neighborhoods that housed White residents while sparsely extending public drinking water sources only to the edges of Black

FIGURE 2.3: Michigan Nurses March in Flint, Michigan, to Proclaim Poor and Black Residents' Right to Clean Water as Humans, 2016. Source: Bill Pugliano, Getty Images.

neighborhoods. And in Charlottesville, Virginia, maps dating from 1920 to approximately 1959 show that water pipes coursed throughout residential neighborhoods in White working-class sections of the city, but near Black neighborhoods, they were sparsely located.[47]

Dr. W. E. B. Du Bois studied living conditions of nine thousand Black Philadelphians in 1896–1897. He found that few Black families had indoor plumbing and that "just under 14 percent of the families he surveyed had access to bathrooms or water closets, and many did not have access to private outhouses."[48]

Similarly, the work of Professor Werner Troesken offers "strong evidence" of how city authorities "provided poorer [water and sewer] service to black neighborhoods than white neighborhoods" during the early 1900s.[49] Dr. Troesken found that the racist denial of essential services like water and sanitation was not as extreme in some cities. This finding, he says, is because most city water systems were built before segregation laws began to emerge in the early 1900s.[50] Troesken also explains that because Black inhabitants of urban city centers had the benefit of access to public water sources there, their mortality rates were better than those of people with worse water access.

Of course, evidence that waterborne diseases such as typhoid fever killed Black people at approximately twice the rate that they killed White people between 1900 and 1920 belies Troesken's overarching claim that Black city dwellers did not suffer the poor health outcomes that other Black groups did. Most American cities managed to offer unequal water quality to Black and White neighborhoods. As the United States became increasingly more segregated by the mid-twentieth century, municipalities became more effective at denying water and sanitation—both basic elements of human health—to Black neighborhoods and to neighborhoods where recent immigrants had settled. While sanitation was generously provided to White neighborhoods, Black neighborhoods were among the last to get indoor plumbing for kitchens and bathrooms. In Zanesville, Ohio, for example, the Black community of Coal Run started requesting water service in 1956, the same year the city built a water main that served their White neighbors but ended just before reaching the Coal Run neighborhood. The residents' requests were denied, even as other neighborhoods received water service. Shamefully, the Coal Run neighborhood did not receive city water service until 2003–2004.[51] Governments and citizens used law to racially segregate access to municipal services nationwide: whether Black people lived in cities or rural settings, whether water sources were public or private, or whether the segregation ordinances preceded or followed installation of public health works did not change the health-destroying role that law played in minority communities. Indeed, legalized dehumanization was the law's defining feature well into the second half of the twentieth century.

The illustrative case on the racist denial of essential services was decided by the US Fifth Circuit Court of Appeals in 1971. In *Hawkins v.*

Town of Shaw, Black residents of a Mississippi town brought a class-action lawsuit to gain equal access to municipal services afforded the White residents in their town. More than half the town's residents were Black. They alleged that the town government violated their Fourteenth Amendment rights because White Shaw neighborhoods had high- or medium-intensity mercury vapor streetlights, while street lighting in Black parts of town was provided by bare bulbs. Moreover, they alleged that virtually all White residences had indoor toilets, but all the areas that lacked indoor plumbing were Black. The *Hawkins* plaintiffs also claimed that surface-water drainage caused frequent flooding in their neighborhoods but not in well-constructed White parts of Shaw. Although all residents of Shaw had water service at the time, the water pipes were smaller, and the water pressure lower, in Black neighborhoods than in White ones.

The District Court refused the plaintiff class the injunctive relief its members sought, deferring to their ability to gain relief at the ballot box for the complaints they brought. But the Court of Appeals reversed this decision, notably focusing on the "clear overtones of racial discrimination in the administration of governmental affairs of the town of Shaw." The appellate court could not be dissuaded from holding town officials accountable because of the lack of evidence that they harbored racist intent. Instead, the court concluded, "In judging human conduct, intent, motive and purpose are elusive subjective concepts, and their existence usually can be inferred only from proven facts. . . . [T]he record proof does clearly establish conduct which cannot be judicially approved."[52] The *Shaw* Court reversed the lower court's decision in 1971. This litigation occurred well past the Jim Crow era and evinces an ongoing history of legalized dehumanizing deprivations against the Black residents of Shaw. The neighborhoods of Shaw had been totally segregated since 1930, and the evidence the court cited pointed to an inequitable public water system since that time. Therefore, *Hawkins v. Shaw* represents one of the most well-documented cases of continuous and tenacious legalized dehumanization.

The Role of Health-Care and Public Health Professionals

An important takeaway from this chapter is the role the medical community has played in propping up the White supremacist ideology that has made legalized dehumanization possible. From the unenlightened scientific racism prevalent during the Enlightenment period that informed Jefferson and the other colonial slaveholders, to the pseudoscience of eugenics that plagued marginalized communities throughout the twentieth century, health-care and public health professionals have been instrumental in supplying the so-called scientific justification for legalized dehumanization.

Some health professionals disavow responsibility for transforming inequitable social structures that contribute to the health disparities they are laboring to defeat. They claim that social problems are beyond their expertise, and they seek to draw clinical boundaries around their work with patients.[53] This mindset is like a farmer who disavows responsibility for a bad crop in a year when she initially planted her seed in a field filled with rocks and boulders, explaining that she is a farmer, not a geologist. The farmer's shortsighted sphere of interest is counterproductive and will not contribute to her ultimate goal of reaping a bountiful harvest. The farmer could point to others who should have removed the rocks and boulders before she planted. And to some degree, the farmer is right; she cannot take sole responsibility for getting the field ready to plant. But neither can a good farmer ignore the condition of the field before planting and expect that her crops will succeed. Even more importantly, the farmer cannot blame the seed for failing to propagate or the heavens for failing to supply enough good weather to make planting profitable. When the farmer realizes that rocks and boulders are interfering with her crop's growth, she must not wait until someone else takes responsibility for transforming the rocky field into healthy soil. If she does, she is acting much like the health providers who argue that the social determinants lie far outside their scientific and clinical spheres of responsibility. Both the provider and the farmer will find that much of their work will be futile or at least underproductive.

Structural racism and, specifically, legalized dehumanization represent massive and multiple rocks strewn throughout patients' lives; providers belong at the center of the effort to eradicate these unethical and unjust obstacles. My argument is based on both history and pragmatism. In addition to their responsibility to reverse the legacy of their historical discriminatory contributions to structural racism, health-care providers occupy central positions in the anchor institutions of many communities. This central position argues in favor of having health providers serve as the hub of healing in America. Achieving health equity will require that we work together to dismantle the dehumanization myths underlying structural racism and the resulting legalized structures built on White supremacist doctrine that these myths spawned. In place of distorted social determinant structures, we must rebuild systems that afford the basic needs of every human being to ensure equal treatment of all people, as mandated by the Constitution's Equal Protection Clause. Therefore, eliminating health disparities will require collaboration between medical, legal, and social service providers and patient communities to honor the humanity of all patient populations.

No discussion of eliminating dehumanization is complete, however, as long as it focuses solely on the psychological effect on the dehumanized. Whether subtle or blatant, the cruel and ironic fact is that dehumanization also harms those who perpetrate the myth. In short, dehumanization dehumanizes the dehumanizer. When an individual or a society strips others of their human identity, they concurrently shed the human emotion and identity that could have and should have protected them from monstrous behavior toward their victims. Dehumanization reduces one's empathic ability to appreciate the pain of others.[54] Denying the humanity of others separates the perpetrator from the person's own humanity as well, dulling and even extinguishing human empathy, compassion, and moral accountability. A sad and brutal irony, dehumanization makes the victimizers their own victims. Herbert Kelman, professor emeritus at Harvard University, summarizes the effect well: "Continuing participation in sanctioned massacres not only increases the tendency to dehumanize the victim, but it also increases the dehumanization of the victimizer himself. Dehumanization of the victimizer is a gradual process that develops out of the act of victimization itself."[55]

Dehumanization arguments to sustain segregation laws work irrationally both ways to degrade victims and victimizers. Take, for example, the case of a defendant, an Iowa cemetery arguing that it had the right to refuse burial to a plaintiff's non-White husband:

> The restriction to members of the Caucasian Race is almost as old as the cemetery business and has come down with the development of the cemetery business. This restriction is in probably 90 per cent of the private cemeteries in the United States. . . . Private cemeteries have always had a right to be operated for a particular group such as Jewish Catholic Lutheran, Negro, Chinese, etc., not because of any prejudice against any race, but because people, like animals, prefer to be with their own kind.[56]

This argument proves way too much—unwittingly arguing that people should behave as animals do, even in death. Dr. Kelman explains that researchers have confirmed this reciprocal aspect of dehumanization:

> [Researchers] have dramatically demonstrated, in a simulated prison study, in which subjects who were randomly assigned to a victimizer role tend to become brutalized by virtue of the situational forces to which they are subjected. In sanctioned massacres, as the victimizer becomes increasingly dehumanized through the enactment of his role, moral restraints against murder are further weakened. To the extent that he is dehumanized, he loses the capacity to act as a moral being.[57]

Angela Onwuachi-Willig insightfully calls for an accounting of the full harms of White Americans' racial dehumanization. She lays out the consequences of believing in White racial superiority, an obviously fallacious notion that produces "unchecked White privilege." She identifies the psychic damage that dehumanization visits on White people at an individual level; the damage includes increased fear, defensiveness, and the anxiety of believing that there is anti-White racism. Moreover, Dr. Onwuachi-Willig explains the costly societal consequences of dehumanization—the overall destruction of the means by which our society might eradicate racial inequality and achieve the elusive goal of equality.[58] Her insights are spot-on. But perhaps Archbishop Desmond Tutu said it best: "When we oppress others, we end up oppressing ourselves." And the archbishop's observation may be the most persuasive reason of all for America to reform the laws that have enshrined blatant and subtle dehumanization and to eliminate legalized dehumanization as a powerful building block of structural racism.

3

LEGALIZED INEQUALITY

And they are lucky that what Black people are looking for is
equality and not revenge.
—Kimberly Latrice Jones, Black Lives Matter activist

The first thing we do, let's kill all the lawyers.
—Dick the Butcher, *Henry VI*, Part 2, Act IV, Scene 2

The notion of *just health* describes the condition in which everyone in
a society has an equal opportunity to be healthy. Equality, therefore, is
a necessary precedent for just health, and structural inequality is the
greatest existential threat to health equity. Importantly, just health does
not depend on everyone's enjoying the same health care or treatment.
It does not even mean that everyone has an equal health outcome. That
would be an absurd objective, since people are different in a myriad of
health-related ways, and countless health-relevant factors contribute to
a person's or a population's health. But just health absolutely depends on
a society and system in which every human, and certainly each population group of humans, is equally valued. When they are, their chances of
enjoying good health are equitable. Just health, then, simply means that
no one person or group of people is unfairly granted or excluded from
the means of pursuing good health. Thus, equity is the chief characteristic of just health. Paula Braveman defines health equity as follows:

> Health equity means that everyone has a fair and just opportunity to be
> as healthy as possible. This requires removing obstacles to health such
> as poverty, discrimination and their consequences, including powerless-
> ness and lack of access to good jobs with fair pay, quality education and

housing, safe environments, and health care. For the purposes of measurement, health equity means reducing and ultimately eliminating disparities in health and its determinants that adversely affect excluded or marginalized groups.[1]

Just health, the ideal that I introduce in this book, enlarges Dr. Braveman's health-equity definition by identifying justice as the indispensable prerequisite for health equity. I apply a Rawlsian notion of justice—incorporating the American philosopher's theory of justice as fairness—to define just health as the moral mandate to protect and advance an equal opportunity for all to enjoy the greatest health and well-being possible. In so doing, I embrace the role of law—in particular, the law of human equality—to either create or destroy the "fair and just opportunity" that is necessary for health equity. Moreover, to show why just health, and therefore health equity, has yet to be achieved in this country, I point squarely at circumstances in which the law has failed.

For Americans with low wealth, little power, or few resources, there can be no health equity apart from laws that protect their equality. Laws that either fail to protect or explicitly destroy any aspect of equality also drive health inequity. For example, equality laws that prohibit discrimination could be useful tools in removing health-equity obstacles such as poverty, where poverty arises from unfair wage, employment, or labor practices. Laws that prohibit discrimination and its consequences can help address the powerlessness that excludes marginalized groups from enjoying equal access to the good jobs, fair pay, quality education, safe housing safe environments, and health care, all of which, according to Braveman's definition, are required for health equity. Thus, a society can achieve just health by legally protecting equal access to all the social determinants of people's health, regardless of their race, religion, ethnicity, sexuality, age, gender, or ability. In contrast, a society that tolerates underenforcement of antidiscrimination laws also tolerates inequality that prevents some people from living healthy lives while privileging others to enjoy good health. Unjust health will prevail in such a society, and the damage to health equity will be far-reaching. Again, my parents' lives provide a useful example.

The Multigenerational Effect of Structural Racism
(Or "Children Should Know their Grandparents—
But Health Behavior Is Not the Point!")

Mae and Vincent Bowen were born in the United States, Mae in 1931, and Vincent in 1930. Because they were Black, my parents they lived in a society where they were not afforded equal access to the same healthy housing, basic education, well-paying jobs, safe working conditions, healthy environments, or recreation choices that were available to their White counterparts born at the same time. Indeed, in this country, African American populations have never enjoyed an opportunity to be healthy in the same way that White populations have. Had my parents been born White, their chances of living longer and healthier lives would have been substantially greater. Equal opportunities to be treated fairly in school, housing, and public transportation and at work, the grocers, restaurants, movies, all forms of lodging (including motels, hotels, and inns), and elsewhere would have meant healthier and probably more prosperous lives for my parents. As I have described earlier, it is easy to see and even quantify the extent to which structural inequality contributed to my parents' early deaths. Put another way, the cost of structural racism to them as individuals and to other individuals of their generation is great and clear. The cost to my brother and me as their children is also great, though more difficult to quantify.

The structural racism that took my parents' lives prematurely changed my life irretrievably. Some research suggests that it changed my life from the moment I was conceived.[2] Gratefully, I did have my parents in my life during childhood and adolescence. During that time, they sacrificed their lives to make me the well-educated woman I am today. But I could speculate about what losing my parents early to structural racism has meant in other terms. I can base these judgments on the lives of my many close friends who are White. An experience I had this year is illustrative.

One recent New Year's Eve, a dear friend texted a celebratory message to me. We attended high school together. We have stayed in touch over the years, and both of us have made careers in the legal academy. He is brilliant. He is kind. He is White. He texted:

> In Manhattan this evening with [famous person we both admire] and [their] amazing nonagenarian parents.

My vivid imagination immediately traveled to the swankiest, *cozy* Manhattan apartment I had ever visited on a play date with my Fieldston classmate to try to guess what this experience must be like. I imagined a candlelit dinner table. In my mind's eye, I saw my friend, the famous author, and two white-haired intellectuals having an animated, stimulating conversation about history, current events, the books they read recently, and, of course, lessons from almost a century's worth of life experiences. This image I conjured up was warm and delightful—and gave me a tinge of envy. Oddly, it was not the swank or the author's status that I longed for. It was the contrast between that holiday experience and my own.

This same holiday season, my husband, my brother, and I decided to diagram our family tree. We began taking oral histories of the seniors in our family, in an effort to piece together the various names and relations and to hear the narratives they would share. It has been great fun. But it has also illuminated the costs of structural racism. Among us—three African American adults, together with all our four siblings, we have only one living parent to interview. We have no living aunts or uncles to interview. While my brother and I only had one aunt—my father's sister, who died at age thirty-four—my husband's father had eight siblings, and his mother had one. Seven of these ten aunts and uncles married. All might have been nonagenarians today. But none are alive today. We have no living aunts or uncles to interview. Our research led us to extended family members—people who were close friends of our parents. These are people who were always present for holidays and milestones and had earned the endearing title of "Aunt or Uncle So-and-So," though we shared no blood relationship. That list has proved fruitful—there are still a few octo- and nonagenarians to interview, but not a single one is male. My husband, my brother, and I are not unique in this regard; this is the story of living and dying Black in America. Our women die younger than White people; our men die the youngest of all. This is the immeasurable cost of lost wisdom, family history, security, and sense of belonging that structural racism has visited on my generation of African American adults.

As I imagine my high school friend's New Year's Eve dinner, I can imagine the lost advantages of the wisdom, counsel, and love from parents, aunts, and uncles who died younger than their White counterparts. I can speculate about my unrealized prospects for wealth and income transfers; think, for example, of the possible savings in childcare costs for my three children alone! When I look at my White friends— because the overwhelming majority of people who live to age ninety in the United States are White—most of them still have at least one of their parents alive and many have two living parents. Of course, the precise extent of my loss is speculative. I cannot say for certain that my parents would be alive or healthy today if America had been true to its promise of equal opportunity. I cannot say just how much I would have been helped by their experiences if I could have sought their perspective for my scholarship or asked for their help when I hit rough patches as a parent. Could they have given me strength and encouragement when I faced discrimination in the workplace? I can only guess at how much they might have multiplied my joy if they could have been present with me when I celebrated life's victories. Nor can I know how I would have managed the burden of their aging if they had lived long enough to need my help as their health declined. The exact nature of these losses is uncertain. But other costs of structural racism are not.

I do not have to guess or speculate about the enormous loss of benefits that structural racism has visited on my three children and others of their generation. Research confirms the benefits my children would have realized if my parents—their grandparents—had been treated equally to those who were born White in America. From the research literature and what I know of my parents, these elders would have served as role models. They would have encouraged academic and other success and would have given their wisdom, advice, and emotional support to my children had structural racism not cut their lives short. Moreover, research shows that my children would have had the benefit of increased resilience, social cohesion, and increased protection from the risk of depression if their grandparents had lived longer.[3]

These losses to my children anger me the most of all because they demonstrate the essence of what is structural about racism in the United States. It does not simply hurt populations of minority children disproportionately—White children are much more likely to have their grandparents and therefore to have better physical and mental health outcomes than are African American children. But structural racism's devastations reach out to decimate the lives of multiple generations. I feel this inequity acutely when a friend tells me how they treasure a Bible or another book that has an inscription their grandfather wrote for them. Or when a peer describes their tradition of taking each of their grandchildren on an outing or a vacation to celebrate a milestone birthday. I long for Black, Latino, and Indigenous children to know this security and stability as frequently as White children do.

In my family, as in the majority of African American and other minority families in the United States, structural racism has not only deprived my parents and me (as one of their children) but has also visited long-term adverse impacts on my children as well. Three generations in my family, at least, have been harmed by the structural racism that cut short my parents' lives. This long-term, widespread impact of structural racism underscores why we need to dismantle structural inequality and racism; failure to do so dooms every successive generation of minority children to the replication of inequitable, unjust, and avoidable adverse outcomes forever.

In 1974, the Association of Black Cardiologists (ABC) launched a campaign titled Children Should Know Their Grandparents. The drive aimed to address the fact that disproportionate death rates among African Americans from cardiovascular disease, including hypertension, heart failure, coronary heart disease, and stroke, had reached crisis proportions. With grant money and well-orchestrated communications fanfare, the ABC put out books, videos, website content, and countless educational programs. Black celebrities joined as spokespersons. And the quality of the medical information was exceptional, as one would certainly expect from an organization of professionals, scholars, and experts who define the exceptional caliber of the ABC. But here is the problem. The ABC campaign did (and continues to do) a beautiful job of providing information to Black families about steps they can take to reduce their disproportionate risk for cardiovascular disease. The information is vital and useful—lifesaving tips for diet, exercise, and treatment. Yet as important as this campaign is, it completely misses the point, which is that *structural change*—not changes in individual health behavior—is required to defeat the tragic racial disparities in mortality from the leading cause of death in the United States.

In fact, the gap between Black and White death rates from heart disease has gotten worse, not better, since the 1974 ABC campaign began. The best available evidence shows that although absolute rates of death from heart disease decreased from 1968 to 2015 for the US adult population overall, they decreased slower among Black people than among White. According to the National Vital Statistics System data on US deaths, note Dr. Miriam Van Dyke and colleagues, "at the national level, heart disease death rates for blacks and whites were similar at the start of the study period (1968) . . . [but] nationwide, the black-white ratio of heart disease death rates increased from 1.04 in 1968 to 1.21 in 2015, with large increases occurring during the 1970s and 1980s."[4] State-level data throughout the country concur with this finding, and certainly in New York, where my parents and grandparents were residing when they died. Figure 3.1 shows the heart disease rates and annual percentage

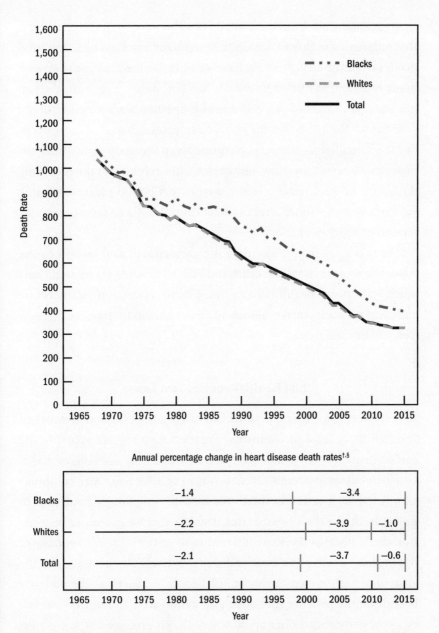

FIGURE 3.1: Black and White US Death Rates from Heart Disease, 1968–2015. Source: M. Van Dyke et al., "Heart Disease Death Rates Among Blacks and Whites Aged ≥35 Years: United States, 1968–2015," *Morbidity and Mortality Weekly Report, Surveillance Summaries*, 67, no. 5 (2018):1–11.

changes among adults in the United States between 1968 and 2015. Note that although the three lines on this graph for Black, White, and total death rates from heart disease have steadily declined, the gap between Black rates and White or total rates has not. In some periods, the gap has widened, showing that racial health disparities worsened until the year 2000.[5] Note also that the annual percentage change in these death rates was smallest for Black people throughout the study period until approximately 2009. Arguably, one explanation may be that the economic downturn of the Great Recession during that period presented White Americans with similar structural conditions to those facing minority families throughout history.

The takeaway from these data is clear: with all due respect to the ABC, the world's most elaborate and effective health promotion campaign to improve health behavior may be necessary but will never be sufficient to defeat structural racism. Structural racism must be dismantled structurally.

Just Health Requires Just Laws

In the United States, structural racism has been erected and maintained through three legal mechanisms. Together they restrict access to the resources and power that people need to live healthy lives (figure 3.2).

This chapter presents the data showing that this legal combination is lethal. It also lays the foundation for an enduring solution to unjust health in the United States. The fact that we profess to be a nation that embraces the Rawlsian notion of justice—the fair equality of opportunity—offers us a clear pathway to actively pursue the end of the structural racism that causes unjust health in America. The pathway is built on the premise that if we as a nation were to radically reform our laws and compel their alignment with our professed aspiration for equality, the United States would be transformed—not overnight, but fundamentally and sustainably transformed—into a society that enjoys just health.

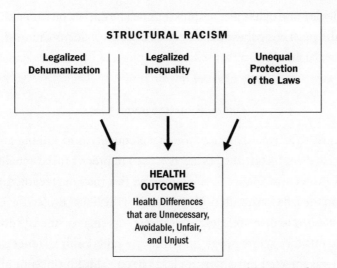

FIGURE 3.2: Relationship Between Law, Structural Racism, and Unjust Health in the United States.

This chapter calls for the United States to finally and truly live up to its promise of equal justice for all. In the past, whenever US lawmakers attempted to do this by reversing legalized dehumanization and inequality, they failed. Ever since the Equal Protection Clause was ratified in 1868 and Congress subsequently enacted civil rights laws to implement the Fourteenth Amendment's equality principle in 1870, 1875, 1965, and 1965, White supremacy has instead prevailed as the foundational ideology that informed US law, with recurring success. By 1868, the foul doctrine had so saturated the national psyche that racism had wicked up through all fibers of American society with a relentless resilience that eventually overwhelmed all attempts to legalize racial equality. Indeed, the hope and aspiration for African Americans to experience equal justice under the law has thus far been unrealized. I am convinced this sad state of injustice can change with a new understanding of the role law has played in producing pervasive inequality. With this understanding, our laws can be reformed. Toward that end, I will demonstrate how law, as the chief tool of Black dehumanization, has fashioned structural racism and yielded one of its chief outputs—unjust health. By outlining this history and presenting these data, I aim to accurately document the human cost of structural racism and thereby inspire and compel its demise.

*Un*equal Justice under Law

The most effective way to destroy racial equality is to kill the law that purports to protect it. The US law designed to protect racial equality, the Equal Protection Clause, is contained within the Fourteenth Amendment to the US Constitution. When ratified, the Equal Protection Clause was intended to dismantle legalized White supremacy—the vile doctrine that asserts that White people, as a race, are superior to all other races— which has infected the American legal system since its inception.[6] As a result, the Equal Protection Clause and the laws passed to implement it have been resisted, outright reversed, or restricted over the past 153 years since the Fourteenth Amendment became law. Thus, instead of living up to our nation's aspiration for equality, our courts, judges, legislators, and lawmakers have allowed legalized White supremacy to flourish. This is the ideological genesis of structural racism. Distortions, obfuscations, and outright attacks on the principle of human equality have proved so influential that, rather than protecting all people, our nation's laws have, for the past century and a half, protected the rights of governments and private parties to perpetuate racial inequality. To understand why, let us begin with the text of the Constitution itself.

Colonial America

The language of the US Constitution laid the foundation for legalized racial inequality from the beginning of our national government. It did so by embedding legalized dehumanization into our nation's charter. Though both the Constitution and the Declaration of Independence were signed in Philadelphia's Independence Hall, by 1787 the Constitution had drastically departed from the egalitarian document that had accomplished America's independence just over a decade earlier. When the original Constitution was adopted, nowhere did the text mention equality or include the word *equal*. Instead, the Constitution codified racial inequality by assigning an inferior status to Black human beings in multiple provisions. For example, in Article I, section 2, when the framers reached a compromise to bring the Southern states back into the Union, they did so by reducing the legal value of an African American life to only three-fifths the value of all other persons. In Article I, section 8, clause 18, the United States constitutionalized the trade of Black human beings as slaves, setting the tax it would accept into the nation's coffers for importing people as chattel property "not exceeding ten dollars for each Person." Elsewhere in the Constitution, Article 4, section 3, established federal protections for property rights in Black human beings under the Fugitive Slave Clause. Although Frederick Douglass famously argued that the Constitution is an antislavery document, his assertions are contradicted by the fact that in 1793, Congress enacted, and President George Washington signed, a national Fugitive Slave Act. The act was inspired by the constitutional provision that Douglass had defended.[7] Also, several states thereafter followed the constitutional model to make it legal to viciously hunt down Black people who sought freedom.[8]

> No Person held to Service or Labour in one State, under the Laws thereof, escaping into another, shall, in Consequence of any Law or Regulation therein be discharged from such Service or Labour but shall be delivered up on Claim of the Party to whom such Service or Labour may be due.

To reach this brutal result, the founders had to know *and reject* the shared understanding of equality of their day as it was set forth in the Declaration of Independence. They had to conclude that this understanding of equality did not apply to Black people.

In addition to the constitutional text, the historical record confirms this dichotomous understanding. In 1776, the Continental Congress, without dissent or disagreement, declared that "all men are created equal." The members borrowed the phrasing from sources that made clear that their pronouncement spoke to the essential equality of humankind. They wrote these words not merely to assert their political equality with the English crown but also to affirm that the colonists were equal in their humanity to members of the British monarchy. They fashioned the Declaration to assert that the crown and the colonists all shared the same creator, using the concept of equality that had been defined by British philosopher John Locke. In 1690, Locke had argued that "God is the creator and he did not grant superiority to any individuals in modern day society. . . . In races of mankind and families of the world, there remains not to one above another."[9] This Lockean argument provided the early inspiration for the Declaration's preamble. Furthermore, the Constitution's drafters also found contemporary confirmation that all humans are equal in Thomas Paine's pamphlet *Common Sense*, published in 1776. There, the political philosopher argued for American independence:

> Mankind, being originally equals in the order of creation, the equality could only be destroyed by some subsequent circumstance: the distinctions of rich and poor may in a great measure be accounted for, and that without having recourse to the harsh ill-sounding names of oppression and avarice. Oppression is often the CONSEQUENCE, but seldom or never the MEANS of riches; and tho' avarice will preserve a man from being necessitously poor, it generally makes him to timorous to be wealthy.[10]

Paine went on to explain that it was the unbiblical *government by kings* that was the means by which "a race of men came into the world so exalted above the rest, and distinguished like some new species, . . . As the exalting one man so greatly above the rest cannot be justified on the equal rights of nature, so neither can it be defended on the authority of scripture."[11] Paine's pronouncements, however, were apparently not seen as an impediment to the oppression of Black mankind.

Samuel Johnson's *Dictionary of the English Language* (1755)

In 1775, just before the Declaration of Independence was written, Samuel Johnson's *Dictionary of the English Language* published a plain, direct, commonsense definition of the word *equal*:

E'qual. *adj.* [equalis, Latin.]

1. Like another in bulk, excellence, or any other quality that admits compariſon; neither greater nor leſs; neither worſe nor better. . . .
3. Even; uniform. . . .
5. Impartial; neutral . . .
7. Equitable; advantageous alike to both parties . . .
8. Upon the ſame terms

E'qual. *n.* [from the adjective.]
1. One not inferior or ſuperior to another. . . .[12]

This definition is notable for its application to both people and inanimate objects. It provides an incontrovertible contrast to White supremacist notions of hierarchical human value. Remarkably, this 1775 dictionary definition also distinguishes between the quality of being equal—a truism—and equity, an outcome that results from recognizing differences in order to achieve true equality. There was no doubt, then, that in 1787, when the Constitution was written, and by 1788, when it was adopted, the framers had access to these definitions of equality that express the social, political, and moral standing of all human beings. Yet at least with respect to the principle of equality, Associate Justice Thurgood Marshall correctly pointed out that the Constitution and the government it formed were "defective from the start, requiring several amendments, a civil war, and momentous social transformation to attain the system of constitutional government and its respect for the individual freedoms and human rights, that we hold as fundamental today."[13] Justice Marshall's claim is certainly borne out in the legislative record.

The first constitutional corrective came in 1865, after the bloody loss of between 620,000 and 800,000 lives in the four-year-long American Civil War. The US Congress set out to amend the nation's charter by passing the Thirteenth Amendment, which, in its final form, pronounced that "neither slavery nor involuntary servitude, except as a punishment for crime whereof the party shall have been duly convicted, shall exist within the United States." However, even the history of this constitutional amendment reveals the ambivalence with which the nation's lawmakers approached the Constitution's first step toward reversing nearly two hundred years of America's tradition of legalized inequality. Here is the terrible irony: the original Thirteenth Amendment, introduced on March 2, 1861, was proposed not to *abolish* slavery. Instead, it would have added an *unamendable* amendment to constitutionally *permit* slavery and prohibit federal interference with the state-run slave trade. Introduced by Senator William H. Seward of New York and Representative Thomas Corwin of Ohio and endorsed by President James Buchanan, the so-called Corwin Amendment, had it been ratified, would have done the exact opposite of the Thirteenth Amendment that is part of our Constitution today. In its original form, this amendment would have constitutionally and permanently approved the institution of slavery. The Corwin Amendment to the Constitution read as follows:

> Article Thirteen
> No amendment shall be made to the Constitution which will authorize or give to Congress the power **to abolish or interfere within any state**, with the domestic institutions thereof, including that of persons held to labor or services by the laws of said State.
> Approved March 2, 1861[14]

This proslavery version of the Thirteenth Amendment came dangerously close becoming law. The astonishing truth of this historical fact would hardly be of note except that not only did supermajorities of both houses of Congress pass this *pro*slavery version of the Thirteenth Amendment, but the "Great Emancipator" himself—President Abraham Lincoln—spoke with approbation about this version of the Thirteenth Amendment. In his first inaugural address, given two days after the proslavery version passed, the new president declared, "I have no purpose, directly or indirectly, to interfere with the institution of slavery in the States where it exists. I believe I have no lawful right to do so, and I have no inclination to do so." Lincoln opposed only the expansion of slavery but said he could tolerate its continuation by law in states that had chosen the institution. About the proposed Corwin Amendment to the Constitution, President Lincoln was unequivocal:

> I understand a proposed amendment to the Constitution—which amendment, however, I have not seen—has passed Congress, to the effect that the Federal Government shall never interfere with the domestic institutions of the States, including that of persons held to service. To avoid misconstruction of what I have said, I depart from my purpose not to speak of particular amendments so far as to say that, holding such a provision to now be implied constitutional law, I have no objection to its being made express and irrevocable.[15]

Within a year, three of the six states that ratified the proslavery amendment—before it was finally withdrawn in 1864—had voted to legally embed the institution of slavery in the US Constitution.[16]

Before leaving this disturbing saga, we must consider two important points. First, the vast majority of US lawmakers were ambivalent at best about constitutionalizing freedom for the four million enslaved Black Americans over whom the Civil War was fought. Both Presidents Buchanan and Lincoln, as well as the original sponsors of the Corwin Amendment, are remembered in historical accounts as "morally opposed to slavery." Yet the compromise they introduced contradicts this account. The irrevocable constitutional amendment could have permanently enslaved African Americans. We will never know whether the proslavery version of the Thirteenth Amendment would have had sufficient votes to become part of our Constitution, because the ratification was interrupted by war. Instead, the Thirteenth Amendment that abolished slavery was ratified in December 1865.[17] We do know, however, that at the close of the Civil War, even after four years of bloodshed and carnage, there was no moral consensus that the enslavement of Black Americans was wrong. And many of those who opposed the peculiar institution were willing to legalize, indeed constitutionalize, Black inequality.

Second, the version of the Thirteenth Amendment that did become part of the Constitution did not then, and still does not today, end the practice of slavery in the United States. The amendment expressly permits the enslavement as a punishment for crimes once the person has been "duly convicted." Thus, as Professor Michelle Goodwin convincingly argues, the Thirteenth Amendment merely forbade one form of slavery while legitimating and preserving other forms, such as slavery behind prison bars.[18] Again, the historical record reveals this perpetuation of slavery was aimed at Black citizens. Immediately after the Thirteenth Amendment ended chattel slavery, a series of laws called the Black Codes were enacted throughout the South to criminalize conduct common to Black people. These laws were enforced only against African Americans, who, if "duly convicted," became eligible under complex convict-leasing programs to labor on prison farms and in chain gains, providing free labor. Often, the prisoners were working on the same plantations where they had worked before emancipation had purportedly freed them. In effect, the Thirteenth Amendment became a legal loophole for reenslavement.[19] Since the express aim of these convict-leasing systems was to provide "one hundred able bodied and healthy Negro convicts" for a fee paid to the state, it can be reasonably concluded that the amendment did not end slavery and, even today, certainly does not guarantee equal justice under the law for Black Americans.[20]

Reconstruction

Congress next attempted to legalize equality among the races through the Civil Rights Act of 1866. The Republican-controlled Congress believed that the Thirteenth Amendment, ratified in the previous year, only provided "fundamental freedoms" of US citizenship: equal rights to property, contract, and legal remedy. Congress plainly sought to expand these rights, with a broader understanding of equality, when it enacted the Civil Rights Act of 1866. By this statute, the lawmakers intended to codify equal rights to vote and to hold office and equal protection against segregation and discrimination. These rights went beyond the Thirteenth Amendment.[21] Proponents like Senator Lyman Turnbull of Illinois saw the new law as a way to reverse the legal inequality of the Black Codes and every form of discrimination that persisted against African Americans after emancipation. Senator Turnbull argued that the southern Black Codes "still impose upon [African Americans] . . . the very restrictions which were imposed upon them in consequence of the existence of slavery, and before it was abolished. The purpose of the bill under consideration is to destroy all these discriminations."

The 1866 act was passed despite President Andrew Johnson's veto and before the Southern states were officially reintegrated into the Union.[22] Therefore, Republican members of the 39th Congress, well aware that this federal law was vulnerable to repeal, immediately turned next to promulgating the Fourteenth Amendment to place equality for newly emancipated Black Americans on more certain constitutional ground. The drafters of the Fourteenth Amendment held the view that the statement of equality contained in the Declaration of Independence was true and should be part of the Constitution. John Bingham of Ohio repeatedly expressed his belief that the "absolute equality of all" was as "universal and indestructible as the human race" and that, therefore, both equality and equal protection belonged in the nation's Constitution.[23] Abolitionist Charles Olcott advocated for equality because of his

Christian faith, arguing that "genuine Christianity is a system of republican liberty and equality; . . . it grants and guarantees equal rights to all mankind."[24]

Representative Thaddeus Stevens of Pennsylvania introduced the Fourteenth Amendment in Congress with a plain and powerful statement of the intended meaning of the amendment's Equal Protection Clause:

> This amendment . . . allows Congress to correct the unjust legislation of the States, so far that the law which operates upon one man shall operate *equally* upon all. Whatever law punishes a white man for a crime shall punish the black man precisely in the same way and to the same degree. Whatever law protects the white man shall afford "equal" protection to the black man. Whatever means of redress is afforded to one shall be afforded to all. Whatever law allows the white man to testify in court shall allow the man of color to do the same.

Representative Stevens went on to explain that the Fourteenth Amendment was intended to reverse America's century-old tradition of legalized White supremacy:

> These are great advantages over their present codes. Now different degrees of punishment are inflicted, not on account of the magnitude of the crime, but according to the color of the skin. Now color disqualifies a man from testifying in courts, or being tried in the same way as white men. I need not enumerate these partial and oppressive laws. Unless the Constitution should restrain them, those States will all, I fear, keep up this discrimination, and crush to death the hated freedmen.[25]

Lest there be any confusion about the full extent of the racial equality that Representative Stevens sought to achieve between Black and White Americans in introducing the Fourteenth Amendment, he requested that when he died, he be buried in a nonsegregated cemetery. He also wrote his own epitaph, which reads:

> I repose in this quiet and secluded spot, not for any natural preference for
> solitude. But finding other cemeteries limited as to race by charter rules,
> I have chosen this that I might illustrate in my death the principles which I
> advocated through a long life, *equality of man before his creator.*[26]

It is fair to say that the chief proponents of the Fourteenth Amendment regarded the essential equality that it preserved as the same as the ideal proclaimed in the Declaration of Independence. These advocates sought to reverse legalized dehumanization of African Americans and to establish that the US Constitution regard all humankind as equal before their creator and under the law.

Of course, not even all Republicans in the 39th Congress shared this passionate and unequivocally expansive aspiration for legal equality. But Stevens was far from alone. The majority of Congress voted to constitutionalize the equality provisions of the Civil Rights Act of 1866, voting in favor of the Fourteenth Amendment. A statement that John Martin Broomall, another member of the Pennsylvania delegation, made on the floor of the House provides confirmation: "The fact that all who will vote for the pending measure [the Fourteenth Amendment], or whose votes are asked for it, voted for this proposition in another shape, in the civil rights bill (of 1866), shows it will meet the favor of the House."[27]

The Republicans who fought to ensure equality through the Fourteenth Amendment intended to expand and constitutionalize the protection for *political* equality found in the Thirteenth Amendment and the Civil Rights Act of 1866, while also protecting the *civil* equality of Black Americans provided under the Thirteenth Amendment and its statutory progeny. For this reason, the proponents included in the first clause of the amendment the provision that "no State shall make or enforce any law which shall abridge the privileges or immunities of citizens of the United States."[28]

Moreover, the Republicans who dominated the post–Civil War Congress further sought to include a prohibition against denying African Americans *equality of opportunity* under the Fourteenth Amendment. According to Professor Charles Postel, the amendment's drafters "pursued . . . 'the utopian vision of a nation whose citizens enjoyed equality of civil and political rights, secured by a powerful and beneficent national state.'"[29] According to legal scholar and professor Michael McConnell, "the Fourteenth Amendment, at its heart, embraced the principle of equality of civil rights: any civil right to which a white person would be entitled must be extended to all citizens on exactly the same terms."[30] Professor Michael Klarman identifies the tension between the Fourteenth Amendment's Equal Protection Clause (section 1) and the amendment's clear tolerance for racial discrimination in voting (section 2). He thus correctly foreshadows the struggle for full equality—a struggle that would result in ratification of the Fifteenth Amendment, which was needed to outlaw racial discrimination in voting.[31]

Further, the Reconstruction Acts of 1867–1868 were required to grant African American men the right to vote.[32] But when these acts were enacted, the Fourteenth Amendment's legislative history suggests that the meaning of the word *equal* in the Equal Protection Clause refers to essential, equal humanity of all people, reflecting the principle that "all are created equal" before God. At the time of its enactment, the Fourteenth Amendment was an attempt to unite the Declaration of Independence vision that "all men are created equal" with the government's constitutional charter. The work of successive congressional legislation throughout the Reconstruction period confirms that this was the goal. Thus, although historians focusing on the debate that surrounded its passage argues the Fourteenth Amendment did not arise from any "predetermined logic of emancipation," such a proceduralist view misses the moral commitment to "equality in the broadest and most comprehensive democratic sense" that drove the amendment's most ardent proponents.[33]

Congress moved expeditiously within the twelve-month period between 1870 and 1871, passing three laws designed to protect African American equality.[34] First, in May 1870, the 41st Congress passed the Enforcement Act of 1870, also known as the First Ku Klux Klan Act, to enforce the Fifteenth Amendment's prohibition against state actors' denying the right to vote on the basis of race.[35] The Enforcement Act criminalized violent or coercive tactics by individuals such as Ku Klux Klan (KKK) members seeking to prevent African Americans from exercising their right to vote. Thus, by criminalizing such violent acts of intimidation that threatened Black voters, Congress also intended that legalized equality would include egalitarian male suffrage.

The second Enforcement Act, passed in 1871, gave the federal government control over administering national elections and empowered federal judges to supervise local polling places.[36] The act further sought to enforce civil equality and quell the organized criminal campaigns launched to violently thwart Black enfranchisement.

Third, the 42nd Congress passed the Ku Klux Klan Act of 1871.[37] This legislation provided civil penalty against states specifically for aiding in acts of violence or coercion against African Americans to prevent them from achieving equal protection under the law by exercising their rights of property; contracts; legal remedy or participation; and suffrage by commission, omission, conspiracy, or implied acquiescence.[38] This law was a full-throated attempt to reinforce the civil protections provided in the Civil Rights Act of 1866, the Fourteenth Amendment, and the Fifteenth Amendment. The Ku Klux Klan Act of 1871 legislated against state failure or refusal to protect African Americans from violence or threats of harm perpetrated by the KKK and other White supremacists.

Remarkably, opposition to legalized equality for African Americans was not limited terrorist organizations such as the KKK. Opposition was also carefully constructed by other White supremacists, including respected politicians and journalists who wrote for mainstream publications. These visible leaders broadened the support for legalized inequality to White citizens who deemed it their birthright to be superior to Black Americans even if they were poor. One political poster of the time shows a mob of supposedly unruly Black men attempting to vote. The text decries politicians who support extending suffrage to Black men: "They are rich, and want to make The Negro the Equal of the Poor White Man, and then rule them both."[39] "Negro Equality" was the heinously offensive objective of the Fourteenth Amendment and was the reason it was bitterly opposed by its opponents.

In a final effort to legislatively legalize equality for African Americans during the Reconstruction, the 43rd Congress passed the Civil Rights Act of 1875. Senator Charles Sumner of Massachusetts introduced an expansive desegregation bill pursuant to the Fourteenth Amendment's Equal Protection Clause: it forbade racial discrimination that would prevent "the equal and impartial enjoyment of any accommodation, advantage, facility, or privilege" that a state provided.[40] In defending the bill, Senator Sumner and an opponent, Senator Joshua Hill of Georgia, spoke about the nature of legalized equality, definitively pronouncing the injustice of a separate-but-equal alternative to full equality under the law:

> MR. SUMNER. . . . The Senator mistakes substitutes for equality. Equality is where all are alike. A substitute can never take the place of equality. It is impossible; it is absurd. And still further, I must remind the Senator that it is very unjust; it is terribly unjust. Why, sir, we have had in this Chamber a colored Senator from Mississippi; but according to the rule of the Senator from Georgia we should have set him apart by himself; he should not have sat with his brother Senators. Do I understand the Senator from Georgia as favoring such a rule?
>
> MR. HILL. No, sir.
>
> MR. SUMNER. The Senator does not.
>
> MR. HILL. I do not, sir, for this reason: it is under the institutions of the country that he becomes entitled by law to his seat here; we have no right to deny it to him.

MR. SUMNER. Very well; and I intend to the best of my ability
[through my civil rights bill] to see that under the institutions of his
country he is equal everywhere. . . . [Responding to Senator's persistent defense of separate-but-equal]

MR. SUMNER. The Senator does not seem to see that any rule excluding a man on account of his color is an indignity, an insult, and
a wrong; and he makes himself on this floor the representative of
indignity, of insult, and of wrong to the colored race.[41]

For this declaration of Black equality, Senator Sumner was literally and
ferociously beaten within an inch of his life on the floor of the US Senate.

The incident is captured in an artist's wood engraving published in the
Congressional Globe, depicting the caning of Senator Sumner by Representative Preston Brooks of South Carolina.[42] Brooks so opposed
Sumner's position that he challenged Sumner to a duel, but to no avail.
Instead the Democratic congressman resorted to slamming his cane over
Sumner's head, leaving him bleeding on the floor of the Senate chambers
on May 22, 1856. The resulting head trauma kept Sumner from work for
nearly two years. When he did return to his seat in the Senate in 1859, he
resumed his antislavery campaign until his death in 1874.

The 43rd Congress passed the Civil Rights Act of 1875 only after reaching a compromise that construed access to public amenities as a civil
right but viewed desegregated accommodations as a social right, which
lay outside its constitutional authority to legislate and enforce.[43] This
distinction between *civil* and *social* equality eventually fueled a century
and a half of debate and struggle for those trying to achieve full equal
justice under the law for African Americans in this country. Nevertheless, Congress's enactment of the three Reconstruction amendments,
and its relentless pursuit of a full understanding of equality through the
Civil Rights Acts of 1866, 1870, 1871, and 1875, make clear that in US legal
history, Reconstruction was a period characterized by Congress's effort

to provide African Americans full political, civil, and social equality by law.

For a while, this policy of legalized equality succeeded. The Fourteenth Amendment was interpreted and enforced as the antislavery provision that it is, designed to reverse the institution that profoundly violated the equality premises of the Declaration of Independence. During Reconstruction, inequality based on race was viewed as a violation of the natural rights that all men had intrinsically, given to them by a "higher law" or power. The pragmatic results tangibly began to raise the fortunes and status of Black Americans. During Reconstruction, Black people began to exercise their human rights to civil, legal, political, economic, *and* social equality.

But besides being short-lived, the epoch represented a time fraught with contradictions, and it was cut short before African Americans could uniformly find equality under the law. Black-owned businesses emerged and began to flourish in banking, insurance, and manufacturing.[44] To be sure, many Black people continued to suffer abject poverty during Reconstruction, unable to escape the peonage laws that kept them in bondage after slavery. But the undeniably positive impact of their equality under the law could be seen in increasing financial and social equality among the newly freed Black Americans. In some states, African Americans began to acquire land and accumulate property such as farm animals, gold and silver coins, wagons, and buggies. In other states, legislatures enacted laws that prohibited Black residents from owning any real property whatsoever. For example, under a Georgia law enacted in 1818, free Black people could not hold title to real property, whether by direct or indirect purchase, or by being named as beneficiaries under a White person's will.

Fundamental voting rights for Black men (but not Black women) expanded, resulting in the election of sixteen Black male members of Congress and an estimated fifteen hundred elected to public office nationwide. An 1872 Currier & Ives print shows Hiram Revels of Mississippi, the first African American elected to the US Senate, along with six Black representatives elected to the House from the 41st and 42nd Congress.[45]

African American politicians drew Black and White voters and enacted such legal provisions as the homestead exemption, which abated taxes on residences, to protect home ownership. They also sponsored infrastructure projects that rebuilt bridges and hospitals, putting people to work. At the same time, the Reconstruction era continued to be characterized by vicious campaigns of violence against Black Americans to discourage them from exercising the right to vote, own land, or ascend to social equality with White Americans.[46] Lynching, other murders, and various other forms of racial violence were common during the period that was called "dark and bloody" to describe the African American victims' blood that soaked the ground. Rape and other violence against Black women were rampant and occurred without legal consequence on the absurd basis that "colored women are not moral and virtuous" and therefore deserved no redress for crimes committed against them.[47]

One crucial lesson from Reconstruction concerns the powerful primacy of law. Law not only expresses social norms, but also implements them, functioning as a "yardstick by which individuals measure their expectations and their actions."[48] Thus, the constitutional amendment that legalized the same equality that our Declaration of Independence proclaims made it possible to briefly reorder American society to align with the principles for which our Republic stands. When the rule of law commanded equality, it began to constrain the arbitrary exercises of White supremacy. Indeed, one of the most-cited definitions of equality, written by British jurist Albert Venn Dicey, makes clear that equality is central to the rule of law:

> That "rule of law" then, which forms a fundamental principle of the Constitution has three meanings, or may be regarded from three different points of view. . . . It means, again, equality before the law, or the equal subjection of all classes to the ordinary law of the land administered by ordinary law courts.[49]

The equality that Dicey wrote about here certainly pertained to government officials who, he explained, were equally subject to the rule of law as others were. But his remarks also explain that when the law pronounces and is enforced to compel equality of humankind, this law, and not racist ideology, will order social practices and affairs in all spheres because of "the absolute supremacy or predominance of regular law, as opposed to the influence of arbitrary power." Sadly, the rule of law embodied in the Fourteenth Amendment's Equal Protection Clause enjoyed only a brief period during which it sought to ensure that America's legal system promoted liberty, justice, and fairness.[50]

Jim Crow

By 1883, in a decision titled *The Civil Rights Cases*, the US Supreme Court began the legal reversal of congressional equal-rights efforts made during Reconstruction for African Americans. The high court rejected Black litigants' attempts to enforce the Civil Rights Act of 1875 to gain equal access to inns, hotels, and theaters and instead held that the civil rights act was unconstitutional. *The Civil Rights Cases* decision held that the Fourteenth Amendment is not intended to protect private, individual rights but could void only state legislation and only the state laws and actions that subvert fundamental rights specified in the Constitution.[51] The justices significantly narrowed the reach of the Fourteenth Amendment and interpreted it to allow racial segregation and discrimination by private actors.[52] Even in his dissent to this reversal of the congressional provisions, Justice John Marshall Harlan could not conceal his and his fellow justices' presumption that Black Americans were not of equal value to White Americans. Instead, he quoted with approbation cases that described White people as the "superior race."[53]

Later, in 1896, in *Plessy v. Ferguson*, the Supreme Court infamously upheld the constitutionality of separate-but-equal state laws that enforced racial segregation in public spaces. Justice Harlan, credited with the mistaken egalitarian interpretation of a "color-blind" constitution declared, "Our Constitution is color-blind." In fact, then as now, the doctrine of a so-called color-blind Constitution preserves and protects the legalized presumption of White superiority. Harlan himself taught clearly how the color-blind notion should be understood in context:

> The white race deems itself to be the dominant race in this country. And so it is, in prestige, in achievements, in education, in wealth and in power. So, I doubt not, it will continue to be for all time, if it remains true to its great heritage, and holds fast to the principles of constitutional liberty.[54]

By declaring the Constitution of the United States powerless to put the "inferior" colored race on the same social plane as the White race, the *Plessy v. Ferguson* court halted all progress toward racial equality and ended Reconstruction in 1896. Writing for the court, Justice Henry Billings Brown explained that racial segregation did not violate the Fourteenth Amendment's Equal Protection Clause, because the amendment was intended

> undoubtedly to enforce the absolute equality of the two races before the law, but in the nature of things it could not have been intended to abolish distinctions based upon color, or enforce social, as distinguished from political equality, or a commingling of the two races upon terms unsatisfactory to either.[55]

With these words, the *Plessy* decision began the Jim Crow era, when laws reflected this sentiment that nature itself distinguished Black people from White, and no law could be read to change those distinctions or expect these two kinds of beings to "comingle." Moreover, the Equal Protection Clause, written to enforce racial equality, was twisted by this court to instead distinguish political from social equality. Thus, by dividing the concept of equality into categories, the *Plessy* justices set the nation on a course for the legalization of Black dehumanization and inequality that guaranteed Black citizens would receive anything but equal justice under law. In fact, they received the exact opposite.

During the Jim Crow era, local, state, and federal laws were passed across the country to reassert White supremacy through the legal system. These racist laws were ubiquitous and affected an expansive range of societal institutions; hence the term *institutionalized* or *structural racism*. The Fourteenth Amendment no longer protected Black citizens' equal right to vote; to buy, sell, or hold property; or to participate in civil juries. A full recounting of this period in America's legal history lies outside the scope of this book, and many excellent analyses of this period are available. We will, however, examine a few points to better understand the legalization of dehumanization and inequality during Jim Crow.

Legalized political inequality took the form of laws that restricted the right to vote and stripped African Americans of the ability to influence their social and civic inequality through the political process. Between 1890 and 1910, several states instituted poll taxes, literacy tests, and other mechanisms to prevent Black citizens from accessing an equal right to vote.[56] Virginia's poll tax is exemplary not only because it was ensconced in the state's constitution and would remain sanctioned by law until 1969, but also because the legislative history of the provision leaves no doubt about the dehumanizing motivation that inspired these constitutional provisions.[57] The poll tax was enacted to "purify" elections by excluding "that ignorant and trashy population" that the legislators called the colored race. During the Virginia Constitutional Convention in 1901, one proponent of voting inequality declared his view that White Virginians wore the "Divine imprimatur of that intellectual and racial supremacy which gave them the exclusive right of government." As for the purpose of Virginia's anti-Black constitutional provision, that same legislator proclaimed his purpose was to "discriminate to the very extremity of permissible action under the limitations of the Federal Constitution with the view to the elimination of every negro voter who can be gotten rid of, legally, without materially impairing the numerical strength of the white electorate."[58]

Other states passed numerous other constitutional provisions aimed at permanently legalizing Black inequality. According to a compilation of state segregation laws by 1950, more than thirty state legislatures had enacted constitutional provisions to legalize some aspect of African American inequality.[59] In addition to constitutional provisions, states passed numerous and detailed segregation laws, legally prohibiting African Americans from enjoying equality in all aspects of human life, from such necessities as housing, schools, transportation, hospital care, and washrooms to ridiculously detailed other aspects such as access to circuses, cemeteries, and telephone booths.[60]

Beyond state legislature, courts and the highest elected government officials in America enforced these and other inequality laws with the unrelenting undertone of Black dehumanization. Leading the way, Justice Joseph Story infamously pronounced in the *Dred Scott v. Sandford* case that the "unhappy black race were separated from the white by indelible marks, and laws long before established, and were never thought of or spoken of except as property."

When President Woodrow Wilson supported the KKK and the resegregation of federal agencies from the White House, he used the highest elected office in the land to dehumanize Black Americans as inferior beings.[61] President Wilson left no doubt about his intent. Referring to the Reconstruction era, during which lawmakers passed the Equal Protection Clause; the Thirteenth, Fourteenth, and Fifteenth Amendments; and four civil rights acts in pursuit of racial equality, the nation's twenty-eighth president said, "Reconstruction was nothing more than a host of dusky children untimely put out of school [and a period when] the dominance of an ignorant and inferior race was justly dreaded."[62]

During the Jim Crow era, when judges and prosecutors enforced segregationist laws, some did not hide their belief that Black people were more like animals than children. For example, a North Carolina state court judge said, "I cannot distinguish the case of negroes from that of other animals."[63] A Texas prosecutor argued to a jury:

> This negro is a lustful animal, without anything to transform to any kind of valuable citizen, because he lacts [sic] the very fundamental elements of mankind. You cannot gather dates from thorns nor can you get figs from thistles; you cannot get a nightingale from a goose egg, nor can you make a gentleman out of a jackass.[64]

Other courts admitted that when they enforced property contracts, they did so with the understanding that rights to compensation for loses or gains in the value of a Black person were no different from the right to enforce ownership interests in livestock or horses or dogs.

To enforce these laws of racial inequality, courts had to carefully delineate who was and who was not an inferior being.[65] For this purpose, lawmakers often turned to members of the medical profession who espoused a now-discredited and unscientific White supremacist dogma. Eugenics was the pseudoscience of prominent White leaders in the medical and scientific community who worked to promote Calvin Coolidge's assertion in "Whose Country Is This?," an article he wrote as vice president elect in 1921. Explaining that "America must be kept American," President Coolidge praised the eugenicists' faulty, racist claims: "Biological laws show . . . that Nordics deteriorate when mixed with other races."[66]

For the record, modern eugenicists still exist in the American medical community. They profess a scientific basis for ascribing superiority to Europeans and their descendants and genetic inferiority to non-Europeans.[67] Today's eugenicists define eugenics as "the practical application of genetic science toward the improvement of the genetic health of future generations." The original, more reductive definition was the "science of improving the stock" and spoke to the White supremacist goal of eliminating inferior races by "breeding a more gifted race."[68] Eugenicists argued in the past, and still argue today, that the Black population is genetically inferior to the White one. The movement flourished in the 1920s and 1930s, with leading proponents occupying positions of great influence in major universities, foundations, and research institutes. Their influence can be seen in public health and immigration laws, as well as in laws that affect African American inequality. Segregation laws were driven by a White moral panic that feared race mixing—or "amalgamation"—above all else. In response to this fear, legislators installed an elaborate legal structure to maintain White purity and superiority.[69] Providing scientific legitimacy to Jim Crow–era lawmakers constructing the edifice of structural racism, eugenics has thus had an indelible influence for more than a hundred years of American legal history. The movement lost credibility as genetic science advanced and as eugenics' intimate connection to Nazi anti-Semitism was exposed. Nevertheless, the "vicious pseudoscientific activity of [these] so-called scientists" has left an enduring stamp on American law and arguably continues to fuel White racism today.[70]

Unequal Protection of the Laws: A Wholesale Retreat from Equality in America

Two unanimous Supreme Court decisions—one in *Brown v. Board of Education* and the other in *Hernandez v. Texas*—are generally thought to mark the end of the Jim Crow period of legalized inequality.[71] These decisions returned the nation's jurisprudence to another brief era during which lawmakers strived to enact laws that preserved racial equality. Antidiscrimination laws were promulgated under the Equal Protection Clause at local, state, and federal levels throughout the Civil Rights era, which extended approximately twenty-two years, from 1954 to 1976. During this period, the US Supreme Court handed down several unanimous landmark decisions, such as *Garner v. Louisiana* (1961), *McLaughlin v. Florida* (1964), and *Loving v. Virginia* (1967).[72] These decisions reversed Jim Crow segregation laws, legally enforcing equality for African Americans wherever they lived, worked, ate, and went about their daily lives. In addition, Congress returned to the inspired business of passing laws to protect racial equality, reminiscent of the legislative efforts during Reconstruction. The sweeping civil rights legislation Congress enacted to provide equal protection for Black Americans included the Civil Rights Act of 1964, which prohibited segregation in theaters, restaurants, hotels, and public places; outlawed racial discrimination by recipients of federal funding; and banned racial discrimination in employment.[73] The Voting Rights Act of 1965 protected the equal right to vote free of discrimination, intimidation, or other forms of coercion that had continued to suppress Black voters for almost a century after the ratification of the Fifteenth Amendment.[74] Congress passed the Fair Housing Act of 1968, again to pursue the national ideal of racial equality by confronting residential segregation.[75]

During the Civil Rights era, state legislatures also enacted civil rights legislation, and much of it was, in fact, attempts to control blatantly racist activities and therefore included antimask provisions (related to the KKK), antilynching provisions, and laws outlawing slavery.[76] But, as in the Reconstruction period, support for dismantling structural racism was not unanimous. For example, despite a recorded 4,742 lynchings in the United States, Congress has logged more than two hundred failed attempts between 1882 and 1986 to pass legislation making lynching a Black man a crime. As of July 2021, the Emmett Till Anti-Lynching Act remained stalled in Congress; although this bill passed the House of Representatives, it has been blocked from passage by unanimous consent by a single senator—Rand Paul—who claims the bill is overly broad because it could penalize minor bruising.[77] Successful legalized inequality persists, not only where lynching is concerned.

Despite widespread racial violence and massive resistance to integration that immediately followed the Civil Rights Acts and Supreme Court decisions, the United States has made progress toward racial equality under the law. Residential racial segregation has generally declined since the Fair Housing Act was passed. By the early 2000s, segregation levels remained highest in northern metropolitan areas and lowest in southern metropolitan areas. The general decline marks significant progress, but overall segregation levels remain very high in most parts of the nation even today.[78] As a consequence, schools are still highly segregated across the country. The most significant improvement was seen during the late 1960s and early 1970s. Since that time, however, school segregation has changed little and American children continue to be educated separately and unequally nearly seventy years after the Supreme Court's decision in *Brown v. Board of Education*. Minimal progress toward equality for African Americans in housing and education has been the result of slow, uneven progress toward full equality under the law. Despite congressional effort to reverse legalized inequality during the 1960s and the early 1970s, a period when the Equal Protection Clause was interpreted to impel governments to transform discriminatory institutions, by 1976, the Supreme Court's view of equal protection shifted away from the Civil Rights–era presumption of racial equality and returned to the more familiar territory of legalized inequality.

The US Supreme Court's Contribution to Modern Structural Racism

The turning point that began the reversal of the Civil Rights era gains was a decision in a case involving complaints of racially discriminatory hiring and promotion practices in the Washington, DC, police department. In *Washington v. Davis*, the Supreme Court rejected plaintiffs' claim that the department's hiring practices violated the Fourteenth Amendment's Equal Protection Clause by using a test and various criteria that disproportionately excluded a high number of Black applicants. The test, called Test 21, for example, asked questions about where dates grow, colloquialisms related to forestry, and other topics far afield from policing issues—questions that arguably reflected White cultural biases.

The court held that the disproportionate impact of the department's use of this test could not alone prove a constitutional violation. According to the decision, the impact of producing an overwhelmingly White

police force to protect the safety of an overwhelmingly Black community was insufficient to prove an equal protection violation. Instead, the
Washington v. Davis court held that to prove such a violation, the litigants
must prove that the defendant had a discriminatory purpose as well. The
court said that a statute or government activity otherwise neutral on its
face is prohibited only if its purpose is to invidiously discriminate. In
other words, if a law or policy does not *expressly* state an intention to
discriminate against Black people or others because of race or national
origin, then only evidence that the accused defendant had an intentionally racist objective will suffice to prove the Constitution was violated.
A disproportionate impact in and of itself is not irrelevant, the court
said, but no matter how serious a social inequity the disparate impact
produces, the court's holding means that inequitable impact alone is not
enough to trigger the court's close (i.e., strict) scrutiny. Moreover, disproportionate impact, the court held, does not warrant a conclusion of
purposeful intent. In placing its focus on the purposeful intent of state's
actions, the court precluded the possibility that a disparate-impact claim
might succeed even where intentional bigotry is not evident. While its
new standard closed the door to a broad and possibly unlimited number
of claims whenever racial differences or outcomes arose, it also cut off
access to constitutional protection against government actions or inac-
tion that results in repeated, institutionalized, or even morally untenable
racial disparities. In summary, the court narrowed the application of
the Equal Protection Clause so that, since the 1976 *Washington v. Davis*
decision, its protections are limited to the prevention of official conduct
that is *intended to* discriminate on the basis of race.

With this decision, the Supreme Court rejected the notion that the
Fourteenth Amendment imposes an affirmative duty on governments
to ensure that people of all races enjoy an equal opportunity to succeed
in America. The court can be said to have turned its back on the concept embodied in our Constitution, which guarantees that governments
cannot act to withhold or obstruct the opportunity to compete and live

on equal terms regardless of skin color, nationality, or race. The Rawlsian notions of constitutional equality, fairness, and justice died with the *Washington v. Davis* decision. Instead, the Supreme Court turned to the view, still prevalent today, that the Equal Protection Clause is merely a prohibition against deliberate state acts of intentional discrimination. The resulting Fourteenth Amendment *intent doctrine* has meant that when people who allege they have been injured by legalized inequality or subjected to systemic dehumanization, their constitutional claims will only prevail if they can demonstrate that a state acted with the intentional purpose to cause such inequitable outcomes.

The purposeful-intent standard relies on appropriating the appealing sound of a "color-blind constitution" from Justin Harlan's dissent in *Plessy v. Ferguson*. However, the result has not been the equal treatment of all people by the law. Instead, the law has become an instrument to defeat rather than defend all Americans' rights to equal protection. One might say the court has become blind to injustice, not to color. In many cases that followed, litigants found that the Equal Protection Clause no longer provided protection for blatant racial discrimination under the color of law as long as the government could claim it was not guilty of purposeful discrimination. In case after case, veritable mountains of egregious evidence revealing racial discrimination failed to convince the court that Black people were treated unequally because the court found no evidence that the state had selected a particular course of action *because of*, not merely *in spite of*, its discriminatory effect on Black people.[79] In my view, the *Washington v. Davis* case is poorly reasoned and wrongly decided, unless the goal of the decision was to expressly retreat from enforcing constitutional protections for equal justice for all.

Before the *Washington v. Davis* purposeful-intent standard, Black litigants could prevail when the evidence proved the results of discrimination were clear to the court, even if the motive to discriminate was not. The Equal Protection Clause not only prohibited intentional discrimination but also prohibited arbitrary and capricious neglect of Black Americans' equal rights. In the words of the Fifth Circuit Court of Appeals,

> In order to prevail in a case of this type it is not necessary to prove intent, motive or purpose to discriminate on the part of city officials. We feel that the law on this point is clear, for "'equal protection of the laws' means more than merely the absence of governmental action designed to discriminate; . . ." we now firmly recognize that the *arbitrary quality of thoughtlessness* can be as disastrous and unfair to private rights and to public interest as the perversity of a willful scheme.[80]

Under this reading of the Equal Protection Clause, low-income Black and Puerto Rican litigants in Norwalk, Connecticut, prevailed in a challenge to inequitable displacement when gentrification moved them from their homes in the late 1960s.[81] Also under this reading of the clause, Black residents of Lackawanna, New York, successfully challenged segregation in their town when racially discriminatory zoning laws were enacted to exclude them from building homes in White neighborhoods.[82] After the *Washington v. Davis* ruling, the Equal Protection Clause was further neutralized when, in 2001, the Supreme Court decided *Alexander v. Sandoval*. The court ruled that individual litigants no longer have the right to pursue a private right of action to enforce Title VI of the 1964 Civil Rights Act. In short, with the *Sandoval* decision, the nation's return to legalized inequality was complete. Today, instead of the blatantly legalized inequality that characterized Jim Crow, the post–Civil Rights era now protects structural racism by ensuring that the Equal Protection Clause will be interpreted to protect *unequal* protection of the law.

Unjust Laws Produce Unjust Health Outcomes

This derogation of equality under the Constitution has had devastating real-life consequences. The legal choice to minimize the available constitutional protections for equality has hurt population health. Equal protection laws, it turns out, measurably change lives for the better if vigorously enforced—and for the worse if halfheartedly enforced. This relationship borne out by the differences between health outcomes in historical periods of lax or strong enforcement of the Fourteenth Amendment. Although our Constitution guarantees equality in theory, our government has failed to deliver equal protection in practice. The Equal Protection Clause was originally intended to protect equal justice under law for Black Americans. Yet since the moment it became law, there have been efforts to limit, misconstrue, or minimize the meaning of the clause—efforts reminiscent of the treasonous advice given by Dick the Butcher in *Henry VI*. The preceding review of the Fourteenth Amendment's history and reach across all aspects of Black life in America helps explain how population health in the United States could become so inequitable, with Black and other marginalized people stuck so consistently on the losing end of the outcomes.

In this last section of the chapter, I will use population health data to show that our nation's failure to legally protect the equality of African Americans has harmed health and shortened lives for generations. A leading indicator that epidemiologists use to examine the health of a population is the rate at which people die. Therefore, I have aggregated available data showing the death rates of Black and White people in America over approximately a hundred years.

First, the infant mortality rate, defined as the number of infants per thousand live births who die within the first year of life, is presented for the century between 1915 and 2015. The infant mortality rate reflects the health of children in a population before, for example, a decision to smoke or take a job in a coal mine or find a home near a landfill can influence their life chances. The mortality rate is also a useful measure of maternal health.[83] This measure, frequently called the "most sensitive index we possess of social welfare and of sanitary administration," is thus a primary indicator of population health.

Second, I present data at the other end of the life spectrum. The all-cause, age-adjusted death rate is calculated as the rate of death per one hundred thousand standard population for selected causes of death. It captures all the environmental, disease, and social consequences of life that influence how long people live. Selected causes of death included here are such major conditions as heart disease, cancer, and stroke.[84]

The graphs that follow present infant mortality and age-adjusted death rates for Black and White populations over the past hundred years. These data have their limitations. Record keeping during the Jim Crow period was not reliable enough to interpret these data for scientific precision. Yet these data do show trends that provide theoretical support for the conclusion that unjust law is associated with unjust health.

Figures 3.3 and 3.4 compare the infant mortality and all-cause mortality rates for White and Black Americans for roughly a century. To compare the *relative* health of two populations, I have calculated a ratio of these two population groups' death rates (the dark solid line on each graph). Both graphs also show the *absolute* death rates for Black and White populations. These are the lines that trend downward over time, showing that health has improved for all populations during the past century. The absolute death rates have declined for all races of people because the United States has made progress in reducing death and disease through better health care, improved living conditions, and scientific advances in medicine. Regardless of race, this progress has improved health-care access and quality and has reduced death rates over time. Also, individual-level racial attitudes in America have improved substantially over this period.

But the stunning message from these graphs is that despite historical medical and even racial progress, American health outcomes have not become more equal. To the extent that population health reflects social conditions, the disappointing lack of progress toward health equality, as shown by the Black-to-White ratios for death rates in each graph, suggests a similarly disappointing lack of progress toward racial equality. Evidently, the gains of the past century are significantly and disproportionately the gains of White Americans.

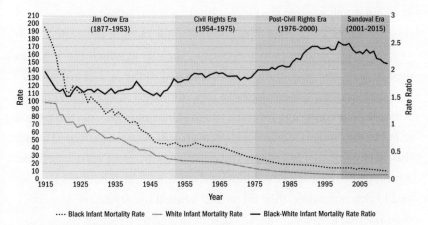

FIGURE 3.3: Black and White Infant Mortality Rates in the United States, 1915–2015. Data from National Center for Health Statistics, "Infant Mortality Rates by Race in the United States, 1915–2013," Centers for Disease Control and Prevention, 2018.

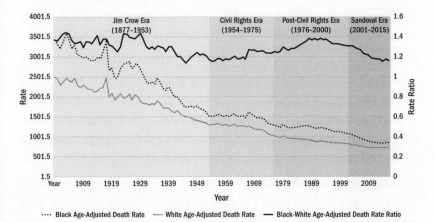

FIGURE 3.4: Black and White Death Rates in the United States, 1900–2017. Data from B. B. Bastian, Vera B. Tejada, E. Arias, et al., "Mortality Trends in the United States, 1900–2017," National Center for Health Statistics, Centers for Disease Control and Prevention, 2019.

Figure 3.3 shows that the ratio of Black to White infant mortality rates (the heavy black line) has trended upward for most of the period from 1935 to 2015. This means that over time, the rate at which Black babies died in their first year of life when compared to the rate that White babies died *increased* even as health care improved in the United States. Notably, that trend has reversed during the Sandoval era (the period after the *Alexander v. Sandoval* Supreme Court decision in 2001), though this decline probably reflects the effect of policies in earlier periods. Again, while these data do not permit a precise match between policies and health outcomes, they do permit general observations. Moreover, the undeniable message here is that health gains were not equally distributed between Black people and White people.

During this approximately hundred-year period, with few exceptions, the ratio of infant mortality rates between Black and White populations has steadily climbed, because the number of Black infants dying per thousand live births has always been greater than the number of White babies dying per thousand live births. Moreover, the evidence suggests not only that the ratio of Black to White death rates has generally climbed for most of the last century, but that it is also *greater* today than it was during Jim Crow. In that era, Black babies died in their first year of life between 1.8 and 1.9 times more frequently than did White babies. By the Sandoval era, when the Supreme Court had completed its retreat from the high goals of equality under the Equal Protection Clause, the ratio of Black infant deaths to White ranged between 2.1 and 2.5. Today, Black babies in America die more than twice as often as White babies do before reaching their first birthday. Social scientists and clinical researchers have been perplexed by the fact that despite substantial improvements to the health and survival rates of US infants overall, there has been little success in reducing the national Black-White differential in infant mortality.[85] The question is, why? Throughout this book, I posit the failure to legally enforce the Constitution's equal protection mandate as an important answer. Because inequality under the law lies at the heart of structural racism, this national failure may be the most important reason of all.

As noted, I have mapped these health data according to the chronological periods of legalized inequality, legalized equality during the Civil Rights era, and unequal protection of the laws in the post–Civil Rights era. Except for two periods in history—the second half of the Civil Rights era and the end of the post–Civil Rights era—the infant mortality rate, a key indicator of African American health, has grown worse over time. Assuming a time lag in the impact that law has had on relative health outcome, this graph suggests that for the brief periods when equal protection law was interpreted to truly protect equality, health differences, as measured by the Black-White infant mortality rate ratio, improved slightly. But because the law has been largely unfavorable with respect to enforcing equality, the relationship between Black and White health has also been unbalanced.

Figure 3.4 tells the same story for all-cause mortality from 1900 to 2017. The top, heavy black line, which measures the Black-to-White ratio of the age-adjusted death rates of populations, is revealing. This line changes little over time. In 1900, during the beginning of Jim Crow, the age-adjusted death rate of Black people was 1.37 times greater than the rate for White people. More than a century later, the Black age-adjusted death rates ratio is barely improved, to 1.23 times greater for Black people than for White—almost the same ratio as it was in 1900. Despite a century of medical and public health miracles such as the control of many infectious diseases, food safety, motor vehicle safety, antibiotics, and vaccinations, Black people did not benefit from these health milestones at the same rate that White people did. As I document through this book, African Americans have poorer health outcomes because their standing as equals under the law, sadly, has changed little over the past 117 years. Though much has changed in America during the twentieth century, structural racism has remained unchanged and persists in destroying health and, ultimately, lives.

As I have shown, laws play a central role in erecting and maintaining structural racism. Whether equal protection laws protect or destroy equality has an inextricable bearing on whether African American people live sicker or die quicker than do White Americans. Having established this association between the theory of structural racism and the empirical evidence of health inequity, the question now becomes, how much does structural racism harm public health? To analyze this question, I turn from the impacts of structural racism on my parents' individual lives to the impacts on the social and environmental circumstances in which they lived. My parents were members of a population group—African Americans who lived in the community of South Bronx. The public health consequences of structural racism had a devastatingly disparate impact on the entire population and community to which they belonged. The impact continues to this day. That is the story told in the next two chapters.

4

UNJUST HOUSING
AND NEIGHBORHOODS

Residential segregation has proven to be the most resistant
to change of all realms—perhaps because it is so critical to
racial change in general.
—Thomas Pettigrew, *Negroes in Cities*

If you sought to advantage one group of Americans and disadvantage another, you could scarcely choose a more grace-
ful method than housing discrimination.
—Ta-Nehisi Coates, *The Case for Reparations*

Nowhere is the reversal of structural inequality and structural racism
likely to do more to produce just health in America than in housing.
Experts have identified racial residential segregation as the "structural
linchpin" of the entire system of racial inequality and stratification
in the United States.[1] Therefore, in this chapter, I quantify the public
health impact of unjust housing and call for the reversal of racially and
economically segregated housing in America to produce just health.
Residential segregation is the degree to which two or more racial groups
live separately from one another in a geographic area.[2] Although segregation levels have shown some improvement since the Civil Rights
era, the United States remains highly segregated in most regions of the
country. Moreover, segregation rates remain extremely high for African
Americans, who are the most segregated and racially isolated group in
this nation.[3]

Residential segregation is a fundamental cause of health disparities.[4] It rigidly maintains racial differences in socioeconomic status and

therefore in health outcomes. Some argue that residential segregation may serve as a protective factor and may actually improve health outcomes for minority residents. However, the great weight of evidence shows that segregation adversely affects minority health. Certainly, African American and Latino respondents who are most often the victims of residential segregation identify it as a negative influence contributing to their poor health outcomes.[5]

Dr. Michael Kramer and Dr. Carol Hogue developed a framework to describe the possible pathways that link segregated housing to poor health outcomes (figure 4.1). The framework offers several important insights explored in this chapter. First, in addition to the adversity (e.g., poor education and diminished employment opportunities) that segregation visits on individuals, it does damage at the neighborhood level. Second, segregation hurts both poor and middle-class residents, especially in the African American community, where even middle-class people are more likely to live in lower-income neighborhoods than are White people at comparable socioeconomic levels. Third, the negative effects of segregation last for generations. Black residents remain excluded from the benefits of wealth accumulation because of depressed housing values and diminished social capital (i.e., fewer benefits derived from professional and other networks).

Achieving just health in America depends primarily on dismantling residential segregation. Above all, this step will require the reform of segregating laws to reverse structural racism; these reforms are described in chapter 6. This chapter makes the public health case for these reforms. Reversing residential segregation would improve outcomes along each of the pathways outlined in the Kramer and Hogan model.

In this chapter, I will focus on three ways in which reversing residential segregation would advance just health in America. First, desegregating housing will have an immediate and transformative impact on improving health outcomes because it will disrupt the disproportionate exposure of marginalized populations to substandard housing conditions. The low-quality housing conditions that contribute to poor health

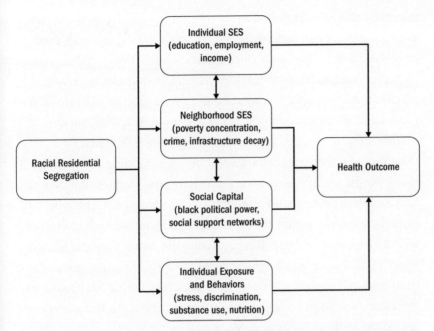

FIGURE 4.1: Pathways between Segregation and Health (SES = socioeconomic status). Source: Michael R. Kramer and Carol Hogue, "Is Segregation Bad for Your Health?," *Epidemiologic Reviews*, 31 (July 2009): 178–194, figure 2.

flourish in segregated neighborhoods but not in racially and economically integrated ones. For this reason, segregation is associated with increased morbidity and mortality for Black people and other minorities. When racial and economic segregation is no longer the defining, legally structured, organizing feature of the American residential landscape, health outcomes will improve and health disparities will measurably decline.

Second, because segregation is the bedrock on which all other structural forms of inequality rest, the reversal of residential segregation would reduce inequality in other major social determinants of health such as education, employment, nutrition, and personal safety. The public health community describes this interconnectedness of social determinants with two words: "Place matters."[6] Another common way to express this neighborhood-based relationship among the social determinants is the observation that "one's zip code more powerfully predicts health outcomes than does one's genetic code." Thus, by dismantling structural inequality and structural racism in housing, segregation in neighborhood schools, workplaces, and social settings will also be disrupted and the health and well-being of communities will improve.

Third, the reversal of residential segregation will gradually unravel the group psychology of dehumanization.[7] Dismantling segregation will bring people of different races, ethnicities, and socioeconomic strata into increased contact with one another. Intergroup contact has been repeatedly shown to reduce racial prejudice and bias. Yet such interactions will not happen overnight. But equalizing the status of people from different racial backgrounds by removing the structures that isolate them from personal contact and cooperation in everyday life has been shown by researchers to provide powerful counterfactuals to stereotypes and prejudices built on ignorance. Moreover, increasing interaction among racial communities will make it more difficult to ignore the structural inequalities that thrive when isolation hides from one group's view the injustices that affect another group. In short, residential segregation will contribute to increasing interaction among human beings from different racial and ethnic backgrounds, challenging the myth of blatant and subtle dehumanization in real time. Therefore, the third and perhaps most important reason to dismantle residential segregation is to help contradict the lie of legalized dehumanization that has undergirded structural racism.

These three reasons for just housing in America make desegregation, quite simply, the right thing to do. But an added advantage to reversing residential segregation is that the empirical evidence shows this reversal will improve health outcomes for all racial groups across the United States.

The adverse health effects of residential segregation have been empirically documented for decades.[8] Likewise, contemporary research continues to confirm these effects. The National Academy of Medicine not only affirms segregation's continuing impact on health today but also importantly distinguishes the harm due to structural *racism* from the harm caused by the more general forms of structural inequality:

> Residential segregation—that is, the degree to which groups live separately from one another—can exacerbate the rates of disease among minorities, and social isolation can reduce the public's sense of urgency about the need to intervene. The effects of racial segregation differ from those of socioeconomic segregation. Lower SES [socioeconomic status] whites are more likely to live in areas with a wide range of SES levels, which affords even the poorest residents of these communities' access to shared resources (e.g., parks, schools) that buffer against the effects of poverty. By contrast, racial and ethnic minorities are more likely to live in areas of concentrated poverty.[9]

It stands to reason, therefore, that our nation needs a comprehensive legal overhaul and bold steps to arrest displacement and gentrification to reverse the effects of racial isolation. Reforms aimed at socioeconomic disparities alone will neither reduce residential segregation nor fix the health disparities that flow from it. Instead, reforms that have meaningful impact on population health disparities must address structural racism specifically and intentionally. Health reforms, therefore must be justice reforms. Said another way, just health will require just housing.

Just Housing and Improved Health

A strong body of evidence demonstrates that access to safe, affordable housing is an essential social determinant of good health. Sadly, extensive data also confirm that African American, Indigenous, and Latino American communities are the least likely of all communities, at every socioeconomic level, to have access to this social determinant.[10] An estimated 10.7 million people live in substandard housing in this country.[11] Of these, approximately 2.6 million (7.5 percent) are African American,

2.2 million (6.3 percent) are Hispanic, and 5.9 million (2.8 percent) are White. Substandard housing describes dwellings in which the physical structure or infrastructure is deficient, defective, or in such ill repair that the home does not meet the basic requirements to provide humans safe shelter. In fact, the substandard conditions present dangers to physical and mental health. What's more, the connection between segregation and poor health has long been known, since well before the Civil Rights era in the United States.[12]

In a seminal article published in 2002, Dr. James Krieger and Dr. Donna Higgins collected evidence that the substandard quality of housing is a key driver of morbidity and mortality.[13] As noted earlier in this chapter, Dr. Kramer and Dr. Hogue also reported numerous studies showing that substandard and defective housing conditions cause major health problems for children and adults.[14]

A growing body of research has more recently confirmed these earlier findings.[15] For example, homes that lack adequate ventilation, lighting, or plumbing have been associated with the spread of communicable diseases such as tuberculosis and cholera. Homes that are infested with roaches or that have inadequate heating are correlated with increased incidence of asthma.[16] The third National Health and Nutrition Examination Survey estimated that 40 percent of childhood asthma is related to a child's home environment.[17] Moreover, moderate to severe housing defects such as dampness, mold, and lack of heat are causally related to other chronic diseases.[18] Substandard home environments are also associated with respiratory disease, neurological disorders, and psychological and behavioral dysfunction.[19] Similarly, both adults and children have been shown to suffer long-term adverse health consequences from living in homes that have lead in paint, plumbing, and water.[20] Researchers have connected the incidence and prevalence of infectious disease with insufficient water supply, leaky plumbing, and insufficient sanitation.[21] Homes that have such structural and design deficiencies as electrical defects, faulty furnaces that emit carbon monoxide, or unstable stairwells are associated with injuries caused by falls and burns each year.[22]

The risk of living in substandard housing has been called a public health crisis, but the risk of this crisis is not visited equally on all communities. Poor rural populations are particularly susceptible to living conditions that lack basic plumbing; in 2012, 30 percent of the nation's rural housing stock lacked piped hot and cold water.[23] Two million people nationally occupy homes with severe physical problems, however, the most recent evidence showed that 7.5 percent of non-Hispanic Black Americans lived in moderately substandard housing, compared with 2.8 percent of non-Hispanic White people. Based on the American Housing Survey, conducted by the US Department of Housing and Urban Development, Black and Hispanic communities are more than twice as likely to face unhealthy housing conditions than are White communities.

These data reflect another housing disparity that disproportionately exposes minority populations to substandard living conditions: the gap in home ownership between Black, Latino, and White people. While 71 percent of White families live in homes they own, only 41 percent of Black and 45 percent of Latino families own their homes.[24] Housing problems that are closely related to poor health (e.g., pest infestation, faulty toilets, mold, lack of heat, and dampness) occur much more frequently in rental than in owner-occupied homes. Tenants in segregated neighborhoods often pay higher rents for these substandard homes and yet have less control over the quality and safety of their homes.[25] As a result, home ownership disparities disproportionately expose minority populations to substandard living conditions, which are yet another cause of health disparities.

Richard Rothstein's excellent book *The Color of Law* catalogs the myriad ways that federal law and policy legalized inequality to construct geographic segregation by race.[26] This narrative of structural racism is well known. But legalized inequality has also more specifically played a role in ensuring that Black, Latino, and Indigenous residents are the populations most exposed to substandard housing. When governments have attempted to aggressively enforce building codes that could require landlords to provide safe, sanitary conditions for renters, the owners have, counterintuitively, sued city governments for violating the antidiscrimination provisions of the Fair Housing Act to resist having to correct unsafe living conditions. In St. Paul, Minnesota, for example, rental property owners fought for the right to continue to rent substandard housing to primarily Black tenants, despite multiple safety violations such as uncollected garbage, dilapidated structures, and roach or rodent infestation, all of which pose serious health concerns. The building owners argued in *Thomas J. Gallagher v. Steve Manger* that their predominately minority tenants were being unfairly targeted for building code enforcement in violation of antidiscrimination provisions of the Fair Housing Act.

All three legal components of structural racism are exhibited in this case. First, the federal government used redlining, zoning, and financing laws to construct public housing projects in St. Paul exclusively for minority families and to construct suburban homes outside St. Paul for White families only; this practice represents *legalized inequality*. Next, city and state governments selectively enforced health and safety building codes, leaving substandard conditions to fester in marginalized communities; this negligence represents *legalized dehumanization*. Finally, rental property owners appropriated the disparate-impact provisions of the Fair Housing Act, which was intended to stop discrimination against minority tenants, to instead escape liability for the hazardous conditions that their properties disproportionately foisted on minority renters. This reverse (and perverse) use of a signature civil rights law to perpetuate discrimination rather to eradicate it is an egregious example of *unequal protection of the law*.

Ending residential racial segregation is an indispensable step to ending structural racism. However, desegregating American neighborhoods will take time and intentionality. The health impacts of desegregation, moreover, will not appear in the data immediately. To reduce the burden of substandard housing that minority families bear disproportionately, governments and community leaders will need to take advantage of zoning laws, building codes, lending laws, and tax credit programs. Moreover, what journalist Tim Henderson calls the "segregated mindset" that has captured American law and life will need to be reformed.[27] An anti-segregation paradigm shift in America will result in better and less disparate health outcomes because racially concentrated exposure to substandard conditions will decrease. An equal opportunity for social mobility will increase. And competition for safe, decent, and affordable housing will make housing more affordable.

Just Neighborhoods and Improved Health

Segregation operates as a systemic mechanism to create and reinforce economic inequality among racial groups. It does so by locating Black communities away from neighborhoods that provide access to the social determinants of health. These determinants include good-quality schools, opportunities for well-paid employment, and healthy food sources. This "spatial mismatch" is deliberate in that minority families would not have chosen these locations without the direct intervention of government and private actors.[28]

My parents, for example, purchased our family home in the South Bronx, joining hundreds of thousands of African Americans who left overcrowded apartments, for which they paid exorbitant rents in Harlem, to low-rise apartment buildings or multifamily homes like mine. The South Bronx represented upward mobility for my parents as one of the designated parts of the city where African Americans and Puerto Rican Americans could become homeowners. My father's work in the Transit Authority gave our family a stable income and the ability to afford housing that service workers and unskilled laborers could not. I remember the large oak trees that lined Ward Avenue. And though they stretched for only one city block, it was *my* block that enjoyed the leafy canopy in summer.

At first I did not realize that the neighborhood was "turning," as my parents began to whisper. We were able to afford our $19,000 home, and obtain a mortgage to finance it, because redlining rules tolerated by law then offered Black families the chance to occupy homes vacated by the

White flight of working-class German, Jewish, Italian, and Eastern European immigrants.[29] No laws forbade the redlining practices that would prevent my family from obtaining a loan to move to similarly priced homes on Long Island. Nor did the law prosecute racially motivated violence that kept us from buying a similarly priced home in adjacent White parts of the Bronx such as Parkchester. No antidiscrimination laws challenged the fact that as the number of Black families displacing White families increased, the quality of public services declined. Hunts Point Hospital, Morrisania Hospital, and the Bronx Eye and Ear Hospital closed. White families fled the public schools, and new public housing projects accepted only Black residents, to further segregate the neighborhood.

The result in neighborhoods like mine across the nation was that marginalized racial groups became geographically bound to inferior schools, with fewer academic and enrichment resources and less experienced teachers for their children. The health-care alternatives near these communities also became limited to inferior facilities with fewer advanced medical resources and a greater percentage of physicians trained in less competitive schools and programs. Evidence has shown that segregated neighborhoods receive lower social service investment in fire protection but excess exposure to police intervention than seen in predominately White neighborhoods. Home values in racially segregated neighborhoods enjoy lower appreciation and therefore convey smaller returns on investments to owners. And therefore, both long-term wealth and social mobility are denied these communities. In sum, residential segregation is responsible for racializing access to the major social determinants of health in neighborhoods.

In their seminal article published in 1999, Dr. David Williams and Dr. Chiquita Collins carefully laid out the numerous pathways through which residential segregation harms health outcomes by choking off access to other social determinants of health.[30] Long before the term *structural racism* became prominent, they explained the difference between an individual's racial prejudice or explicit desire to maintain social distance from others and the structural racism that produced residential segregation through a "complex web of discrimination involving cooperative efforts by the real estate industry, federal housing policy, banking institutions, and vigilant neighborhood organizations." Using mortality data from the National Center for Health Statistics and demographic data from the US Census, Williams and Collins analyzed the relationship between residential segregation and death. Their findings were astounding. Living in a highly segregated neighborhood, they found, is associated with a range of toxic risk factors that increase susceptibility to illness and death for African Americans. Moreover, their analysis showed that for both Black and White populations, though the pattern was weaker for White people, segregation is related to cancer deaths for Black and White males and for Black females, even after adjustment for socioeconomic status. They concluded, "This pattern of findings suggests that there may be some structural characteristics of highly segregated cities that have an adverse impact on all persons who reside there."[31]

The influential work of Thomas LaVeist has demonstrated a statistically significant relationship between residential segregation and higher infant mortality rates among African Americans and White people.[32] Using the multiple findings of this association (reported as early as 1950), Dr. LaVeist added geographic location, poverty, and political power to his analysis to confirm that the disparity between Black and White infant mortality rates is greater in cities that are highly segregated.[33] Importantly, LaVeist also found that Black infant mortality rates declined in segregated cities where Black citizens had greater political power, suggesting that such power could be exercised to mitigate other structural risk factors that contribute to poor outcomes in Black health.[34] Finally, Dr. LaVeist also noted that for both Black and White groups, poverty is also associated with higher infant mortality, so much so that as White poverty increases, the gap between Black and White infant mortality narrows. The gap does not, however, disappear; infant mortality rates for Black babies are higher than for White babies, notwithstanding the mother's education or income level. In fact, Dr. Michael Lu, dean of the University of California, Berkeley, School of Public Health, has declared the belief that racial disparities in infant mortality are due to socioeconomic status are "the biggest myth."[35] National data show that not only are Black infant mortality rates almost three times higher than White rates, but African American mothers with a college degree have worse birth outcomes than do White mothers without a high school education.

Sue Grady's study of 96,882 South Bronx births from 2,095 census tracts, in which she analyzed the relationship between low-birthweight infants and neighborhood segregation at the local level, is, of course, personal to me. According to Dr. Grady's research, my home neighborhood in the South West Bronx suffers from the double jeopardy of high residential segregation and high neighborhood poverty.[36] African Americans are particularly susceptible to this form of *hypersegregation*, a term coined to describe how Black Americans are not only more segregated than other minority communities but also more often segregated simultaneously across several dimensions.[37] In my neighborhood, as with the other low-income areas studied, Dr. Grady found that African American women had a higher percentage (9.6 percent) of low-birthweight babies than did women who lived in nonsegregated neighborhoods (8.7 percent). Low birthweight is associated with poor health outcomes throughout the life course. Using multilevel modeling, Dr. Grady concluded that residential segregation is positively and significantly associated with low birthweight, even after controlling for individual-level risk factors and neighborhood poverty.[38]

Other studies have shown that segregation is associated with poorer adult health. African Americans living in segregated neighborhoods experience shorter life expectancy, higher homicide rates, and greater prevalence of infectious diseases such as tuberculosis, even after controlling for poverty.[39] Delores Acevedo-Garcia has presented an insightful conceptual framework to demonstrate residential segregation's role in the epidemiology of tuberculosis and other infectious diseases.[40] She distinguished the direct and indirect effects that segregation may have on disease transmission. Segregation operates *indirectly* because it concentrates poverty, overcrowding, dilapidated housing, and social disintegration in minority communities with limited access to health care. According to Dr. Acevedo-Garcia's model, segregation operates *directly* to transmit infectious disease by isolating minority communities and thus confining transmission to the segregated group while preventing transmission to the rest of the population. Moreover, by reducing the visibility of infectious disease in segregated communities, segregation increases the likelihood of public health neglect. Dr. Acevedo-Garcia's model not only predicts but also explains the prevalence and incidence of tuberculosis. Between 1985 and 1992, when tuberculosis cases were expanding in segregated urban centers, 50 percent of cases in New Jersey occurred among African Americans who were disproportionately exposed to environmental, population risks of poverty, overcrowded, and dilapidated housing.[41]

Carol Aneshensel and Clea Sucoff found poorer mental health among California youth who lived in segregated neighborhoods than in adolescents living in integrated settings.[42] Yet these researchers misunderstood the association as social selection rather than social causation, saying "families volitionally move into and out of neighborhoods (subject to financial constraints, personal circumstances, and barriers of segregation), and these movements or lack thereof, define the structural attributes of the neighborhood." Dr. Aneshensel and Dr. Sucoff not only underestimated the "barriers of segregation" they described but also wholly failed to appreciate the extent to which minority families have limited financial and personal equality and therefore lack social mobility due to structural inequality and racism.

In another earlier study, Ana Diez Roux and her colleagues somewhat misunderstood the causal relationship between segregation and poor health. Perhaps the misunderstanding was due to their initially faulty premise that framed the outset of their study: "Where a person lives is not usually thought of as an important predictor of his or her health."[43] Instead, Dr. Diez Roux and her team pointed to lifestyle and genetic explanations as the causes of disease. Today, a majority of researchers agree that this causal explanation is incorrect; individual factors are not the primary predictors of poor health. Yet Dr. Diez Roux may be credited with correctly concluding that her study of some thirteen thousand participants showed that neighborhood characteristics are related to the incidence of coronary heart disease and, further, that this finding "suggests that the strategies for disease prevention may need to combine person-centered approaches with approaches aimed at changing residential environments." This wider outlook is an important insight. Another is that changing residential environments requires changing the laws that control them.

The Role of Law

Health-harming residential segregation has endured in America because of structural racism. Laws ranging from direct segregationist directives to implied zoning ordinances and neglected antidiscrimination provisions all contribute to impose predictable and severe health consequences disproportionately on minority communities. The threats to public health that segregated housing presents have been tolerated and significantly exacerbated because federal, state, and local governments ignore discrimination that is in fact a violation of the intended scope of the Constitution's Equal Protection Clause. Worse, the US government has historically engaged in housing discrimination, despite the Constitution's express prohibition, from the beginning of Reconstruction, continuing during the New Deal, World War II, and the post–Civil Rights era of urban renewal.[44] Today, housing discrimination at the hands of state and local governments takes the form of wholesale displacements of minority communities. This is the result of both urban renewal during the latter half of the twentieth century and the inaptly named process of "gentrification" that continues to this day. Whether through exclusionary discrimination that specifically prevented minorities from moving into White neighborhoods, or through nonexclusionary discrimination, through which building owners, tenants, and real estate agents harass or mistreat minority homeowners and tenants, laws enable governmental authorities to tolerate or even facilitate housing discrimination that continues to the present day.[45]

Some evidence suggests that racial prejudice and discrimination has declined since gains of the Civil Rights era.[46] Yet racial prejudice continues to thrive and to contribute significantly to preserving residential segregation in this country.[47] Research shows that homeowners and tenant associations engage in racial harassment and oppose purchases or rentals by minorities. Real estate agents steer minority buyers to homes and apartments that are not located in predominately White neighborhoods. Banking practices that cut off capital investment in neighborhoods on the sole basis of potential borrowers' race violate the antidiscrimination laws on the books but persist nonetheless.[48] Evidence that this type of housing discrimination continues was documented in a 2012 study of the national audits that are conducted to test for adherence to fair housing laws.[49] In that study, Sun Jung Oh and John Yinger used in-person, paired, and internet correspondence tests to evaluate whether sales and rental practices were discriminatory. The study found that real estate agents showed White home buyers 9 percent more houses than they showed equally qualified Black home buyers. It further found that White buyers received information about a greater number of available units than did Black buyers in 13.4 percent of tested inquiries. Similar discrimination marred the market for rental homes. There White renters were treated more favorably than were Black and Latino prospective renters in roughly 28 percent of inquiries. The evidence that persistent racial discrimination continues in the housing landscape confirms that residential segregation does not occur spontaneously. Instead, it thrives without interference from legal prohibitions against discrimination.

As with many cultural phenomena, the evidence of this contemporary racial discrimination in housing may be seen on social media. In 2016 and 2017, *ProPublica* found that Facebook was permitting advertisers for housing to exclude selected racial groups and anyone with an "affinity" for Black, Latino, or Asian Americans from viewing their advertisements.[50] This practice helps explain why residential segregation continues to prevail at high levels in the United States, despite modest declines. Dissimilarity indices remain high, revealing that more than half of the Black or White residents in several of the largest US metropolitan areas would have to move to a different census tract to fully integrate those cities.[51] Persistent discrimination has left African Americans the most segregated population in the United States, and the nation as a whole only barely less segregated than it was at the start of the Civil Rights era.[52]

To explore the changes in residential environments that dismantling residential discrimination and segregation could achieve, an example is useful. The next section looks at my home town—the South Bronx—to examine evidence of how residential segregation affected my family's and my neighbors' access to several social determinants of health such as income, schooling, personal safety, healthy food, and clean air. This examination is intimately related to my father's story told in chapter 1 of this book; it is evidence of the structural racism that took his life before his time.

The Story of Structural Racism in My Home Town:
The South Bronx

As recounted earlier in this chapter, my parents moved into the South Bronx during the 1950s, when it was a neighborhood in transition. The South Bronx was once home to upwardly mobile European immigrants who moved from Lower Manhattan tenements to the "wonder borough." They were attracted to its beautiful parks, tree-lined streets, the Bronx Zoo, the New York Botanical Garden, and the home of Yankees baseball. The Bronx also attracted my upwardly mobile parents for similar reasons when my father got a steady job and they planned to start a family. They were among the hundreds of thousands of Black and Puerto Rican families who similarly left Manhattan for a better life. The difference, however, was that they were Black and Latino, not White. Therefore, the structural racism that followed them pointed to the South Bronx as the allocated space in which they could settle. Furthermore, this racism also settled there with them and turned the neighborhood into a desolate landscape of abandoned buildings, crime-filled streets, and garbage-strewn lots flattened by arson within two decades.

The story of structural racism in the South Bronx is the story my parents lived, as the neighborhood where they hoped to pursue the American Dream changed from two-thirds White in 1950 to two-thirds African American and Latino by 1960 and, according to Professor Evelyn Gonzalez, became a national symbol of urban decay.[53] Of note, my neighborhood today is a symbol of urban recovery; the transformation that is underway, albeit long overdue and excruciatingly slowly, confirms that structural racism *can be defeated*. But when my family lived there, the fact that they and their neighbors were overwhelmingly Black and Puerto Rican dramatically changed the neighborhood's access to resources, services, and political power. That is how structural racism works on geographic spaces. Professor George Lipsitz brilliantly calls this "the racialization of space and the spatialization of race."[54] He explains that neighborhoods are marked with the hierarchical value of the race of the people who live there. At bottom, the beautiful bucolic South Bronx was allowed, quite literally, to burn to the ground once the highly valued White populations departed and my parents and others like them moved in to replace them.

To demonstrate the enduring impact of the historical, legally enabled structural racism on the social determinants of population health outcomes, I analyzed a series of maps from my hometown, the South Bronx. I viewed them chronologically to examine, first, how legalized inequality enabled residential segregation, which initially set off the events that embedded structural racism in the South Bronx. Next, the maps illustrated how this racism affected the resources available in the South Bronx once its residents became predominately Black and Puerto Rican. I also compared historical maps with contemporary ones. Moreover, I examined maps that illustrate the distribution of fundamental social determinants of health. As a result of this analysis, I found graphic support for my analytical observation that structural racism fixes the odds of the inequitable life chances that a segregated community will experience.

The progression toward assuring the probability of poor outcomes seen in the South Bronx today is neither random nor unpredictable. Geographic racial isolation, above all else, depresses wealth, jobs, and wages. Increased criminal activity not only accompanies this income suppression and concentrated poverty but also thrives as the focus of crime control shifts from community safety to property protection. Simultaneously, the resources drained from public schools lock in a multigenerational cycle of poor education. Then, disparately poor health outcomes for the population inexorably follow as the loss of resources and quality of the built environment are ensured by the legalized dehumanization of marginalized populations that live in these segregated spaces. Once Black and Latino populations replaced White ones in the South Bronx, for example, new interstate highways—in my neighborhood, the Cross Bronx Expressway—displaced beautiful homes and parks, to introduce the environmentally hazardous and relentless noise and air pollution. Also, once White people left the South Bronx, healthy food sources and open spaces disappeared and obesity flourished. These are the building blocks of structural racism, and the geographical descriptions that follow show the interconnectedness of each component. Finally, my South Bronx analysis poignantly illustrates how structural racism progresses not only because the data that accompany each layer of change are part of my life story but also because the story changed before my eyes as the race and ethnicity of the South Bronx transitioned from White to Black. The change happened quickly, and the differences were as stark as day and night.

Segregation: Legalized Inequality

Structural racism began in the South Bronx with the legalized inequality of segregation. In 1937, so-called residential security maps of the

South Bronx were created by the Home Owners' Loan Corporation (HOLC). The HOLC, a US federal agency, created these maps of localities throughout the nation to guide mortgage lenders, appraisers, and real estate investors where to invest. When a map was colored red, or *redlined*, that area was described as a hazardous investment area.

Even in 1937, the South Bronx was an area designated as a high risk for investment. This designation set a pattern of substandard neighborhood conditions in place—a pattern that endures to this day. Importantly, race and ethnicity were at the center of the HOLC determination of the neighborhood's suitability for investment. Each HOLC map was accompanied by a summary of its inhabitants. The narratives accompanying the maps reveal the structural racism that informed federal lending standards. Each form had a category to indicate the percentage of "foreign-born" families and the extent of "Negro Infiltration." These categories identified the presence of people from racial and ethnic minority groups as negative attribute that undermined property values and reduced the chances that capital would be directed toward that section of the city. For the South Bronx, the federal government's explanatory narrative with the HOLC map warned against investment, because of the "steady infiltration of negro, Spanish and Porto [*sic*] Rican" people, as well as Russian and Polish laborers. This designation from the 1930s has affected the South Bronx today. Like the nearly three-quarters of the areas the HOLC designated as "Hazardous," the South Bronx remains a low-income, racially segregated neighborhood more than eighty years later.[55] Analysts Bruce Mitchell and Juan Franco explain that the HOLC redlining system ensured persistent economic and racial inequality in cities that would be denied access to capital investment. And, as Mitchell and Franco explain, residents could not access mortgage loans, in no small part because of their race and ethnicity. Some maps went as far as to describe racial minorities as groups embracing unlawfulness, explaining that a neighborhood was undesirable because of the "infiltration of negros and other criminals."

This HOLC map supported lending practices that limited where my parents could consider buying a home. Because racist and xenophobic policies among lenders, real estate agents, and neighbors were supported rather than challenged by law, my parents could not consider suburban neighborhoods on Long Island, in Westchester County, or even in other parts of the Bronx, even if they could have afforded homes there. Today, unsurprisingly, the South Bronx—especially the neighborhoods in the west—continues to exhibit the scars of residential segregation. Without question, one of the most enduring consequences of the redlining program was to suppress employment opportunities in these neighborhoods. As a result, economic and residential segregation have persisted in the South Bronx. Contemporary maps of the South Bronx dated 2018 show that all of the lowest-income zip codes in New York City are in the South Bronx neighborhoods that were redlined in 1937.[56]

In 1979, the year my father died, our household's annual income for our family of four was among the lowest in New York City. We lived just above the poverty line on less than $30,000 per year, which was average for families in the redlined South Bronx. Today the South Bronx, with a population of 1.2 million, remains one of the most racially segregated areas in the nation; according to New York University's Furman Center, the population is 56.2 percent Hispanic, and 43.7 percent non-Hispanic Black.[57] In other words, nearly ninety years after the HOLC designations, the redlined South Bronx remains economically, racially, and ethnically segregated. The next few discussions on the distribution of resources reveal the structural impacts on each of the major social determinants of health available to residents of the South Bronx.

Schools, Jobs, and Crime: Unequal Protection of the Laws

The South Bronx areas that were redlined in 1937 continue to host the poorest-quality schools and, relatedly, the highest crime rates today. The juxtaposition of these low-educational-quality and high-crime regions with the redlined areas of the 1937 HOLC tell this important story about segregation: where legally enabled segregation flourishes, access to the resources necessary to live healthy lives is absent. Schools in the South Bronx are failing. While the district receives one of the city's largest per-pupil allocations in school funding, the concentration of poverty and homelessness is reflected in low attendance, low reading proficiency, and low graduation rates. Moreover, compared with schools in middle-income neighborhoods, segregated schools have fewer advanced placement courses, less-qualified teachers, less access to academic and college counseling, and weaker networks connecting them to employers and colleges.[58] Programs that allow parents to pick any school within the district do not change the fact that the district is economically and racially segregated and therefore all its schools are segregated as well. Similarly, the area continues to have the highest rate of violent crime in the city. This outcome is predictable given the well-described inverse relationship between concentrated poverty, joblessness, low wages, and crime. The income per capita is less than half of other New York areas; the unemployment rate is 56 percent higher than the national average.[59]

Maps of the present-day South Bronx also highlight the relationship between poor schools, low-wage employment, and increased crime. Educational attainment depends on a number of variables, many of which rest with the individual student and family. However, families are less able to contribute to student success if educational options have been inadequate for generations, leading to low-wage jobs and therefore housing in neighborhoods where the opportunity costs of crime are low. In other words, just as health behaviors are influenced by an individual's or a family's environment, so too are the choices that create educational achievement. As my own story attests, the educational options have been limited for the majority of South Bronx residents for decades.

Food and Health Care: Legalized Dehumanization

The same areas redlined by the HOLC in 1937 as having an infiltration of "negro . . . and Porto Rican" people today suffer the greatest food insecurity, where more than 2.9 million people report missing meals.[60]

This widespread food insecurity is, predictably, associated with the same Bronx regions that have the greatest prevalence of obesity.

Living in food deserts—areas that lack healthy food alternatives and whose primary food sources are fast food and convenience stores—can lead to poor diets. Research has shown that neighborhoods with few healthy food options but several sources of unhealthy foods are frequently correlated with areas that have high rates of obesity and chronic diseases.[61] This inequitable access to healthy foods is compounded by the evidence that segregated neighborhoods have fewer recreational facilities and open spaces than do other settings. Thus, the lack of opportunity and a concern for personal safety are likely to discourage healthy exercise behaviors. Moreover, in contrast to the scarcity of healthy food alternatives, segregated neighborhoods see an abundance of alcohol and tobacco advertisers and retail outlets. This exposure is positively correlated with increases in such unhealthy behaviors as smoking and excessive alcohol consumption.[62] In fact, researchers have recently shown that unhealthful food and beverage advertisements for sugary beverages, candies, processed foods, alcohol, and beer are disproportionately located in subway stations that serve the South Bronx.[63] Other data show that 25 percent of subway riders are Black, Latino, or low-income laborers of all races. Finally, the South Bronx has been designated a Medically Underserved Area for having too few primary care providers, and a Health Professional Shortage Area since 1978.[64] This means that the US Department of Health and Human Services has identified this population as having insufficient access to primary care physicians, dentists, or mental health providers. The South Bronx, like other segregated neighborhoods across the nation, is served by health-care institutions that have fewer financial and clinical resources, providers with inferior clinical qualifications and educational training, and poorer outcomes for patients than do health-care institutions in nonsegregated communities.[65]

The confluence of these conditions in segregated neighborhoods largely explains why more than 30 percent of adults in these redlined areas of my South Bronx neighborhood are obese. In 2006, researchers reported that the death rate for diabetes among women in the South Bronx is twenty times that for women with diabetes in the predominately White Upper East Side of Manhattan, a mere ten-minute subway ride away.[66] A 2015 paper reported that South Bronx residents suffered one of the state's highest rates of premature death due to heart disease—the condition that took my father's life at age forty-nine. Finally, in 2020, the Bronx was declared the "coronavirus capital" of New York City, recording some of the highest numbers of COVID-19 cases, hospitalizations, and deaths. The structural conditions that make residents of this community susceptible to premature death due to these multiple underlying comorbidities were in place long before these health data were collected. The numbers provide evidence that structural racism is a fundamental cause of health disparities.

The Environment: Legalized Dehumanization and Unequal Protection of the Laws

The disproportionate assault of pollution on the health of South Bronx residents cannot be overstated. The lack of access to clean air to breathe, another key social determinant of good health, has been denied the residents of this segregated neighborhood. The South Bronx has become home to multiple air pollution hazards. Traffic from three major interstate highways crisscrosses the area daily, depositing carbon monoxide, nitrogen dioxide, and fine particulate matter ($PM_{2.5}$ and PM_{10}) into the air. Long-term exposure to high concentrations of these toxins is associated with asthma and other chronic lung diseases, respiratory illnesses, and cardiovascular disease. The South Bronx also has become home to over half of New York City's waste transfer stations, where garbage trucks from all over the city dump their waste.[67] In contrast, the predominantly White Upper East Side of Manhattan contains no waste transfer stations though it is located right next to the South Bronx. Waste transfer stations are industrial locations where garbage is brought in, sorted, and then shipped to the appropriate locations such as landfills for disposal. The South Bronx records the highest number of garbage and other trucks per hour—one every twenty-four seconds—of any location in the city. It also records the highest concentration of asthma-related pollutants in the city. Residents complain of the odor, and studies confirm that the high diesel emissions from garbage truck traffic in the area pose a significant public health risk.

Not only is the sheer number of trucks that pass through the South Bronx hazardous, but the location of the roads that carry these trucks can also jeopardize children's health. A study conducted by the New York University Wagner Center concluded that approximately half of children who attend prekindergarten to the eighth grade in the South Bronx attend schools located within 150 meters of a highway or truck route. Moreover, elementary schools, hospitals, and nursing homes are all located near industrial manufacturing facilities throughout the South Bronx.[68]

In the South Bronx, as in much of segregated America, Black Americans are much more likely to live within one mile of a polluting facility than is any other racial group.[69] Indeed, the area is unremarkable among segregated neighborhoods in that there, Black and Latino children are more likely than White children to attend schools located near polluting facilities.[70] The result in these neighborhoods is poorer student health and academic performance.[71]

The Outcome: Public Health Disparities

The South Bronx analysis discussed here is proof positive that the result of injustice is health inequality. This impactful relationship is seen in the dramatically disproportionate disease burden from asthma borne by minority residents of the South Bronx because of segregation. Asthma is a chronic lung disease that is linked to air pollution from vehicular traffic, power-generating facilities, and waste disposal industries, all pollution sources that have found homes in the South Bronx. Asthma affects people of all ages, diminishing their quality of life and sometimes causing premature death. In the South Bronx, asthma fatality rates are three times the national average, and hospitalization rates due to asthma are five times the national average.[72]

The disease is especially dangerous to children's health. Research has shown that children from the Bronx are particularly susceptible to asthma that is related to their housing conditions. In 2009, Dr. Karen Warman, a pediatrician in the Bronx, and her colleagues studied more than 1,700 children between five and eleven years old with persistent asthma. The researchers compared the responses of parents from 265 Bronx children with the responses from parents of 1,500 children from seven other locations. Dr. Warman and her team found that the parents of children from the Bronx, more than the other parents from the other locations, were significantly more likely to report aeroallergens in their homes; more likely to report cockroaches, mice, and rats in their homes; and more likely to report visible mold in their homes.[73]

It is no wonder, therefore, that pediatric asthma rates in the Bronx far exceed national pediatric asthma rates. Not only is the prevalence of disease greater in children who live in the Bronx (15.5 percent of young Bronx children have asthma, compared with 9.2 percent in New York City and 8.9 percent of US children ages two to seventeen overall), but the severity of the disease is also greater. Children in the Bronx are twice as likely to be hospitalized and more than twice as likely to die from asthma than are children anywhere else in the United States. In the South Bronx specifically, in 2013, 0.03 percent of children aged five to fourteen were hospitalized for asthma in New York City overall, while 1.2 percent of children in South Bronx neighborhoods were hospitalized for asthma.[74]

Recent data from the New York City Department of Health on the prevalence of asthma among adults show that the highest rates occur in the South Bronx. While New York City as a whole persistently registers among the highest asthma rates in the country, the South Bronx neighborhoods, followed closely by the predominately Black neighborhoods in Brooklyn and Queens, are the worst affected in the city.

We must understand that the story of structural racism and its effects on the social determinants of health in the South Bronx is not unique.

The same cascade of deteriorating events has been initiated by the laws that institute and maintain residential segregation across the nation. These conditions disproportionately burden African American, Latino and Indigenous communities around the nation, from small towns like Charlottesville, Virginia, to large metropolitan areas like Baltimore, Detroit, Chicago, Milwaukee, and Kansas City. Although residential segregation has declined most dramatically in the South, famous strongholds of segregation like Pine Bluff, Arkansas; Jackson, Mississippi; and Birmingham, Alabama, remain divided and are in states that sit atop the list of those with the largest Black-White wealth gaps in the country. The deliberate segregation techniques used by the US government during the first half of the twentieth century has produced racially divided access to the social determinants of health today.

Segregation has declined somewhat across the nation since the Fair Housing Act of 1968 outlawed housing discrimination, but racial segregation, especially between non-Hispanic Black people and White people, remains persistently high across much of the nation.[75] Using the US Census Bureau data between 2013 and 2017 as the most commonly cited measure of segregation, the dissimilarity index for the United States overall has declined from 0.70 in 1990 to an estimated mean of 0.60 as of 2014.[76] The dissimilarity index ranges from 0 (complete integration) to 1.0 (complete segregation) and describes the proportion of the Black population that would have to move in order to eliminate segregation. The national dissimilarity index of 0.599 means that today, nearly 60 percent of Black or White people would have to move to another location to evenly distribute Black and White residents, in light of their share of the population. Despite its common use, the dissimilarity index is not a perfect measure of segregation.[77] But it is widely adopted and therefore useful to evaluate segregation trends over time and among localities. Segregation levels vary across the country. Dissimilarity indices range from a low of 0.15 in California to a high of 0.80 in Milwaukee and the tristate area that includes New York, New Jersey, and Pennsylvania. Segregation between Black and White residents is the lowest in the South and western parts of the United States and the highest in the Northeast and Midwest.

The coincidence of residential segregation, poor social conditions, and poor health outcomes in the South Bronx vividly illustrates that structural racism generally, and residential segregation specifically, are fundamental causes of racial health disparities throughout the nation. Only interventions aimed at these fundamental causes will reverse the aggregated deprivations of the social determinants of health. This insight was first highlighted by David Williams and Chiquita Collins in their important paper delineating evidence that residential segregation is a fundamental cause of health disparities.[78] Noting that substantial differences in Black and White health persistently occur in the United States with large Black and White differences in socioeconomic status, Dr. Williams and Dr. Collins explain that residual differences in health and social outcomes among racial groups are attributable to long-term consequences of racism.[79] The encouraging news is that the residential segregation and even its associated dehumanization can be reversed.

Structural Racism in Housing

The laws that establish and maintain residential segregation are dehumanizing because they treat people in a manner inconsistent with their value and status as human beings. Segregationist laws represent dehumanization by commission, and the failure to enforce laws that prohibit discrimination in housing represent dehumanization by omission. In both instances, the law imposes conditions and operates from assumptions that disregard the humanity of others. But the reverse is also true. Disrupting laws and legal processes that support residential segregation will not only have a juridical impact—making laws more just—but also a constitutive one as well by creating an environment in which people can experience the humanity of people unlike themselves. While laws do not in their own right establish the status of a person or group of people as human, they can create an environment that makes dehumanization less likely to flourish.[80] Therefore, legally disabling residential segregation will also disable the conditions that enable dehumanization. Ending residential segregation will reverse the physical isolation and separation of racial groups and help equalize their access to social resources among racial groups. Most importantly, dismantling residential segregation will increase interaction between different groups. This increased intergroup contact, therefore, makes it easier for people to view one another as fully coequal humans. This syllogism is based on the intergroup contact theory.

Simply stated, intergroup theory hypothesizes that increasing personal contact and acquaintance between members of different racial groups can reduce prejudice.[81] The positive effects of intergroup contact on cross-racial attitudes have been studied and repeatedly validated in multiple settings. While contact alone is not enough to significantly reduce negative attitudes, empirical studies have revealed a good deal about the environments in which intergroup contact does work to reduce bias. For example, researchers have confirmed a list of necessary conditions, such as sharing common goals, engaging in cooperative ventures, and having the support of external authorities, that combine to make group interaction an effective mechanism for reducing racial prejudice.[82] We also know that intergroup contact can occur vicariously through the experiences of another and still have a positive effect on reducing prejudice and bias. In 1997, groundbreaking studies of extended group contact showed that even without personal interaction, knowledge that a person in one's racial group had a friendship with a person from another group resulted in less negative attitudes toward the other racial group overall.[83]

Most importantly, intergroup contact decreases racial bias when it occurs in settings that present the opportunity to build friendships across groups. When the contact allows for more intimate interaction, it can produce both direct and indirect results. Remarkably, research conducted during the period when my parents moved to the South Bronx showed that this is exactly what happens when racial groups live together in desegregated neighborhoods. In a 1952 study conducted among public housing residents, researchers found that direct and intimate contact between Black and non-Black residents led to attitudes that were more positive about Black people in general and to indirectly positive attitudes about potential relationships among the races. Older studies focused on the attitudes of White people and how integrated living changed their attitudes toward Black people. Participants described changed racial attitudes of housing residents this way:

> The women who live closer to Negroes, it appears, are not only more likely to have the more intimate types of contact with Negroes; having *more opportunity to observe other white women associating with Negroes* [italics added], they are also more likely . . . to believe that interracial activities are socially approved.[84]

Similarly, in another study, researchers compared attitudes toward African Americans in segregated and integrated housing in the northeastern section of the country. They found that White people who live near Black people have more contact with, and thus more favorable attitudes toward, Black people. The difference could not be accounted for on the basis of initial favorable attitudes. Nor could the improvement be the result of a favorable social climate at the time of this 1952 study. Yet the researchers found that "nearness of residence to negroes 'increases the likelihood that the white resident will observe interracial association of negroes and whites as a normal part of the social processes of the community.'"[85] Researchers registered lower levels of racial anxiety and increased group-based empathy for people of different races.[86] In other words, White people began to see Black people as human. Of course, this is only one side of the interracial relationship. Later studies found less improvement in attitudes that minority group members had about White people. Black biases toward White people are real, though these biases should not be falsely equated with structural racism. Anti-White biases are not historically enabled through legal mechanisms that control educational, governmental, residential, criminal, and civil justice systems to exclude or disadvantage White groups. On the other hand, a robust and accessible literature describes the psychological evidence that supports my conclusion that intergroup contact generally, and integrated housing specifically, will reduce dehumanization.[87]

One final observation warrants attention: the question of whether race or socioeconomic status better explains the structural inequality seen throughout this chapter. Without question, the structural deprivations shown here are mediated by race—not income, education, or any other measure of socioeconomic status. The South Bronx story ideally demonstrates this answer because of the marked transformation the neighborhood underwent when disfavored *White* immigrant populations lived there, as compared to the conditions that prevailed when disfavored *Black and Latino* populations arrived. In 2015, Jo Phelan and Bruce Link published a groundbreaking paper that generalized and advanced the Williams and Collins thesis. Dr. Phelan and Dr. Link asserted that racism is a fundamental cause of health inequality. Their theory delinked differences in race, as a biological construct, and socioeconomic status from observed racial inequalities:

> We conclude that racial inequalities in health endure primarily because racism is a fundamental cause of racial differences in SES [socioeconomic status] and because SES is a fundamental cause of health inequalities. In addition to these powerful connections, however, there is evidence that racism, largely via inequalities in power, prestige, freedom, neighborhood context, and health care, also has a fundamental association with health independent of SES.[88]

Their assertion means that the secondary effects of residential segregation will only be eradicated when we disrupt structural racism as root cause.

5

UNJUST EDUCATION

A person who lacks basic elements of an education is not fully healthy.
—Robert Hahn and Benedict Truman

The deprivation of public education is not like the deprivation of some other governmental benefit. Public education has a pivotal role in maintaining the fabric of our society and in sustaining our political and cultural heritage; the deprivation of education takes an inestimable toll on the social, economic, intellectual, and psychological wellbeing of the individual, and poses an obstacle to individual achievement.
—*Plyler v. Doe,* 1982

Mine were one of the four sets of parents, out of the eleven families I knew well from the block where I grew up, whose children escaped the cyclical grip of systemic racism in the South Bronx. In each case, the quality education they obtained for their children is the compelling factor in their success. Also, in each case, the parents' fight against structural racism to gain equal access to the better education is the main reason that only one women out of those eight parents is alive today. The Green, Ince, and Harris families, like my parents—the Bowens—pulled us out of our neighborhood public schools in the South Bronx before fifth grade. When they did this, we kids were not altogether sure that this was a good decision. For one thing, the daily commute was brutal and seriously cut into our time hanging out on the front stoops and playing sewer-to-sewer touch football until the streetlights came on. For another thing, we soon drew unwelcome attention from the neighborhood's toughest kids who stayed behind.

I wish I could say I appointed myself well. While I distinctly remember marveling that one of the Harris boys had a strong Christian faith as well as a powerful right jab, the Green girls and I were not so gifted in the art of physical combat. Luckily for us, however, Mrs. Green was a ringer. I recall one encounter in particular that featured Mrs. Green coming to break up a fight one of the Green girls and I had gotten into but surely were not going to win. I vaguely remember that Mr. Green—a dear man with the warmest of smiles and a killer sense of humor—also came to our defense. But not before Mrs. Green arrived. As far as I could tell, her feet must not have touched a single step as she descended from her second-floor apartment, because she was down on the street in an instant. Nor did she bother to waste the time to drop whatever implement she had been using to do her housework before she arrived just in time to promise to deploy that implement to another purpose on our behalf. It does not always work out well when your mom steps in to fight for you, but Mrs. Green was apparently persuasive. We never again had any encounters with those girls. To this day, I love to recall that story with Mrs. Green. We still laugh aloud about her speed. And we love to reminisce about her wonderful husband, whose story was much like my father's, from its hardworking beginning to its early and untimely end. But the point of the story for this book is to underscore the difference that having access to a quality education made in our lives, and the price our parents had to pay to get it.

The Bowen, Harris, Ince, and Green kids all did well in life. But when we were young, nothing exceptional about us distinguished us from most of the other kids in our neighborhood. We all played together on our block. Some of us owned our family homes, others rented. All our parents were laborers. Some of us went to church and some did not. All of us stayed to witness the chaos of our South Bronx neighborhood's storied transition from a bucolic to bellicose landscape. But the urgent message of this chapter is this: There is a reason the Bowen, Green, Ince, and Harris kids got out of the South Bronx to come dance at one another's weddings, visit each other's newly purchased homes, send holiday photos of our kids who got to college, and all while working one rather than multiple jobs. It is because none of us went to school in the South Bronx beyond the fifth grade. We enjoyed these advantages because we got high-quality educations *outside* the South Bronx—education that should be available to all kids equally, including those *within* the South Bronx. However, we all traveled, and paid dearly for these schools. All of our parents scraped together the money to send us to private or parochial school. If good local public schooling had been available, then the Harrises, Greens, Inces, and Bowens would not have prematurely lost all the men and most of the women in their families. Instead, the adults died early deaths, due in no small part to what they had to do to pay the taxes that financed the neighborhood schools that failed all the other kids, as well as the fees for their own kids to go to the schools that changed their stars. For all the families in my neighborhood, and for America overall, the human cost of structural racism has been unfathomably high.

Much of the debate about structural racism in education has been about affirmative action in higher education. While I firmly believe that without affirmative action in post-secondary schools, I also believe that I would not have the privilege to be the dean of a top American law school, without the Fieldston School's extraordinary commitment to affirmative action in elementary, middle, and high school. Fieldston's commitment to making a great education accessible to minority families made an enormous difference in the academic preparation and social networks that led me to graduate from Harvard College, the University of Virginia Law School, and the University of Colorado Graduate School. I will go further and say that Fieldston's commitment to educational equality in my early years enabled me to obtain advanced degrees that are a nontrivial part of the reason that I have now outlived both of my parents.

The Fieldston School approached affirmative action as an ethical imperative. That meant the school admitted a critical mass of students

from Black and Latino families in each grade. This approach eliminated tokenism, exceptionalism, and isolationism. No individual
failure or success was racialized. It also meant the school made a long-
term commitment to engage in the ongoing struggle that comes from
the inevitable clashes that occur when an educational institution com-
mits to dismantling societal structures of inequality—whether those
structures are racism, sexism, anti-Semitism, homophobia, or other
histories of oppression. Fieldston's full name is the Ethical Culture
Fieldston School to reflect that it was founded by, and governed under
the auspices of, the humanitarian organization the New York Society
for Ethical Culture in 1878. Originally, the school was called the Work-
ingman's School. The core premise of the school then and now is to
ensure that all children have access to a quality education. Fieldston
stands out for its principled commitment to actively pursuing equality of educational opportunity to achieve a better society. And today,
many of the most remarkable leaders fighting for equity and justice in
a myriad of sectors around the world are my classmates and the friends
I made at Fieldston. The school taught me that a quality education is
life-determinative.

Considering the evidence that not only place but also education matters, this chapter will recount the salient features of a quality education
that are lacking for most minority children in this country because of
structural racism. First, structural racism robs Black, Latino, and Indigenous children of the access to the quality teachers, curricula, and
counselors I had at Fieldston. Second, structural racism infects tracking
policies to steer minority students into low-performance, stigmatizing
programs that did not exist at Fieldston. And third, it disproportionately
disciplines Black children especially severely, introducing them to the
criminal justice system that was unheard-of at Fieldston. The chapter
then examines the empirical evidence that lifelong disparities in health
and criminalization flow directly from these three aspects of structural
racism in education. In this chapter, I aim to unmask this form of racism

that plagues our nation's education system, from preschool to college. I conclude that reversing it is the single most effective guarantee of a just society, where all will have an equal opportunity to experience just health.

Copious empirical evidence confirms that well-educated people enjoy better health than do less-well-educated people. As people attain higher levels of education, they generally report better health and physical functioning, while self-reported health is worse among people who have achieved less education. The scientific record offers multiple reasons for this well-established relationship between education and health. The story is complex but crucial because each level of complexity reveals a layer of structural racism that operates in public school systems to deny an equal opportunity for African American, Indigenous, and Latino American children to enjoy good health. The inequities set forth here are not incidental by-products of an otherwise fair system. Instead, they come from pervasive discrimination that effectively rigs a system of educational inequality.

Law plays a central role in the rigging. In 1971, the Supreme Court recognized this role and approved broad judicial power to remedy legalized inequality in schools. In *Swann v. Charlotte-Mecklenburg Board of Education*, Chief Justice Warren Burger explained that the court's decision was to remedy the "loaded game board" that American school districts represent.[1] The court has since reneged on that view. Thus, a "loaded game board" remains a signature result of structural racism in the United States. To extend the analogy, think of a game in which one group of players alone has advance knowledge of the rules, double the resources for playing the game, multiple turns during each round, and lighter consequences for mistakes made. You have just imagined the loaded game board that Chief Justice Burger referred to and that accurately describes the US education system.

In this chapter, I emphasize the urgency of reversing legalized racial inequality and segregation in American schools as a vital part of the effort to achieve just health. The chapter proceeds in four parts. First, it summarizes the evidence that a good education is a social determinant of good health. The data that connect educational attainment to health outcomes are unassailable. A clear, positive gradient clearly shows that as people become more educated, they live healthier, longer lives. However, these data raise an important question of causality. Does a good education cause one to experience good health, or is it the other way around? That is, are good education and good health statistically related because healthier people can do better in school? The answer is that both observations are accurate. Individual health predicts a person's ability to attend school and learn while there. But strong evidence also proposes that in many ways, the extent and quality of education influences how healthy individuals and populations can be.

In the second part of this chapter, I challenge the fallacious notion of an "achievement gap" between students of color and White students. The very term *achievement gap* is a form of dehumanization. It focuses attention in ways that incorrectly suggest individual deficiencies, using White students as a reference group. Instead, the evidence in this section reveals that performance disparities are much less about achievement than they are about *opportunity gaps* due to persistent, pervasive structural racism in schools and school systems. These include troubling differences in the quality of education available to minority students. We see, for example, shortfalls in instructional resources, teacher quality, curricula, and enrichment programs and abhorrently biased discipline disparities. These deficiencies, among others, all but guarantee that beginning in preschool and throughout their education, minority children will be systematically excluded from the chance to compete for the American Dream. The health consequences are devastating and last beyond a lifetime, for generations.

The third part of this chapter empirically shows how the police violence that begins in schools has a harmful impact on mental and physical health in Black and Latino communities as well as White ones nationally. This section supports the conclusion that eliminating disciplinary discrimination in the education system is likely to have far-reaching benefits for population health. Moreover, to the extent that educational opportunity is distorted by racial discrimination, the inequity runs afoul of the Equal Protection Clause and produces unconstitutionally variable health outcomes. These health disparities ultimately exacerbate racial gaps in employment, income, and wealth.

The last part of the chapter demonstrates the employment, income, and wealth impacts of discriminatory education. The evidence shows that the monetary value of improved educational attainment is reflected in significantly higher earnings, which are associated with both improved health status and health behaviors over a lifetime. Thus, by reversing educational inequality, we could improve access to all other resources needed for an equal opportunity to participate and succeed in life overall. In short, decreasing educational differences that are due to racial discrimination will increase health equity.

Good Education Produces Good Health

The relationship between health and education has long been described by social scientists. In their seminal article on these links, Catherine Ross and Chia-ling Wu discuss how inequality in education harms health, refuting the naive notion that personal choices about job and lifestyle operate independently of education and social context to produce health outcomes.[2] Dr. Ross and Dr. Wu confront the "social inequality" and "individual responsibility" dichotomy and assert that individual-level psychosocial resources and health behaviors occur within, and because of, socially structured environments. Precisely hitting the proverbial nail on the head, they explain how education fits into the theory of structural inequality explored in chapter 1 of this book:

> Stressors, hardships, and health behaviors are not randomly distributed; they are socially structured. Smoking, exercising, drinking, or a sense of personal control are not *alternatives* to socially structure inequalities like

unemployment, poverty unfulfilling jobs, or economic hardships faced disproportionately by those with little schooling. On the contrary, they link education-based inequality to health.[3]

Ross and Wu used data from 2,031 respondents to a 1990 telephone survey to test three links between education and health. First, they theorized that education determines work and economic opportunity. Employment shapes work conditions, which also influence personal health and well-being, and in turn determines one's ability to maximize income and minimize levels of economic hardship. Second, education also shapes the health-improving protective resources such as a sense of personal control and access to social support. Both personal control and social support improve health and mortality. Third, as educational attainment and, therefore, income increase, so does the likelihood of engaging in such healthy behaviors as exercising, eating healthy foods, and refraining from smoking or excessive drinking. The researchers' cross-sectional and longitudinal data confirmed these three assumptions. Ross and Wu found that education is strongly and positively associated with measures of health. It improves health indirectly by improving work and economic conditions as well as psychosocial factors like health behavior.

Researchers Robert Hahn and Benedict Truman add to this work by providing an evidence-based explanation of the pathways through which education and public health are linked.[4] Whether the information is based on self-reported or administrative data reporting rates of major circulatory diseases, diabetes, or liver disease, health outcomes are associated with education. Several psychological symptoms as well as mortality and life expectancy are inversely associated with educational attainment.[5] In light of this empirical evidence, Dr. Hahn and Dr. Truman acknowledge that educational attainment and health are reciprocally related, while their data also strengthen the causal claim.

Health is clearly a prerequisite to obtaining education. A sick child cannot learn as well as a healthy child can. But the reverse is also true in that education is a fundamental, upstream social determinant of health during childhood and throughout the life course. According to Hahn and Truman, good education causes good health:

> We argue that education—the product and personal attribute acquired—is both a critical component of a person's health and a contributing cause of other elements of the person's concurrent and future health. . . . Attainment of a certain level of formal education by young adulthood affects lifelong health through multiple pathways.

Figure 5.1 illustrates these multiple pathways. As shown, the process of education and its results (e.g., knowledge, skills, and capacities) are all *contributing causes of health.* Hahn and Truman conclude that the association between education and health meets most of the criteria required to infer causality: Studies throughout the literature consistently replicate the association; they often test and confirm the temporal sequence in which education precedes health outcomes. Moreover, the association is plausible and coherent and fits with the views of education expressed by the US Supreme Court in *Plyler v. Doe* and in *Brown v. Board of Education.* In the latter case, the court declared, "In these days, it is doubtful that any child may reasonably be expected to succeed in life if he is denied the opportunity of an education."[6]

This model identifies three major pathways linking education and adult health outcomes: the psychosocial environment, a person's work life, and a person's health literacy and behaviors. The *psychosocial* pathway speaks to the health-enhancing impact that education has on a person's socioeconomic status. For example, higher educational achievement introduces students to other high achievers with whom they can form social networks, share social resources, and gain social support. From these psychosocial benefits, families may also enjoy improved economic prospects that contribute to family stability. The second pathway describes how education benefits one's *work* and, therefore, a person's economic conditions. Unemployment rates decline as education levels improve. Wages also increase with education levels. As discussed in chapter 4,

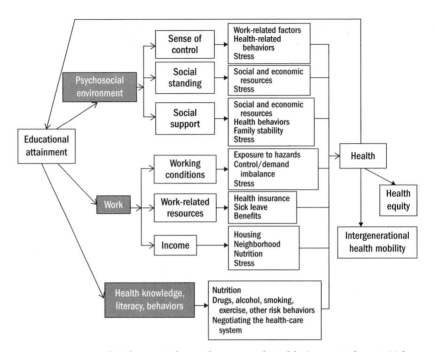

FIGURE 5.1: Causal Pathways Linking Education and Health. Source: Robert A. Hahn and Benedict I. Truman, "Education Improves Public Health and Promotes Health Equity," *International Journal of Health Services* 45, no. 4 (2015): 657–678.

these two outcomes strongly influence other salient determinants of health, such as which residential and neighborhood options are available. Finally, the model identifies education's positive influence on the third pathway: an individual's *health literacy and behaviors.* Through this pathway, education is connected to health by fostering such individual-level changes as increasing leisure time to engage in healthy behaviors and having discretionary income to eat better food. Overall, however, the strength of this model is that it captures the structural impacts that education has on population health outcomes.

Dr. Emily Zimmerman, Dr. Steven Woolf, and Dr. Amber Haley provide another comprehensive model to explain the connection between educational attainment and health. They argue that "education is one of the key filtering mechanisms that situate individuals within particular ecological contexts. Education is a driving force at each ecological level, serving as a determinant of everything from our choice of a life partner to our social position in the status hierarchy."[7]

The Zimmerman model thus offers a theoretical understanding of the way education influences health. Moreover, the model contextualizes the economic factors at a societal level that influence the increasing importance of education as a (structural) social determinant of health:

> Research based on decades of experience in the developing world has identified educational status (especially of the mother) as a major predictor of health outcomes, and economic trends in the industrialized world have intensified the relationship between education and health. In the United States, the gradient in health outcomes by educational attainment has steepened over the last four decades . . . in all regions.[8]

Finally, this model further elucidates how individual and community effects of education work together. Individuals with higher levels of education are less likely to engage in risky behaviors and more likely to pursue healthy ones. Research shows this propensity arises partly because a higher level of education tends to lower the stress associated with economic or relative deprivation.[9] Independent of individual- and family-level factors, education modestly affects community-level resources and institutions required for good health outcomes. These requirements include physical features such as recreational space, access to healthy food, and a strong economic base that produces jobs. Education is also positively associated with stronger community services such as improved access to, and quality of health-care options, and sociocultural features such as neighborhood reputation. Moreover, neighborhood characteristics driven by education tend to make communities more resilient and better able to work collaboratively to recover from disasters or protect against crime. The empirical data are consistent with the models showing that increased education improves health.

A well-known and well-respected study conducted by Jennifer Montez, Robert Hummer, and Mark Hayward analyzed longitudinal data collected over a nineteen-year period for more than a million respondents
to the National Longitudinal Mortality Study.[10] Their analysis measured
the impact of various stages of educational completion on mortality for
different racial and ethnic groups. The results, notably, were not linear,
and although they were generally similar among racial groups, the results
were not entirely uniform. Three important findings from this study bear
highlighting here. First, educational attainment, though determined early
in life, is predictive of opportunity and status throughout the life course.
Second, although a modest decline in the risk of death for adults between
ages twenty-five and sixty-four is associated with education through high
school, the risk of death declines sharply for all races that pursue schooling beyond high school. A high school diploma has a strong association
with life expectancy because this diploma is the most basic requirement
for decent employment and is a prerequisite for higher education in the
United States. As a policy matter, Dr. Montez, Dr. Hummer, and Dr.
Hayward conclude, this analysis strongly supports aggressively reducing
the high school dropout rate among all populations to improve health.
These results are shown in figure 5.2, which compares the risk of death
with years of education for non-Hispanic White and non-Hispanic Black
males and females. (The log-odds coefficient is a mathematical operation
that makes the comparison easier to see; the higher the coefficient, the
higher the odds of death.) All lines trend downward, showing a reduced
risk of death as education increases. But the sharpest decline in all cases
is after high school graduation.

Third, even after high school graduation, for Black and White males
and females, each additional year of education is associated with a lower
mortality risk, and there is no ceiling effect on the longevity of educational benefits. However, for Black people, unlike White people, what
matters for improving mortality after high school are credentials. Black
people receive less reduction in their mortality risk from attending

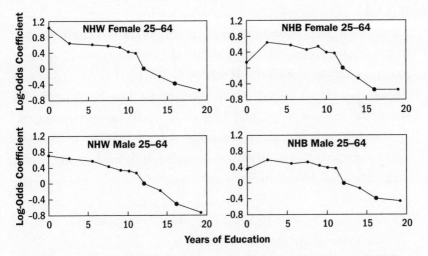

FIGURE 5.2: Risk of Death at Progressive Levels of Educational Attainment (NHW = non-Hispanic White; NHB = non-Hispanic Black). Source: Jennifer K. Montez, Robert A. Hummer, and Mark D. Hayward, "Educational Attainment and Adult Mortality in the United States: A Systematic Analysis of Functional Form," *Demography*, 49, no. 1 (2012): 315–336.

college without earning a bachelor's degree, whereas White people experience lower mortality from attending college even without earning a credential. Insightfully, Dr. Montez and her colleagues interpret this finding in light of the structural differences that affect Black and White populations in America:

> Our finding that credentials are what matter most for blacks is likely a manifestation of structural conditions, such as residential segregation, school quality, early family environments, and employment discrimination. For instance, smaller mortality risk reduction for each year of schooling may reflect the fact that black youth are more likely to attend inner-city, poorer-quality schools; and disparities in school quality explain a substantial portion of the black-white achievement gap during schooling and the wage gap after schooling.[11]

These researchers conclude that the policy implications include the commonly agreed-upon need for early childhood education, smaller class size, and promoting early childhood well-being, as well as more controversial solutions such as school vouchers. However, they also identify the need to facilitate access to college for more Black youth, not just the academically select, and the need to promote and enforce equality in employment hiring and promotion to improve health outcomes.

Dr. Zimmerman and her team compiled updated evidence of the health impact of education. The results are startling:

- At age 25, U.S. Adults without a high school diploma can expect to die 9 years sooner than college graduates.
- According to one study, college graduates with only a Bachelor's degree were 26 percent more likely to die during a 5-year study . . . than those with a professional degree.
- Americans with less than a high school education were almost twice as likely to die in the next 5 years compared to those with a professional degree. . . .
- By 2011, the prevalence of diabetes had reached 15 percent for adults without a high school education, compared with 7 percent for college graduates.[12]

The scientific literature that documents the inverse relationship between education and individual adult death rates in the United States has been described by experts as vast. In light of this information, we must confront the evidence that the opportunity to obtain an education is not distributed equally throughout the population. Racial and ethnic discrimination erect barriers to minority populations who seek an equal opportunity to get a good education. To better illustrate the lasting impact of structural racism, the next section explores how education discrimination contributes to minority communities' disproportionately poor health.

Unequal Protection of the Laws in Education

Until 1954, the allocation of inferior education opportunity and resources to African Americans while awarding superior access and quality of education to White students was explicitly the law of the land in the United States. But in *Brown v. Board of Education*, the Supreme Court issued a unanimous decision to declare that racially segregated educational facilities are inherently unequal and violate the Equal Protection Clause of the Fourteenth Amendment.[13] Ten years later, the US Congress passed the Civil Rights Act of 1964, a sweeping legislative effort to reverse legalized dehumanization and inequality in this country. This chapter of the book lays out the mechanics of how the Supreme Court retreated from the goal of providing equal educational opportunity to all US students, regardless of race, color, or national origin.

Unequal Opportunity

Section 402 of the Civil Rights Act of 1964 called for the Commissioner of the Office of Education to conduct a survey and report to the president and to Congress the results "concerning the lack of availability of equal educational opportunities for individuals by reason of race, color, religion, or national origin in public educational institutions at all levels in the United States." The result, a 1966 report by James S. Coleman, was titled "Equality of Educational Opportunity."[14] The Coleman Report became the first comprehensive dataset gathered nationwide to document school segregation. At that point—more than a decade after the *Brown v. Board of Education* decision—American schools remained separate and unequal. Almost 80 percent of all White students in the first grade attended schools that were between 90 and 100 percent White. More than 65 percent of all Black students in the first grade attended schools between 90 and 100 percent Black. In the South, most students attended schools that were 100 percent White or Black.

Brookings Institution researchers Grover J. "Russ" Whitehurst, Richard Reeves, Nathan Joo, and Edward Rodrigue have updated these data in two of the most comprehensive studies of school segregation in the United States.[15] Consistent with many studies, their research shows that immediately after the *Brown* decision, school segregation within school districts declined sharply during the 1960s and 1970s, despite massive resistance to implementing the legal requirements for equality in public education. However, the Brookings researchers also measured racial segregation between school districts and found that segregation actually increased slightly during the 1960s and 1970s as White families fled to the suburbs, leaving inner-city schools to minority students. Since the *Brown* ruling, school segregation has declined somewhat in America, but largely because of the growth in the Latino population, not because the separation that isolates students by race has significantly improved. In fact, both Black and White students are now more likely to attend school with more Hispanic students, but Black and White children are barely more likely to attend school with one another. Moreover, since school segregation by income has increased since the 1990s, both within and between school districts, Black students are four times as likely to attend a high-poverty school as they are to attend a low-poverty school, while for White students, the numbers are exactly the reverse. Still, when examining the stubborn resilience of segregation and its impact on educational quality, we must remember that most Black families in the United States are not poor and most poor families are not Black.[16] We also need to understand what each of the many indices used to measure segregation tells us. For example, simply measuring the drop in the number of White only schools in the United States—a decrease that is significant—says little about racial segregation, since much of the decline is attributable to increased numbers of Latino and Asian students in predominately White schools.

We also have to examine the correlation between racial segregation, school quality, and students' academic outcomes by race. One Brookings study notably points out that the relationship between racial segregation and educational outcomes is largely explained by economic segregation. That is, Black children's lower scores are because of the poor quality of the schools they attend and the fact that they attend those schools— whether the students are poor or not—more often than White students attend low-quality schools, even when they are poor. The Brookings team summarizes its conclusions:

> Black kids are not scoring worse because they are black, but because they tend to be poor. . . . The weight of evidence suggests that, at least in the context of the education system, the worse educational outcomes for minority students are the result not of the racial composition of their schools but the economic backgrounds of their fellow students, and the quality of the school itself—both of which are strongly correlated with race.[17]

Finally, the Brookings reports shed considerable light on the relationship between residential segregation and school segregation. It turns out that school segregation is directly related to neighborhood segregation. When it comes to the racial composition of schools, most look like the neighborhoods in which they are located. The takeaway, therefore, is that repairing racial inequality in education will require repairing racial inequality in housing and neighborhoods. This conclusion becomes especially important in light of the evidence that the poorer-quality schools attended predominantly by minority children are causing the achievement gap plaguing Black and other minority children.

We need to keep in mind, however, that structural racism segregates elite public schools, regardless of neighborhood characteristics. Admissions criteria maintain the advantage that privileged families are able to give their children.[18] Expensive test preparation, attentive and strategic academic counseling, equipment-dependent sports, arts, and music skills as well as access to parents and others who are savvy—these help maintain abysmally low rates of enrollment at elite public magnet schools such as the Bronx High School of Science (which admitted 12 Black students out of 803 in 2019) and Stuyvesant High School (where 29 of 3,300 students are Black).[19] The segregation of the nation's schools remains a major contributor to the differences in Black and White achievement.

The "Achievement Gap" Myth

Analysts and journalists are regularly seduced by the ease of pushing out statistics about the "Black-White achievement gap" in education. They cite the gap to highlight academic performance differences between Black and White students. The problem with these statistics is that they tell exactly the wrong story. The data are most often used to tell a narrative of disparately poor individual performances in higher education, employment, and the criminal justice system. Here is a typical example:

> Among people 20 to 24 years old, blacks are far less likely to complete or be in the process of completing college, far less likely to work, and far more likely to be in prison or other institution. The rates of incarceration and non-employment for young black men paint a particularly dire picture.[20]

This individualized interpretation, however, is wrong. The real question is *why* these different probabilities exist. The answer is laid bare by the stories of the kids I grew up with in the South Bronx. As I recounted at the beginning of this chapter, most of the low-income kids from my neighborhood had to attend the low-quality schools in my neighborhood and therefore received low-quality educations. Those who escaped the South Bronx neighborhood schools also escaped poverty. Moreover, the structural answer to this question is revealed in the fact that the same was true for my parents, for both my sets of grandparents, who were born at the turn of the century, and for their parents, who were born into slavery. The so-called achievement gap is in fact a multigenerational and highly racialized opportunity gap.

The telling indicator of the gap's true cause is the fact that a child's social class is the single most significant predictor of educational success. In fact, children are sorted even before they enter kindergarten, research shows. Children from socially disadvantaged families are far behind their wealthier counterparts even from the moment they enter kindergarten.[21] This pattern replicates the social gradient that is the hallmark of structural inequality. The empirical record shows that the storied "achievement gap" is not tragic evidence of individuals' failure to achieve but is, to a much larger degree, evidence of structural barriers that selectively limit some populations' access to resources. Specifically, the gap is primarily the result of the consistent difference between the inferior quality of schools that Black and Latino children are most likely to attend and the superior quality of schools that White children attend. These patterns of disparate school quality are not random and have long-term consequences. They are the predictable, cumulative effect of administrative and pedagogical decisions that repeatedly disfavor children from marginalized racial and ethnic groups.

A practice that significantly influences the so-called achievement gap is tracking. This is the practice of steering Black students with and without disabilities toward inferior or nondiploma programs, while allowing White children with and without special needs to earn a high school diploma. Another contributor to the racially disparate educational outcomes is the much harsher school disciplines meted out to Black, Latino, and Indigenous students than are given to White students for similar behavior. This systemic difference lays the foundation for racially disproportionate exposure to the criminal justice system and its well-documented disparities throughout the life course. Taking each instance of systemic discrimination in turn, we can easily see why the so-called achievement gap between Black and White students is less about deficient students and more about deficient structures. Let us examine these structures in more depth.

Unequal Quality

Strong evidence shows that the so-called Black-White achievement gap is influenced by the unequal quality of schools that students attend, rather than by their race. The Coleman Report, released in 1966, was the first major published account of the association between school quality and student achievement by race.[22] The report provided detailed data on the differences in school quality afforded to Black and White students. Conducting a survey of more than 645,000 students, the Coleman team of researchers found that Black children attended poorer-quality schools than White students did. The physical features of schools for Black children were also inferior to the schools for White children:

> Negro pupils have fewer of some of the facilities that seem most related to academic achievement: They have less access to physics, chemistry, and language laboratories; there are fewer books per pupil in their libraries; their textbooks are less often in sufficient supply.

The study did find that Black students had more cafeterias than did White students nationwide. But in every category directly related to academic achievement, White students attended better-quality schools overall nationwide:

> Just as minority groups tend to have less access to physical facilities that seem to be related to academic achievement so too they have less access to curricular and extracurricular programs that seem to have such a relationship. . . . Finally, white students in general have more access to a more fully developed program of extracurricular activities, in particular those which might be related to academic matters (debate teams, for example, and student newspapers).

The pattern of inferiority found in facilities and programs was also present in the quality of instructional personnel, but to a much lesser extent.

In other words, Black teachers in predominately Black schools had only slightly fewer credentials, such as highest degree earned, years of experience, or verbal scores, than did White teachers in predominately White schools. Today, the gap in the quality of mostly Black and mostly White schools is more pronounced.

Despite similar teacher credentialing in most schools, studies have consistently shown that teacher quality is unevenly distributed among schools, to the detriment of minority students and those from low-income families.[23] Moreover, teachers in predominately African American schools often have lower salaries and less experience. The curricular content offered at segregated minority schools is also inferior to that at segregated majority White schools. Black, Latino, and Indigenous students attend schools with fewer Advanced Placement and honors courses that prepare students for college. Nationwide, 25 percent of high schools with the highest percentage of Black and Latino students do not offer Algebra II, 30 percent do not offer chemistry, and fewer than half of Indigenous high school students have access to a full range of math and science classes.[24] Figure 5.3 shows that only 57 percent of Black students and 47 percent of Indigenous students attend schools where they have access to the science and math courses that prepare them for admission to competitive colleges, whereas 81 percent of White students have this access.[25]

Finally, college and career counseling professionals who are essential to academic planning to promote college admission and readiness are remarkably unavailable to majority Black and Latino schools. Experts recommend a student-to-counselor ratio of 250-to-1. Smaller, more affluent schools have much lower ratios to provide individualized attention to students and families. Although the high schools with the largest Black and Latino enrollments have close to the same ratios as do large, majority White schools, the US Department of Education notes that "an astounding" 20 percent of high schools have no school counselor at all.

Using school data from the Texas School Project and the Early Childhood Longitudinal Survey, Eric Hanushek and Steven Rivkin in 2006

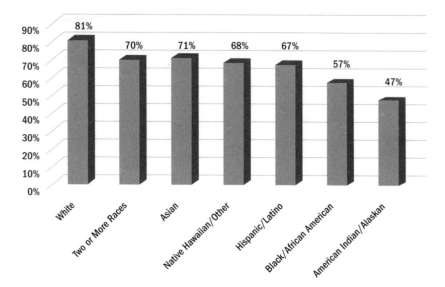

FIGURE 5.3: Students with Full Access to Math and Science Courses by Race and Ethnicity, 2014. Source: From US Department of Education, Office of Civil Rights, "Civil Rights Data Collection: Data Snapshot (College and Career Readiness)," Issue Brief 3, March 21, 2014, https://cdn.uncf.org.

showed that the widening achievement gap that occurs largely in the early elementary school years, between the third and eighth grades, is influenced primarily by three school characteristics.[26] Dr. Hanushek and Dr. Rivkin listed these three influential factors: the level of student turnover in a given school, the proportion of teachers with little or no experience, and the level of racial segregation (i.e., startlingly, they found that the higher proportion of Black-only peers diminishes Black student achievement especially).[27]

We need to understand this last factor—the concentration of Black enrollment—in a structural, social context to avoid the serious error of interpreting the results to convey an intrinsic negative characteristic of Black students. For example, the concentration of Black enrollment in a school is also correlated with the concentration—that is, the segregation—of resources and living conditions for students in the neighborhood where the school is located. As discussed earlier, this neighborhood effect of living in a predominately Black neighborhood will influence access to healthy food, the quality of health care, household income, and many other structural elements that affect school performance and for which the enrollment demographics are no more than a proxy indicator. Moreover, the association that Hanushek and Rivkin show does not account for the subtle but pernicious message Black students glean from their isolation in lower-resourced, lower-income schools, as well as from the atmosphere that discourages them from taking higher-level classes and activities when attending well-resourced schools. As Zyahna Bryant, a fierce and outstanding student activist in Charlottesville, Virginia, recently explained, "No matter how high your scores are or how many hours you put into your work, you are still black. . . . There's a whole system you're up against. Every small victory just cuts a hole into that system reminding you how fragile it is. But it's still there."[28]

Finally, in this discussion of unequal equality, I take strong issue with researchers who focus on the correlation between individual- and family-level differences between Black and White students and their respective academic performance. Research that points to the number of hours a parent reads, while ignoring the disparities in employment that inform the availability of those hours, or the number of books in a home while giving no consideration to gaping income disparities that allow wealthy families to purchase books, travel abroad, engage tutors, enroll in the best preschools, and invest in enrichment activities, is shortsighted and misleading. This blaming of victims is common among some educational theorists and completely misses the structural influences that shape individual and family characteristics. The great weight of the empirical evidence suggests that structural drivers, which are significantly influenced by racial discrimination in the social determinants of health, play a major role in the differences in school quality—structural differences that are the true basis of the inaccurately named "Black-White achievement gap." Indeed, the influence of structural discrimination is likely larger than the empirical record reveals, as Hanushek and Rivkin explain:

> All in all, the central finding is that school quality plays an important role in the determination of achievement and racial achievement differences. Indeed the impact of schools is almost certainly much larger than we show here . . . [because] easily quantifiable variables do not explain the bulk of the variance in teacher and school quality.

Today, when more than half of US students attend school in racially concentrated districts that are more than 75 percent White or non-White, the difference between the quality of Black and White schools remains a sadly powerful and salient component of structural racism.

There is a silver lining to the data on disparate school quality and racial discrimination presented here. Evidence suggests that a change in equal protection laws can improve schools and reduce educational discrimination. For example, after the watershed decision in Brown v. Board of Education, when school opportunities were equalized for both Black and White students, the achievement gap virtually disappeared. After passage of the civil rights legislation of the 1960s, progress toward racial convergence was evident.[29] This improvement stalled, however, around the 1990s. Some attribute this reversal to changes in postindustrial economy: the loss of jobs and similar economic depressants. Notably, however, the reversal also coincides with the end of US commitment to equal protection in education. Therefore, consistent with the core conclusion of this book, a change in law is the first and most important step required to end structural racism.

Unequal Intraschool Segregation

Thus far in this chapter, I have explored educational discrimination and segregation that separates children by placing different races in different school districts or school buildings. We will now explore discrimination that segregates students within a single school. Recently, even as racial segregation between schools and school districts has declined somewhat in the United States, racial isolation within the classrooms and programs has increased. Indeed, ability grouping—also known as *tracking*—has been called a silent and oblique method of achieving racial school segregation in an ostensibly integrated school.[30] While within-school tracking has a much smaller influence on the degree of overall segregation than does interschool and interdistrict segregation, the health impacts of within-school segregation are nontrivial.

The origins of the practice are bigoted and discriminatory. Between 1920 and 1950, educator Lewis Terman imported the Stanford-Binet IQ test and urged its use for ability grouping to separate new immigrants who were from ethnic groups that he deemed "feeble minded" from Anglo-Americans in schools.[31] The pros and cons of tracking today are bitterly disputed, and the research on its effectiveness is divided.[32] A detailed analysis of this issue lies outside the scope of this book. Instead, we will consider the evidence that tracking has a disparate and adverse health impact on minority students.

Studies show that tracking disproportionately isolates and stigmatizes minority students, lowering their self-esteem as well as teacher expectations of them. Minority students in schools using tracking participate in fewer extracurricular activities and drop out at higher rates than do minority students in untracked schools. Because tracking often excludes minority students from classes required for college, the adverse consequences can be long term. For example, Black students are significantly underrepresented in Advanced Placement and other higher learning opportunities.

Students from minority backgrounds are often steered into lower-level courses instead of the college-preparatory classes, partly because they lack the preparation afforded White students in earlier grades and partly because of low teacher expectations.[33] Within-school segregation is most common and severe in middle and high schools nationally but also begins early in the elementary school years. The early labeling can therefore establish inferior study habits, performance patterns, peer networks, and educators' expectations that are difficult to alter in later years.

Dylan Conger studied segregation across elementary school classrooms in New York City.[34] His study addressed the tracking of students according to their academic performance and the separation of students according to the ability assessments given by gifted and talented programs. He examined the possibility of unfair or discriminatory treatment of Black and Latino children in the distribution of students among classrooms within each school. Dr. Conger concluded that placing students from different racial groups into the same school does not ensure they will also share the same teachers, classrooms, or resources. Moreover, Dr. Conger's study revealed that current levels of within-school segregation could not be explained by random processes, "suggesting that more systematic forces may be at play."[35]

In a recent study of schools throughout North Carolina, researchers from Duke University and the University of North Carolina at Chapel Hill found that school segregation has generally increased in North Carolina between 1998 and 2016 and that within-classroom segregation accounted for up to 40 percent of all of this racial segregation in the state's high schools.[36] Students in this study started to isolate by race in middle school, with a pronounced split in the seventh grade.[37] Classroom segregation was greatest in high schools and between White and Latino students. Where the schools in their study had larger populations of Black students, segregation increased across classrooms. The data showed that White students were more likely to be enrolled in advanced courses than were Black and Latino students.

Within-school segregation can significantly affect students' opportunities to prepare for college. For example, the US Department of Education found that the 2,500 Black students in a New Jersey school district were awarded only 18.7 percent of the seats in Advanced Placement classes, though they represented 51.5 percent of the district's high school student population.[38] In many schools, White students are more likely to graduate with advanced high school diplomas that provide the advanced credits that many competitive colleges require. In Virginia, for example, starting as early as middle school, honors and accelerated courses put some students on track to receive advanced high school credits so that in Charlottesville, 75 percent of White students graduate with an advanced diploma, compared to 25 percent of Black students who have this credential on graduation.[39] Black and Latino students are more likely to be placed in tracks to receive alternative rather than full high school diplomas. In Wisconsin, for example, White children with special education needs are 31 percent more likely to receive traditional high school diplomas than are children from minority backgrounds. The upshot of these within-school disparities is that minority children have a higher chance of leaving high school ill prepared for college and the job market. Both these educational deficiencies present uniquely disproportional health risks that could be avoided through nondiscriminatory educational policies.

Unequal School Discipline

A disturbing pattern of discrimination emerges from the data concerning the treatment of students in US public schools. Specifically, Black, Indigenous, and Latino children receive strikingly more punitive treatment than do White students. Because the differences are so dramatic and consistent between Black and White students especially, this section will focus on these two groups. Black students are 2.5 times as likely to be suspended as White children are. Although they represent 15.5 percent of students overall, Black children account for 39 percent school suspensions and, in 2015–2016, 31 percent of school arrests.[40] Figure 5.4 shows that Black children receive the greatest disproportionate share of disciplinary actions in all recorded categories, whereas White children are the most underrepresented in each category. These disciplinary differences funnel straight into the criminal justice system, where Black youths are again treated differently from White youths. The result is a

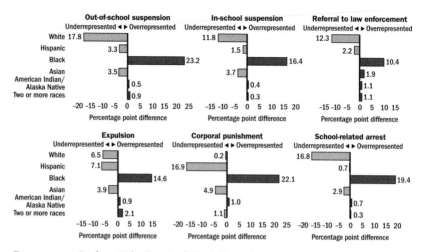

FIGURE 5.4: Students Who Received Disciplinary Actions Compared with Overall Student Population, 2013–2014. Source: US Government Accountability Office, "K–12 Education: Discipline Disparities for Black Students, Boys, and Students with Disabilities," March 2018, 14, www.gao.gov.

pattern that systematically removes Black children from the educational system at a disproportionately higher rate than other children, creating a population of uneducated or undereducated children. The population effect of this pattern creates a structural difference in health. Black children are less likely to be well educated and therefore enjoy good health than their White peers are.

Important evidence suggests these disciplinary differences begin at the earliest possible moment that children are in school. Further, the inconsistencies are due in large part to biased adult decision-making rather than to genuine differences in behavior by children. In 2014, the US Department of Education released data on suspension and expulsion of preschool students from 97,000 of the nation's public schools and 16,500 school districts across the country:

The results showed profound racial disparities in the administration of preschool discipline. While black students represented 18% of preschool enrollment, they made up 42% of students suspended once, and 48% of students suspended more than once. The statistics were even bleaker for [Black] boys, who were the recipients of three out of four preschool suspensions.[41]

These data tragically suggest that the dehumanizing presumption of guilt and treatment of children as criminals begins for Black children even before they enter kindergarten.[42] Studies have shown that teachers and others in authority tend to overestimate the age of young African American boys, prompting the suggestion that this error may partly explain how teachers develop age-inappropriate expectations for Black children's behavior. Other research suggests that teachers' biases unconsciously influence how they interpret actions of children at play, causing them to see the same behavior differently, depending on the race of the child.[43]

A recent report by the Yale Child Study Center confirms that unconscious racial bias may be a factor in this distressing pattern. The Yale study asked early childhood educators to watch videos of preschoolers engaging in typical activities for their age. The teachers were asked to look for "challenging" behavior from the children, though none was in fact present. The videos were standardized, and each group of teachers was balanced by gender and race. As the teachers watched the videos, researchers tracked the participants eye gazes as they searched for challenging behaviors. In a second part of this study, teachers read a standardized vignette describing a preschooler with challenging behavior. Along with each vignette, the teacher participants were told names that implied either a Black boy or girl, or a White boy or girl, and some teachers also received randomly distributed information about the child's family background.

The research produced several important findings, of which two are relevant here. First, when the teachers expected challenging behavior, they gazed longer—looking for that behavior—from Black children, especially Black boys more than from other student groups. Second, providing family background generally lowered the severity of teachers' discipline—but only when the child's race matched the teacher's expected narrative. Whenever the child's appearance did not match the family narrative that the teachers would have expected by race, the knowledge was correlated with increased severity of discipline. This second finding suggests a more complex layer of teacher biases directed toward family structures that may also operate to influence disciplinary disparities.

For our analytical purposes, these data demonstrate how far unconscious racial bias—a prejudice that presumes blameworthy behavior according to racial stereotypes—can hurt the educational opportunities and therefore the health of a child from the start. According to one report by Travis Riddle and Stacey Sinclair, "Overall, there is consistent evidence that black students' behaviors are both perceived as more problematic and are punished more harshly compared with White students."[44] Nationally, Black boys and girls are the only racial group for which both genders are disproportionately disciplined across all six forms of disciplinary actions, whether their schools were located in high- or low-poverty areas. These data were remarkably consistent for Black children regardless of gender. Indeed, Black girls were suspended from school at a higher rate than girls of every other racial group and at higher rates than all groups of boys of most racial groups.

In their study of how racial bias may affect disciplinary disparities, Dr. Riddle and Dr. Sinclair showed that county-level estimates of racial bias, using data from 1.6 million participants in the Implicit Association Test website, are associated with disciplinary disparities across almost 96,000 US schools and 32 million Black and White students during 2015–2016.[45] Their analysis considered five types of disciplinary actions. They found that counties with higher levels of explicit racial biases in favor of White people had greater disciplinary disparities between Black and White students in all five categories. However, they further found that implicit biases were associated positively only with out-of-school suspensions that year. Despite the possibility that these results could possibly be explained by another variable such as the absence of positive

African American role models in each county studied, the size of the study and the consistency of its results with other research strongly suggest that racial bias helps drive discipline disparities.

Discriminatory Discipline Hurts Children for Life

The tragedy of disciplinary disparity is even more unconscionable considering that Black students do not, in fact, misbehave at higher rates than White students do, even though Black children receive harsher penalties for the same behavior.[46] Nationwide, student suspensions for less serious offenses have increased. In one well-constructed study, researchers Johanna Lacoe and Matthew Steinberg documented suspensions in the School District of Philadelphia for incidents such as "willful defiance," failure to turn off a cell phone, not wearing the required school uniform, or failure to remove a hat. These nonviolent, relatively minor infractions represented more than half of all suspensions in Philadelphia schools during 2011–2012.[47] Here is the problem. These minor infractions are the types of behavior that not only are common among youth of all races but, because of unconscious racial bias, are also frequently misinterpreted as more threatening and serious when done by Black or Latino students than by White students.[48] Thus, the differences in discipline that students receive are not only discriminatory but also devastating to the life chances for students of color.

This type of disciplinary discrimination that Black children especially face during their school years has a well-documented effect throughout their lives. Disparate school suspensions exponentially increase the chances that a student will not succeed in school, for several reasons. Absences represent interruptions in learning. Being away from school disrupts students' chance to engage in the important social networks with students experiencing success in school. As a result, the most reliable peer-reviewed research concludes that disparate student suspension decreases students' educational achievement.

Studying student performance before and after suspension in California schools, researchers found that multiple suspensions lowered students' English scores even after controlling for student differences.[49] In Philadelphia schools, suspensions diminished math and reading achievement.[50] Expulsion and suspension create opportunity to fill idle time unproductively. It is not surprising, then, that research reveals suspended students in New York City have weaker attendance, test scores, and course completion rates and ultimately are more likely to drop out before they graduate.[51] And students who are suspended not only return to lower teacher expectations in school but also have lower self-esteem wherever they are.[52] By 2017, Black and Latino children represented all but 5.2 percent of those jailed in New York City's student detention facilities. These children were in jail rather than in school. There, instead of learning to read, complete math problems, think critically about history and language, create art or music, and develop social networks that would lead them to college, the overrepresentation of these students in detention exposed them disproportionately to police brutality and harassment.[53]

Overall, the data presented in this chapter thus far underscore the devastating truth that unequal protection for educational opportunity is a key driver of unequal health. Not only do differences in education lead to differences in health, but the education-related gap in life expectancy between Black and White populations is actually getting worse in the United States. For all races, adults with less than a twelfth-grade education today have life expectancies comparable to adult people in the 1950s and 1960s. In other words, less educated people of all races have not enjoyed the benefit of better health over the past decades. But the story is worse for minorities. S. Jay Olshansky reported in 2012 that the disparities between Black and White life expectancy appear to be related to educational attainment and the impact education has on income and socioeconomic status. He reported that while White people with more than fifteen years of education had life expectancies far greater than did Black Americans with fewer than twelve years of education. Moreover, these gaps have widened over time, as shown in Figure 5.5.

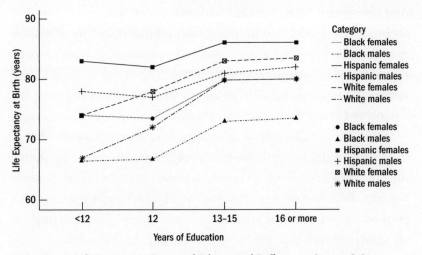

FIGURE 5.5: Life Expectancy, Race, and Educational Differences. Source: S. Jay Olshansky et al., "Differences in Life Expectancy Due to Race and Educational Differences Are Widening, and Many May Not Catch Up," *Health Affairs*, 31, no. 8 (2012): 1803–1813.

According to Dr. Olshansky, the life-expectancy differences between races is stark:

> Differences in longevity between subgroups of the US population are so pernicious and systemic that it is now reasonable to conclude that at least two Americas have formed, with notably different longevity prospects. The two are demarcated by level of education and its socioeconomic status correlates, and related to race or ethnicity.[54]

This is the reason that educational discrimination is so abhorrent. Simply put, it kills.

The discrimination that leads to segregation between schools and school districts consigns minority children to lower-quality schools than what their White peers attend. To the extent that schools themselves are integrated, segregation within schools further isolates children by race and reserves the best educational resources for White children.

And shockingly, wherever Black children attend school, they are disproportionately subjected to suspension, expulsion, and incarceration in a tangle of racial discrimination that all but guarantees what has been misattributed as an achievement gap between Black and White students. Instead, what we are actually seeing is a pervasive *equality gap* in our schools and in our nation. Where educational opportunity is concerned, White students still enjoy an advantage over Black students. To link these inequalities to the disparately poor health outcomes that are the subject of this book, in the next two sections, I describe the relationship between discrimination in education and two lifelong impacts of this poor education: criminal justice and income inequality. Both impacts are associated with racialized disparities in population health.

Criminal Justice Inequality: The Lifelong Injustice of Educational Discrimination

To confirm the lifelong consequences of an unjust educational system, this section explores how the racial inequalities in school discipline are disturbingly similar to, and appear to predict, the disparate treatment that youth receive in the criminal justice system. In 1998, Black youths with no prior criminal records were six times more likely, and Latino youths three times more likely, to be incarcerated than were White youths for the same offenses.[55] The tragic connection between unequal education, inequitable discipline in schools, and disproportionate representation of minority youth in the criminal justice system has been called the *school-to-prison pipeline*. Researchers Johanna Wald and Daniel Losen explain the phenomenon this way:

> This get-tough approach to discipline in schools is mirrored in the treatment of youths in the criminal justice system. Since 1992, forty-five states have passed laws making it easier to try juveniles as adults, and thirty-one have stiffened sanctions against youths for a variety of offenses. . . .

The racial disparities among those most severely sanctioned by these laws and policies are startlingly similar to those found in student discipline data. . . . In fact, the racial disparities within the two systems are so similar—and so glaring—that it becomes impossible not to connect them.[56]

The connection has been termed a *pipeline* to call out the inevitability of outcomes once the initial patterns are set. A pipeline evokes the image of water being induced to travel in a predetermined direction, at the insistence of a directive set of circumstances set in motion by an external hand to turn on the faucet, as it were. The pipeline imagery drives home the involuntariness of the travelers in the pipeline and the isolated nature of their journey. And though there may be leaks in the pipeline—a few individuals escaping the dark journey here and there, the overarching pervasiveness of the narratives and data irrefutably connects the discipline disparities in school with injustices in the criminal justice system.

The presumption that minority children are criminals begins to manifest itself in school. Data from the state of Connecticut provide an example of this presumption across the nation. In 2014, White children in the state were more likely to get mental health treatment for bad behavior, whereas Black and Latino children were more likely to be sent to jail (figure 5.6).

Wherever these discipline disparities punish similar behavior dissimilarly, racial discrimination in education contributes to structural racism by guaranteeing the adverse economic and social aftereffects of early criminalization will disproportionately hurt Black and Latino populations over the life course. This structural racism that plagues minority children with disciplinary discrimination from preschool through high school can follow them to replicate racially unjust outcomes in the criminal justice system when they become adults. Structural racism in the criminal justice system is the subject of numerous outstanding books.[57]

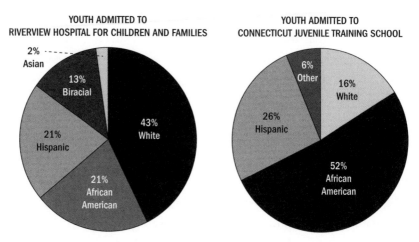

YOUTH ADMITTED TO
RIVERVIEW HOSPITAL FOR CHILDREN AND FAMILIES

2% Asian
13% Biracial
21% Hispanic
43% White
21% African American

YOUTH ADMITTED TO
CONNECTICUT JUVENILE TRAINING SCHOOL

6% Other
16% White
26% Hispanic
52% African American

FIGURE 5.6: Disparate Treatment of Juveniles by Race in Connecticut, 2014. Source: Jacqueline Rabe Thomas, "Boys in Jail in Connecticut at a 10-Year High (Part I)," *Connecticut Mirror*, February 19, 2014.

Multiple studies have confirmed the association between bias and incarceration rates; studies have shown that Black men are more likely to be employed and less likely to be incarcerated if they live in counties with less racial animus.[58] This chapter will not repeat the full discussion of mass incarceration inequities found in other literature. For our purposes, it is sufficient to recognize that the unequal disciplinary treatment of minority children in schools has a long-term impact: it places these children at higher risk than what White children face for unequal treatment in the criminal justice system as adults.

Despite the similar rates at which Black and White people engage in criminal conduct, the structural racism that begins in schools is replicated throughout the criminal justice system. At every stage, whether during initial police stops, searches, charges, and arrests; in the exercise of prosecutorial discretion in charging or negotiating plea agreements; in the conduct of criminal trials in the jury selection during the sentencing phases; and in incarceration rates, similarly situated people of different races receive unequal treatment at the hands of the law.[59] These successive disparities result in *cumulative* disadvantages by race and ethnicity throughout a person's lifetime.[60] In one very well-designed study, for example, Professors Andrew Gelman, Jeffrey Fagan, and Alex Kiss analyzed the racially disparate impact of policing practices in New York City. They found that Black and Latino people were stopped more often than White people were "in comparison to both the populations of these groups and the best estimates of the rate of crimes committed by each group."[61] Their evidence also showed that minority motorists are disproportionately stopped by police and that, once stopped, Black and Latino motorists are more likely to be searched and arrested by police.

Other studies have documented the unjustly disproportionate sentencing, plea bargaining, and overall incarceration rates for those who are Black and Latino, especially for nonviolent drug offenses, where the incidence of offending behavior does not differ by race in proportion to criminal justice involvement. In a 2000 study, Jamie Fellner wrote about the disparity that has captured not only the criminal justice system but also the national imagination:

> Cocaine use by white Americans in all social classes increased in the late 1970s and early 1980s, but it did not engender the "orgy of media and political attention" that catalyzed the war on drugs in the mid-1980s when smokable cocaine in the form of crack spread throughout low-income minority neighborhoods that were already seen as dangerous and threatening. Even though far more whites used both powder cocaine and crack cocaine than blacks, the image of the drug offender that has dominated media stories is a black man slouching in an alleyway, not a white man in his home.[62]

To underscore this point, consider the striking differences between Black and White arrest rates for marijuana use in the United States from 2014 to 2018, despite the striking similarity between the two groups' use of marijuana (figure 5.7).

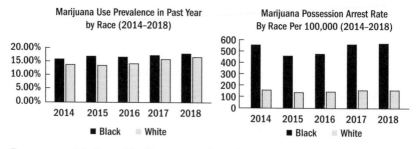

FIGURE 5.7: Marijuana Use (Percentage of Population Using Marijuana) and Incidence of Arrests in the United States, by Race, 2014–2018. Source: National Survey on Drug Use and Health, conducted by the Substance Abuse and Mental Health Services Administration.

The left-hand graph in the figure shows clearly that the prevalence of marijuana use by Black and White people is nearly the same, year after year. Yet the right-hand graph shows wildly disparate arrest rates for marijuana violations for Black and White people. The glaring lesson from these data on marijuana use and arrests is that structural racism produces young minority students' disparate exposure to the disciplinary gaze of their teachers in preschool, to the disparate referrals to juvenile detention as adolescents, and to the gaping wide differences in arrest rates as adults. In short, unequal access to quality education generates consequences that last a lifetime.

The disparate criminalization that results from the discriminatory disciplinary consequences faced by Black students in school will ultimately have devastating public health consequences.[63] First, high-incarceration neighborhoods experience an increased incidence of mental illness such as depression and anxiety disorders as well as increased infant mortality among family members left behind.[64] Second, criminalization of minority youth subjects them to disproportionate health risks. As we have seen during the COVID-19 pandemic, incarcerated populations live in isolated, close quarters and therefore are at greater risk for transmission of infectious diseases such as viral hepatitis, sexually transmitted diseases, and tuberculosis.[65] Third, the communities that receive formerly incarcerated family members after release are therefore at risk of greater exposure to communicable diseases than are communities that escape the overcriminalization of their youth populations. The economic impact of these three health outcomes is a final concern raised by structural racism in education and is one we will examine next.

Income Inequality: The Lifelong Health Burden of Educational Discrimination

As we have seen in this chapter, minority children lack equal opportunities for a good education in the United States because racial and ethnic discrimination impedes their access to good schools, good teachers, good courses, and fair disciplinary treatment. As a result, a larger percentage of minority children than White children are poorly prepared for the workforce. The minority workers will be more limited to low-wage, low-quality jobs, while their White peers are more likely to land higher-paying, higher-quality jobs. Socioeconomic status, typically measured by income, education, and occupation, is intimately linked to a broad range of health disparities. This is why two prominent researchers, Dr. Nancy Adler and Dr. Katherine Newman, perceptively note, "Policies that affect the health of the labor market are perhaps the most important medicine we can apply."[66] That is, to improve disparate population health outcomes, America must remove from its education system the structural racism that locks in disproportionate employment outcomes by race.

Racialized differences in income levels and income earning opportunities are important to health outcomes because they determine one's means for purchasing most other social determinants of health such as food, housing, health care, and recreation. Education disparities lead to income inequality primarily because in the United States, education largely predicts what kind of job and, therefore, the earning potential and occupational status one will enjoy over a lifetime. Conversely, racial disparities in education also predict the racial composition of the unemployed. Unemployment is a health risk; research has shown that the mere threat of unemployment can adversely affect one's health.[67] Clearly, the evidence shows that those who are employed in the United States generally have better health than do unemployed people. So, having a job improves health. But the kind of job seems to matter as well. Lower-status jobs, where workers have less control, less ability to protect themselves from strain or injury, or greater exposure to hazardous materials like lead or asbestos, are associated with higher risk of heart disease and other poor health outcomes. Higher-status and therefore better-paying jobs, where workers exercise greater control over their working conditions and perform a larger variety of tasks, are associated with better mental and physical health outcomes. To the extent that racial disparities in education better prepare White populations for the higher-status jobs and predispose minority population to the lower-status ones, structural racism further ensures disparities in population health.

The best research on the association between education and income and, consequently, health in the United States has been conducted by Nadarajan "Raj" Chetty and his colleagues. In a brilliant analysis of 11,571 students randomly assigned to classrooms in Tennessee schools from kindergarten to third grade, Dr. Chetty's team followed those children into adulthood to investigate how the quality of education affected the children in later life.[68] The results are remarkable. The researchers found that the quality of elementary classroom environments can raise test scores, improve college attendance, and raise income in adult life. More specifically, the data confirm several important associations. First, students in small classes are significantly more likely to attend college than are students from larger classes. Second, students with better-experienced kindergarten teachers have higher earnings. Third, classroom environments significantly impact adult earnings. And finally, students in higher-quality kindergarten through third-grade classrooms have higher earnings, college attendance rates, and other life outcomes. Dr. Chetty and his coauthors also report their findings in qualitative terms:

> Increasing class quality by 1 standard deviation of the distribution within schools raises earnings by $1,520 (9.6%) at age 27. Under the preceding assumptions, this translates into a lifetime earnings gain of approximately $39,100 for the average individual. For a classroom of 20 students, this implies a present value benefit of $782,000 for improving class quality for a single year by one (within-school) standard deviation.[69]

These statistics mean that removing discriminatory differences in the quality of schooling could increase adult income by nearly 10 percent. Figure 5.8 shows this relationship graphically, with class quality indicated on the x-axis by kindergarten test score percentile. In this study, the average test scores for students at the end of their kindergarten year are a proxy for the kindergarten class quality because the scores capture peer, teacher, and other classroom characteristics that affect test scores.

Then, in 2016, Dr. Chetty and his colleagues produced a pathbreaking study to show the relationship between income and life expectancy in the United States between 2001 and 2014.[70] Using income and health data from 1.4 billion Americans, the researchers compared income tax records with death records from the Social Security Administration. Among their most important findings was the extent of the difference that income made: "First, higher income was associated with greater longevity throughout the income distribution. The gap in life expectancy between the richest 1% and the poorest 1% of individuals was 14.6 years for men and 10.1 years for women."

In a later study, Dr. Chetty and his team analyzed the sources of racial and ethnic disparities in income throughout the United States. After capturing the fundamental relationship between income and life expectancy, the researchers showed why the gaps are so enduring.[71] Their findings are noteworthy: the income gap between Black and White groups—the

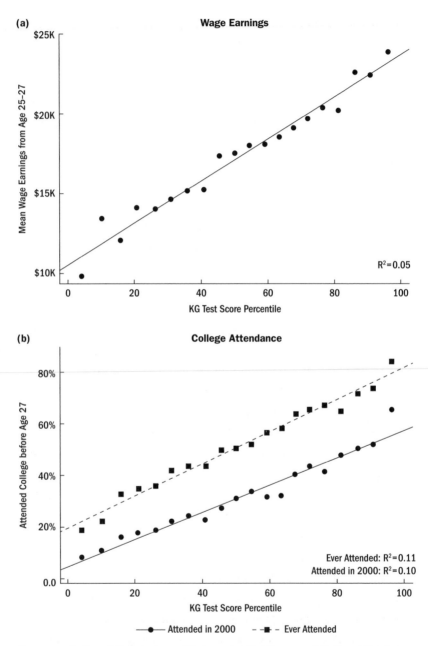

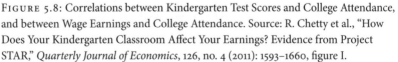

FIGURE 5.8: Correlations between Kindergarten Test Scores and College Attendance, and between Wage Earnings and College Attendance. Source: R. Chetty et al., "How Does Your Kindergarten Classroom Affect Your Earnings? Evidence from Project STAR," *Quarterly Journal of Economics*, 126, no. 4 (2011): 1593–1660, figure I.

largest racial difference they found—affects Black children for generations. Dr. Chetty's team describes the cause: Black Americans have "substantially lower rates of upward mobility and higher rates of downward
mobility than Whites, leading to large income disparities that persist
across generations." Notably, several other findings by the research team
offer hope. All children, the team explains, have a degree of social mobility
if the social environment around them has three characteristics: (1) low
poverty, (2) low racial bias, and (3) high participation from fathers:

> Closing the gap in opportunities between black and white children at a
> given parental income level could therefore eliminate much of the black-
> white income gap within two generations. Second, the black-white gap is
> significantly smaller for boys who grow up in certain neighborhoods—
> those with low poverty rates, low levels of racial bias among whites, and
> high rates of father presence among low-income blacks. Black boys who
> move to such areas at younger ages have significantly better outcomes,
> demonstrating that racial disparities can be narrowed through changes
> in environment.

The Chetty team's work demonstrates the potential power of removing structural racism in education to change the environment in the
United States within two generations. Dismantling structural racism
will decrease racialized concentrated poverty, decrease the rate at which
mass incarceration removes Black fathers from families, and mitigate
racial bias overall.

Ending once and for all the US legacy of segregated education, which
extends well beyond the Supreme Court's unanimous *Brown v. Board of
Education* decision, offers a policy path forward to end structural racism.
Again, my family story illustrates the potential benefits of such a policy
if it were systematically replicated to affect families on a population level.

The best information I have suggests that not one of my four grandparents finished high school. My paternal grandfather left home and
school to learn a trade making and repairing shoes at age fourteen; it

was always a point of pride in my family that I too got my first paying job as a swim instructor at the same age. My maternal grandfather's education equipped him to work as a laborer first on Works Progress Administration construction crews revitalizing Harlem's Mt. Morris Park during the Depression and then driving a food delivery truck for the city's public school system. Though I am less certain of whether my paternal and maternal grandmothers received high school diplomas, I know that both my parents finished high school. Although the school systems they attended steered them toward low-paying trades, both my mother and father valued education so highly that they struggled to return to college at night while working and raising a family. My father graduated with a bachelor's degree from City College of New York's evening program. This degree allowed him to add a white-collar job to his other jobs. His efforts enabled him to embark on the journey to leave the legacy of education that would allow me to escape poverty.

It is no overstatement to say that both my parents worked so hard that they quite literally gave their lives to make sure that their children—my brother and I—obtained a college education. Their determination and hard work have made all the difference for generations to come. Both my brother, Vincent Bowen III, and I graduated from Harvard University; we hold three graduate degrees between us. My three children are similarly well educated, having completed college and at least one graduate degree. But more to the point of this book and chapter, my brother has lived longer than my father did, and I have lived longer than my mother. The good news is that our educational attainment makes it very likely that my children's children will know their grandparents. Their grandparents will engage in healthy living and will leave generational wealth that will increase the opportunities my great-grandchildren will have to escape the outcomes predicted by structural racism. Without question, the fight to enforce our Constitution's guarantee of equal protection of the laws will give all Black and other minority families a better shot at enjoying the same equal opportunity to enjoy just health in a just United States.

6

A CALL TO NATIONAL ACTION

An improvement in Negro health, to the point where it would compare favorably with that of the white race, would at one stroke wipe out many disabilities from which the race suffers, improve its economic status and stimulate its native abilities as would no other single improvement. These are the social implications of the facts of Negro Health.
—Louis I. Dublin, "The Health of the Negro," 1928

The face of your Petitioner, is now marked with the furrows of time, and her frame bending under the oppression of years, while she, by the Laws of the Land, is denied the employment of one morsel of that immense wealth, apart whereof hath been accumulated by her own industry, and the whole augmented by her servitude.

WHEREFORE, casting herself at your feet of your honours, as to a body of men, formed for the extirpation of vassalage, for the reward of Virtue, and the just return of honest industry. . . .
—Belinda Royall, 1783

This chapter is dedicated to solutions. It outlines the most basic legal and policy reforms the nation needs if it is to dismantle the mechanisms supporting structural racism that prematurely ended my parents' lives. The recommendations contained in this chapter seek first to restore and strengthen existing legal rules that uphold the constitutional guarantee of equal protection of the laws. They then aim to create new legal rules that will ensure that African Americans, the nation's least healthy population, as well as all other groups in America, can enjoy an equal opportunity to pursue healthy lives. The plan offered here is straightforward and can be set into motion immediately. Simply put, the most efficient way to dismantle structural racism is for legal and health experts to collaborate in the fight to align US laws with our expressed moral commitment to the ideal that all are created equal and endowed with inalienable rights by their creator. The plan is to finally and fully enforce the law of the Constitution's Fourteenth Amendment.

This chapter does not argue that legal reform is all that is needed to eradicate the effects of structural racism. Legal reform can, however, powerfully influence a fundamental shift in our social norms. This chapter does not purport to offer a quick fix. The legal reform I propose will set the stage for societal change, and the reforms are best if implemented immediately to halt the tragic waste of human lives that structural racism is causing today. But the full realization of the changes recommended here will occur over time. Finally, this chapter does not propose reforms that legal experts can accomplish alone. Reversing the public health impacts of legalized discrimination and dehumanization will require the same historical cooperation of law and health professionals that gave rise to the inequities we see today. Nevertheless, societal change cannot happen without these reforms. They are necessary but not sufficient to remove the legal backbone of structures that have institutionalized racism. Once these structures are destroyed, the United States will be left as a society with the moral obligation to address the personal prejudices and biases—whether conscious or unconscious—that inspired us to erect the legal structures in the first place. This is no small task. Although that project lies beyond the scope of this book, the steps recommended here will go far toward that goal.

Ironically, Chief Justice John Roberts may have best described the required reversal in our nation's approach to the core value of equality to dismantle structural racism when he led the Supreme Court to upend two school districts' democratically and locally constructed plans to end segregation. When the chief justice pronounced in 2007 that "the way to stop discrimination on the basis of race is to simply stop discriminating on the basis of race," he spoke from a privileged perch that skewed his vision of discrimination in America. He did not appreciate how deep, how wide, and how relentless the scourge truly is. The indisputable progress in reducing overt discrimination had sadly lulled Chief Justice Roberts into believing that the solution to the vitriolic vestiges of four hundred years of structural racism lay in a simplistic syllogism.

Since then, however, a global pandemic has intervened. Confederate-flag-toting terrorists wearing anti-Semitic insignia attempted to violently overthrow a democratic election by storming the nation's Capitol to stop a congressional vote to certify the 2020 election. And hundreds of social media communications have revealed the open wounds of racial animus fueling the most recent examples of the centuries-old practice of murdering Black people as of George Floyd, Breonna Taylor, and Ahmaud Arbery. Even the shocking ease with which ordinary White Americans weaponize their privilege and power has been displayed in a viral video of Amy Cooper's decision to threaten an innocent Black man's life by bringing the full force of the New York City Police Department to bear in defense of her right to walk her dog unleashed in a leashed-only zone. These events certainly have awakened many others. Perhaps now, Chief Justice Roberts will understand that his remedy asserted a false equivalence aiming to stop the wrong discrimination. The right way to stop discrimination is not to stop those who are fighting to dismantle it. The way to stop discrimination is to stop enabling those who enjoy the privileges it has institutionalized. The way to stop discrimination is for legislators to enact, and courts to fully enforce, laws that prohibit discrimination in all the institutions and systems that constitute the social determinants of health. The way to stop discrimination is for this nation's highest court to commit fully, for the first time in US history, to the words inscribed above its door: The way to stop discrimination is to guarantee all people, of all races and of all ethnicities, *equal justice under law*. Therefore, this is chapter proposes an antidiscrimination, antiracism plan to achieve just health.

The Case for Structural Antiracist Reform

It has been estimated that only 10 percent of health outcomes are determined by access to, and quality of, health care.[1] According to the best estimates, between 10 and 30 percent of health outcomes depend on individuals' genetic and biological makeup.[2] Health behaviors are estimated to be responsible for up to 30 percent of what determines health outcomes, while the social and environmental characteristics make up approximately 40 percent—the most important influence by far—of the determinants of health. Moreover, because a person's social environment exerts a crucial influence on health behaviors, social and environmental conditions are an even greater determinant of health outcomes.[3] These social and environmental conditions occur in housing, education, employment, and other settings in which people live their lives. Importantly, as we have seen in prior chapters, each of these settings is organized and distributed by law. Therefore, any effort to advance equality in the places where people live and work and play must reach not only the social determinants of health themselves but also the underlying laws that organize and distribute access to the social determinants of health. Transformative interventions must address structural racism—the fundamental cause of racial disparities in each of the social determinants of health—to eradicate racial health disparities. Figure 6.1 summarizes the possible interventions that can reduce the effects or foundations of structural racism and lead to just health. This chapter—indeed this book—focuses squarely on the interventions that attack structural racism at the very foundation of the pyramid pictured in figure 6.1.

The personal and organizational interventions depicted at the top of the diagram were the subject of my first book, *Just Medicine*. They are an important part of accounting for the individual motivations that inform structural racism, but research has shown that they are insufficient solutions on their own. The midlevel interventions noted in the middle of the figure aim at reforming social and health-care institutions

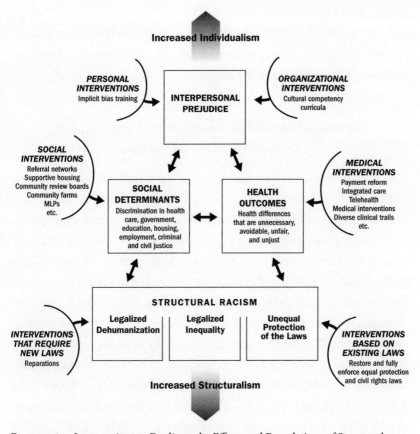

FIGURE 6.1: Interventions to Eradicate the Effects and Foundations of Structural Racism. (MLPs = medical-legal partnerships.)

that discriminate because of racism stemming from explicit and implicit biases. These interventions help produce limited and episodic improvements in health outcomes and in people's physical environment and daily circumstances. However, neither individual nor midlevel interventions can sustainably end health inequality without disrupting the foundation. The foundation—structural racism—must be dismantled by reforming its three core legal mechanisms set forth in chapter 1 (legalized dehumanization, legalized inequality, and unequal protection of the laws) that created and sustain this public health crisis. Legal interventions to reverse structural racism fall into two categories: those that will require the reform of existing law, and those that will be accomplished by the enactment of new laws. Each category of fundamental structural reforms is discussed in turn in the sections that follow.

Reversing Legalized Dehumanization, Inequality, and Unequal Protection of the Laws

As a first step toward addressing our current public health crisis, we urgently need to halt the systematic decimation of the Civil Rights Acts promulgated in the 1960s to dismantle structural racism in America. Dehumanization occurs when US law fails to protect the civil rights—indeed the *human* rights—of racial and ethnic minority populations to the basic necessities of life. Therefore, enforcing legal protections for the right to clean, safe, decent housing, air, and drinking water, for example, will reverse legalized dehumanization. Reviving the goals of antidiscrimination laws will reverse legalized inequality and restore the intended goal of the Fourteenth Amendment. The focus of reforms I recommend here, therefore, addresses the Fair Housing Act, Titles VI and VII of the Civil Rights Act, and their enabling laws and regulations, all of which have been weakened or neutralized. Importantly, the dismantling of structural racism also depends squarely on restoring the equal protection of laws provided by the Voting Rights Act of 1965. This signature legislation of the Civil Rights era is currently under attack by state and federal government actors as never before. This law is an essential weapon against the resurgence of structural racism and the best offensive weapon to ensure equal political participation in the fight against it. Voting rights reform is the subject of other exceptional works, and the data connecting the association between these rights and public health outcomes—the subject of this book—are still emerging.[4] Therefore, this important civil rights reform is not covered here.

In this chapter, I do call on courts to be held accountable for the resegregation of education. This societal regression has been made possible by the courts' wholesale refusal to acknowledge that separate elementary, middle, and secondary schools and higher education institutions for Black, Latino, Indigenous, and White students are inherently unequal. Finally, I invite lawmakers to enact reparations legislation to responsibly employ the expressive value of law to reflect the highest social ideals on which this nation was built.

Housing Reforms

As seen in earlier chapters, the history of housing segregation in America follows the well-established pattern of structural racism: segregation is above all the product of legalized dehumanization, codified by legalized inequality, and maintained by unequal protection of the law. After slavery ended, residential segregation had to be invented by laws that were fundamentally motivated by the psychology of Black dehumanization, as explained in chapter 2. Locally enacted segregation ordinances initially operated after the Civil War to pry apart racial groups that had settled largely without regard to race. Residential ordinances were promulgated during the period from 1910 to 1915 to establish racial boundaries by neighborhoods, streets, or even individual buildings. For example, newly passed laws forbade owners to sell or lease homes if the transaction did not comply with racist isolation goals. When the Supreme Court held these zoning ordinances unconstitutional in 1917, lawyers wrote, and courts enforced, racially restrictive covenants embedded in real estate deeds of sale to do the work of segregation.[5] In 1948, the Supreme Court in *Shelly v. Kraemer* held these covenants unconstitutional. In response, the federal government stepped in to use laws such as the National Housing Act of 1934, the Housing Act of 1937, and the Servicemen's Readjustment Act (GI Bill) of 1944 to accomplish segregation through redlining, home mortgage lending restrictions, and racially segregation housing development projects.[6] In his book *The Color of Law: A Forgotten History of How Our Government Segregated America*, Richard Rothstein provides a comprehensive account of the federal government's explicit policies and practices that legalized housing inequality during the first half of the twentieth century. Rothstein calls these practices "the most powerful force separating the races in every metropolitan area, with effects that endure today."[7]

Strengthen Enforcement of the Underperforming Fair Housing Act

The Fair Housing Act of 1968 is the sole federal legal intervention enacted to reverse the structural racism that has segregated American neighborhoods since the turn of the twentieth century. It represented a coordinated policy to reduce the state-sanctioned racial residential discrimination and segregation of the preceding fifty years. At best, the act's success and scope is incomplete. According to researchers, "there were small, but steady declines in racial residential segregation between 1970 and 2000," and by some measures, those modest, micro-level gains have continued in some parts of the country.[8] But overall, the macro-level measures of segregation have remained unchanged. This is especially true for African Americans, who remain the most segregated minority group in the United States today.[9] As a legal weapon against segregation, the Fair Housing Act has never been fully enforced. Fully enforcing the plain language of the act, as Congress intended, is the first step toward dismantling structural racism.

The Fair Housing Act of 1968 purported to outlaw racial discrimination in the sale and rental of housing.[10] It prohibited discrimination "against any person in the terms, conditions, or privileges of sale or rental of a dwelling, or in the provision of services or facilities in connection therewith, because of race, color, religion, sex, familial status, or national origin."[11] The law applies to all levels of local, state, and federal government, as well as to private defendants.[12] When the law was enacted, its purpose was clear, as Senator Walter Mondale, the law's primary sponsor, explained fifty years after its passage:

The law was Congress's effort to remedy a great historical evil: the large-scale exclusion and isolation of blacks from white communities. In the

Jim Crow South, white and black citizens were kept apart to confirm and reinforce the idea of white superiority. Residential segregation accomplished the same result elsewhere, but on a much larger scale. The Fair Housing Act was intended to prevent and reverse all this.[13]

Mondale lamented that the country remained segregated despite the law's highest aspirations. Its goals remain unrealized, and instead of progressing toward an integrated American society, the law faced what Mondale called fifty years of "gradual progress and frequent setbacks."[14] The tragic divergence of the law from its original intent must be rectified in three ways, which will examine in the next three sections.

To accomplish its intended purpose, the Federal Housing Administration (FHA), the agency charged with enforcing the Fair Housing Act, must first be dramatically streamlined and strengthened. Currently, the FHA is mired in bureaucracy, offering no real or robust opportunity to challenge segregation or discrimination that violates the law. Moreover, the agency lacks strong enforcement capabilities for the Department of Housing and Urban Development (HUD), placing the burden of enforcement on the victims by requiring them to either file a formal complaint with the HUD or sue in federal court.[15] Efforts to strengthen the agency's authority to enforce the law have failed under multiple administrations. After the passage of the Fair Housing Act, HUD secretary George Romney tried to mandate that a White Detroit suburb include affordable housing before it could receive federal funds through his Open Communities initiative. However, President Richard Nixon canceled Romney's initiative, which would have increased integration, and drove Romney out of his administration.[16]

The Fair Housing Act saw no better results in later presidential administrations. In 1998, under President Bill Clinton's administration, HUD secretary Andrew Cuomo tried to follow in Romney's footsteps, denying federal housing money to communities that did not comply with fair housing laws. Local governments were incensed, but President Clinton lacked the political capital necessary for a fair housing fight after his impeachment.[17] In 2015, during President Barack Obama's second term, HUD settled on new regulations that allowed for enforcement of the Fair Housing Act's requirement for communities to promote integration. These regulations held communities and the HUD accountable with strict timelines while also promoting access to integrated schools, employment opportunities, transportation, recreation, and social services.[18] Yet under President Donald Trump, HUD secretary Ben Carson postponed the Obama administration's requirements.[19]

Without strong enforcement measures, local, state, and federal policies have, since the law's passage in 1968, continued to support de facto housing segregation, allowing redlining, refusing to insure mortgages for Black homeowners, and obstructing affordable housing through local zoning rules.[20] Therefore, to expand the isolated pockets of progress that, unfortunately, have still left African Americans as the group most often concentrated in racially and economically segregated neighborhoods, the FHA must enforce and strengthen its lender oversight, making swift use of penalties for noncompliant lenders.[21] Moreover, the agency must swiftly act on complaints of housing discrimination and reinstate and rigorously enforce AFFH rules (rules related to affirmatively furthering fair housing based on race) for state and local governments.[22]

Aggressively Enforce Disparate-Impact Law

Second, in addition to streamlining and strengthening the Fair Housing Act, the FHA and other fair housing advocates must aggressively but strategically bring disparate-impact claims to challenge the discriminatory effects of unfair housing policies. The 2015 Supreme Court decision in *Texas Department of Housing and Community Affairs v. Inclusive Communities Project, Inc.* (*Inclusive Communities*) and the HUD discriminatory-effects standard provide a basis to aggressively pursue civil rights actions that can remedy discriminatory housing policies.[23] In *Inclusive Communities*, the court held that parts of the Fair Housing Act have a disparate-impact liability standard, allowing for liability based on a challenged practice's indefensible discriminatory effect "even if the practice was not motivated by a discriminatory intent."[24] The court held that suits focused on housing restrictions like zoning laws that essentially segregate residential areas "reside at the heartland of disparate-impact liability."[25] The Supreme Court emphasized that the "heartland cases," that is, the cases supporting this holding, vindicate the Fair Housing Act's objectives by preventing municipalities from continuing to enforce "arbitrary, and in practice, discriminatory ordinances barring the construction of certain types of housing units."[26] In its decision, the court considered the results-oriented language of the Fair Housing Act and its own interpretation of the text of Title VII of the Civil Rights Act of 1964 and the Age Discrimination in Employment Act of 1967: "Antidiscrimination laws must be construed to encompass disparate-impact claims when their text refers to the consequences of actions and not just to the mindset of actors, and where that interpretation is consistent with statutory purpose."[27] Moreover, the court held that Congress, through its 1988 amendments to the Fair Housing Act, ratified disparate-impact liability. According to the court, Congress amended the statute while aware that all nine courts of appeals had unanimously concluded that disparate-impact liability was available, and Congress included three exemptions that would effectively "assume the existence of disparate-impact claims."[28]

As Morgan Williams and Stacy Seicshnaydre discuss in "Legacy and the Promise of Disparate Impact," the Supreme Court in *Inclusive Communities* delivered three major takeaways. First, under the "robust causality requirement," disparate-impact liability is not to be "based solely on a showing of statistical disparity," but successful claims must point to a defendant's specific policy or policies causing that disparity.[29] Second, although both public and private defendants have always had leeway to escape liability by identifying a valid interest served by their policies, fair housing advocates must compel the Federal Housing Administration to ensure that legitimate policies and practices do not arbitrarily perpetuate segregation.[30] Third, and perhaps most important, the *Inclusive*

Communities court held that "revitalizing dilapidated housing in our Nation's cities" and "ensuring compliance with health and safety codes" are legitimate priorities. The natural result is the need for a nationwide priority on aggressively and systematically using this law to eliminate substandard housing conditions that disproportionately hurt Black and other minority communities.[31]

Recent case law supports even wider application of the Supreme Court's decision. Since *Inclusive Communities*, courts have applied disparate-impact analysis to uphold prima facie claims that challenged restrictions on developing multifamily housing.[32] Disparate-impact claims can improve housing and health by challenging policies that restrict housing services for individuals who receive subsidized housing support, such as voucher programs, and policies that place excessive credit-score restrictions on mortgage lending.[33] Voucher programs today often concentrate the participants in high-poverty areas, sustaining residential racial segregation.[34] Credit-scoring mechanisms typically evaluate the environment in which an individual used credit and the riskiness of products used in that environment. Such mechanisms fail to measure the risk characteristic of an individual consumer, instead focusing on the situation they are forced into by structural racism.[35] Because their credit scores are based on the lending environment, communities of color often experience disparate impact, as these communities have historically been denied access to affordable mainstream credit.[36] Tough enforcement of the disparate-impact standard would make enforcement of the Fair Housing Act a powerful weapon against structural racism in housing—one of the most important social determinants of health.

Stop Resegregation through Gentrification

The third way to rectify the divergence between the law and its original intent is to have state, local, and federal governments aggressively pursue affordable-housing policies that stop wholesale displacement of minority communities through so-called gentrification. Across the nation, communities have an unprecedented opportunity to intentionally prevent segregation by employing policies that create and protect affordable housing in Black and Latino communities that are attracting investment withheld from them for decades. *Gentrification*, the regrettable name given to a community development process, transforms marginalized, low-wealth residential communities into predominately White, high-income neighborhoods by investing resources previously unavailable to existing residents and displacing them as housing becomes unaffordable.

The phenomenon and inequitable outcomes produced by gentrification are well known and well documented; I will not review all the literature here.[37] Also well documented are ways to use zoning, vouchers, rent control, and tax laws to resist this discriminatory process and encourage investment in well-integrated neighborhoods that include affordable housing for existing minority residents.[38] Although I will not summarize all the literature in this regard, either, I want to recast the reversal of gentrification and displacement as the work of enforcing the Constitution's Fourteenth Amendment mandate to provide equal protection of the laws for minority communities. The objective is to see in a new light—as a civil rights issue—the laws that will reverse the ongoing, massive displacement of existing African American and Latino families from gentrification. Under this view, applying laws and policies such as rent control to limit condominium conversions; enacting inclusionary zoning programs; freezing property taxes for existing homeowners; and generating tax credits or stabilizing voucher programs are properly seen as the reversal of legalized dehumanization and inequality. The payoff, as the data have shown throughout this book, is a society characterized by just health for all.

Fully Enforce Title VI to End the Public Health Harms of Environmental Racism

Dismantling structural racism will also require reform and full enforcement of the Title VI of the Civil Rights Act of 1964. Title VI, enacted to prohibit racial discrimination by recipients of federal funding, is one of the most underutilized tools in the fight to protect equal access to healthy, pollution-free environments and to health care for marginalized communities. Taking each of these two protections in turn, the recommendations that follow suggest revitalization of this signature civil rights legislation.

Achieve Environmental Justice

The plain language, legislative intent, and regulations available to enforce Title VI give governments the legal authority to prohibit the inequitable distribution of environmental pollution that disproportionately harms health in minority communities. However, the federal government's Title VI enforcement record is dismal. The EPA dismisses or rejects more than 90 percent of Title VI complaints filed. The agency currently takes an average of 350 days to determine whether it will investigate newly filed civil rights complaints.[39] Moreover, according to a recently released report from the US Commission on Civil Rights, until 2017, the EPA had never in its history made a formal finding of discrimination or denied or withdrawn financial assistance from a recipient.[40]

But on January 19, 2017, twenty-five years after the initial complaint was filed, the EPA made a rare finding of environmental discrimination in a case involving a Michigan power station.[41] Notwithstanding this record of nonenforcement, the agency defines environmental justice as "the fair treatment and meaningful involvement of all people regardless of race, color, national origin, or income with respect to the development, implementation, and enforcement of environmental laws, regulations, and policies." "Fair treatment," according to the EPA, "means that no group of people should bear a disproportionate share of the negative environmental consequences resulting from industrial, governmental and commercial operations or policies." The agency further states that its goal is for all people to enjoy "the same degree of protection from environmental and health hazards and equal access to the decision-making process to have a healthy environment in which to live, learn, and work."

Full enforcement of the laws intended to accomplish these goals is an imperative for dismantling structural racism.

Ensure Equal Access to Quality Health Care

The steps to dismantling structural racism must address discrimination in health care as vigorously as they attack housing, education, and criminal justice disparities. The weapon of choice to ensure equal access to health care is a provision of the 2010 Affordable Care Act. As part of this act, Congress enacted a nondiscrimination provision, Section 1557. It is the most important civil rights legislation enacted since the 1960s. Section 1557 provides,

> Except as otherwise provided or in this title . . . an individual shall not, on the ground prohibited under title VI of the Civil Rights Act of 1964, title IX of the Education Amendments of 1972, the Age Discrimination Act of 1975, or section 794 of title 29, be excluded from participation in, be denied the benefits of, or be subjected to discrimination under, any health program or activity, any part of which is receiving Federal financial assistance.

This provision extended the discrimination provisions of the seminal civil rights laws to the health-care industry. Importantly, the law restored a an individual's right to sue under Title VI, and enhanced federal protections for health equity. But like Title VI itself, Section 1557 remains under attack from civil rights detractors and is underenforced by civil rights proponents. Republican-led Justice Department proposals, for example, would eliminate privately enforced disparate-impact claims. Democratic-led administrations favored using the law to enforce all-important prohibitions against gender discrimination while wholly neglecting antiracism enforcement. In addition to the structural reforms in civil rights laws themselves, therefore, dismantling structural racism will require a renewed commitment to aggressively enforcing Title VI and Section 1557 by swiftly investigating and resolving complaints filed. Moreover, the Department of Health and Human Services must proactively use compliance authority to enforce equal protection standards using inspection and enforcement capability under the law.

Three Reforms to Fix Title VI

In other publications, I have discussed the need to reform Title VI of the Civil Rights Act of 1964.[42] I reiterate that recommendation here because giving full effect to the Constitution's Equal Protection Clause depends on this imperative. I recommend three reforms to Title VI law. First, the Supreme Court should restore the individual's ability to sue to enforce disparate-impact cases. Second, the court should expressly reform Title VI to reach unconscious as well as conscious bias under its disparate-impact provisions. Third, Title VI should be broadened to include claims of negligence where unconscious bias claims are concerned.

Congress originally intended to empower private parties and public officials to root out racial discrimination in the United States through Title VI. However, the Supreme Court has retreated from Congress's original intent, effectively neutralizing the title as a weapon against structural racism. In 1974 and again in 1983, the court confirmed that Title VI applied to disparate-impact cases.[43] However, in the 2001 case *Alexander v. Sandoval*, the court reversed nearly three decades of disparate-impact precedent.[44] Justice Antonin Scalia delivered a majority opinion announcing that Title VI permits only private lawsuits that rely on disparate-*treatment* arguments, where a plaintiff can demonstrate that a defendant exhibited *intentional* discrimination, but not private lawsuits that rely on disparate-*impact* arguments. Justice Scalia's argument creates a prohibitive problem of proof. Plaintiffs cannot easily find evidence of explicit racial animus to prove intent. Indeed, evidence that a government action is intentionally racist can seldom be found today. This reinterpretation of the law hinders efforts to achieve environmental justice, for example. The *Sandoval* decision has left minority communities powerless to bring lawsuits that oppose a party's repeated patterns of locating pollution sources near these communities. This new interpretation also limits the marginalized communities' political participation and power to object, while a polluter can assiduously avoid locations near wealthy neighbors and defer to the protests against pollution in their communities. *Sandoval*'s elimination of the disparate-impact grounds thus perpetuates structural racism.

A second needed reform is to correct Justice Scalia's erroneous holding in *Sandoval*. The justice extended the reading of opinions from *Regents of the University of California v. Bakke* (1978), in which the Supreme Court upheld affirmative action admissions in the case of a White male applicant to medical school.[45] Justice Scalia's holding is misguided because the main opinion in *Bakke* cannot be read as a majority opinion on the intentionality issue. Of the five justices who joined the majority to conclude that Section 601 of Title VI only encompassed intentional discrimination, two later wrote to denounce this view in *Guardians Association v. Civil Service Commission* (1983), a case involving the disparate impact that minority officers experienced when taking police examinations.[46] After *Guardians*, various members of the Supreme Court repeatedly reaffirmed that *unintentional* discrimination is within Title VI's reach. For example, in *Alexander v. Choate* (1985), a case in which Medicaid recipients lost their challenge to revisions in Medicaid reimbursement rules, Justice Thurgood Marshall explained that *Guardians* should be interpreted to approve Title VI actions to remedy unintentional discrimination arising under the statute's regulatory scheme.[47] In his concurrence in *Guardians Association v. Civil Service Commission* (1992), a case holding that Mississippi's failure to dismantle its segregated higher education system violated both Title VI and the Equal Protection Clause, Justice Clarence Thomas affirmed that Title VI reaches unintentional-discrimination disparate-impact claims falling under its regulatory scheme.[48] Thus, various Supreme Court justices holding different jurisprudential ideologies in several cases, have admitted that even when a harm is caused unintentionally, Title VI actions can remedy the harm through disparate-impact litigation and enforcement.

In numerous opinions, justices have noted that unconscious biases should be included in disparate-impact claims under Title VI. Justice Ruth Bader Ginsburg has most explicitly articulated this idea. For example, she wrote in her *Grutter v. Bollinger* concurrence: "It is well documented that conscious and unconscious race bias, even rank discrimination based on race, remain alive in our land, impeding realization of our highest values and ideals."[49] The plain language of Title VI should be amended to cover unintentional structural racism, which is often fueled by such unconscious biases. We need this reform to hold government contractors fully accountable for their discriminatory actions. Title VI must be restored to its full usefulness as a weapon against structural racism and to update the law to comport with the changing ways in which racism is manifest today.[50]

Finally, building on the two prior recommendations, I recommend that Congress amend Title VI to expressly add language to Section 601, that expands the provision to permit individual lawsuits for *negligent disregard*— not merely *intentional disregard*—for health harms caused by structural racism. This reform would prohibit discrimination based on unconscious or implicit bias in a way that will drive change by immediately providing incentives for health providers and others to effectively address the effects of implicit bias in health care. Recognizing a negligence cause of action would simultaneously empower the government and private victims harmed by implicit biases to challenge discriminatory policies while encouraging would-be defendants to take reasonable, evidence-based steps to prevent biased decisions. This reform would provide an affirmative defense to federal aid recipients who could show they took reasonable steps to combat discrimination based on unconscious or implicit biases. They could use scientific evidence of which interventions are most effective to plan new policies and thereby avoid liability. Additionally, to restore the public-private enforcement model for all Title VI lawsuits that Section 601 authorizes, enabling language should be added to the end of Section 602.

By changing the statute's plain language, Title VI can better meet the goals of recovery and relief that Congress originally intended when it created the Civil Rights Act of 1964. Moreover, by adding a negligence-based claim to prohibit discrimination rooted in implicit biases and by encouraging all who receive government funding to combat discriminatory injustice, Title VI can be reformed to better reach its overarching goals.[51] In sum, Title VI must be reformed to restore a private cause of action for disparate-impact claims, create a cause of action for plaintiffs to recover against defendants who unintentionally or unconsciously contribute public health harms caused by structural racism, and apply a negligence standard to the unconscious bias claims in order to place reasonable limits on these types of claims while incentivizing the health-care industry to seriously combat the health harms that structural racism causes. While marginalized communities cannot litigate their way to pollution-free neighborhoods and will not achieve health equity solely through equitable access to care, they must be equipped to use equal protection of the laws to remove disproportionate barriers to health. Moreover, they must find powerful partners among legal and health professionals to join them in the battle to achieve public health equity through full enforcement of the civil rights laws.

Education Reforms

Ending structural racism in the nation's school systems will fundamentally destabilize the deadly and diffuse effects of structural racism. The first step is to restore the Supreme Court's enforcement of the Equal Protection Clause, as applied to education.

Restore Equal Protection Law to Reverse Resegregation of Elementary, Middle, and High Schools

After the Supreme Court's landmark decision that declared separate and unequal education unconstitutional in *Brown v. Board of Education*, the court decided a series of cases that affirmed state and local governments' authority to provide equal protection of the laws. For example, the court's 1971 opinion in *Swann v. Charlotte-Mecklenburg* endorsed a broad interpretation of the authority given to local school boards to remedy racial discrimination that had segregated schools. The *Swann* court held that affirmatively acting to remedy school attendance zones that had been discriminatory did not violate the Equal Protection Clause.[52] Nevertheless, the Supreme Court beat a hasty retreat from that position most dramatically in *Milliken v. Bradley* (*Milliken I*) and, later, in *Parents Involved in Community Schools v. Seattle School District No 1* (*Parents Involved*).

This retreat left room for the trend of resegregation that has played out in schools over decades. The court began to undermine the *Swann* approach to desegregating schools in 1974, only three years after the landmark decision, with *Milliken I*.[53] The case's reversal of multidistrict remedies restrictively seeks to find and remedy only specific discriminatory acts rather than regionally remedying discrimination maintained by structural residential patterns. In *Milliken I*, the court reviewed a desegregation plan designed to address the lower courts' decision that the Detroit Board of Education and the State of Michigan intentionally created and maintained residential and school segregation. The lower courts had determined that schools could only effectively be desegregated if predominately White suburban districts were included in the remedy, as the predominately Black population in the City of Detroit had become increasingly isolated. The desegregation plan the Supreme Court considered in *Milliken I* thus involved crossing boundary lines between the Detroit School District and nearby school districts, as the lower courts had found that the state had sustained racial segregation along school district lines. However, the Supreme Court overturned the lower courts' interdistrict desegregation plan. The court held that plaintiffs are required to prove an interdistrict constitutional violation before a court could order an interdistrict remedy, as the remedy's scope must be determined by the scope of the constitutional violation at hand. Consequently, the plaintiffs would have to show that each district included in an interdistrict remedy had intentionally segregated students between districts.

Not only did this decision contradict *Swann's* broad grant of judicial authority, but it also ignored the lower courts' finding that an intradistrict remedy would be ineffective because of how the state and the Detroit school board purposefully segregated schools. By eradicating interdistrict relief, *Milliken I* eliminated opportunities to desegregate school districts that lacked enough White students to do so. Consequently, while segregation within districts decreased from 1970 to 2000, interdistrict segregation increased.

In *Board of Education of Oklahoma City Public Schools v. Dowell* (*Dowel*; 1991), the court continued its departure from construing the Equal Protection Clause to support desegregation efforts.[54] In this case, the court ended a desegregation order and found that a school district had reached unitary status—a term meaning that integration had occurred—despite its admission that the district still contained vestiges of past discrimination and despite evidence that the segregation would resume. Chief Justice William Rehnquist, who as a law clerk recommended upholding *Plessy v. Ferguson* and opposed striking down the odious separate-but-equal doctrine in *Brown v. Board of Education*, wrote for the *Dowell* court. He found the district had spent a "reasonable" period of time making a "good faith" effort to desegregate to the "extent practicable" to protect "local control."[55]

Yet in 2006, the Supreme Court completely reversed "local control," obliterating two school districts' carefully crafted desegregation plans in *Parents Involved*. In that case, the court made it nearly impossible for school districts to use race-based student assignment plans that could survive strict scrutiny.[56] Chief Justice John Roberts wrote for the court to hold that student assignment plans locally designed and used by the Seattle and Jefferson County school districts, which considered student race when placing students in schools, violated the Fourteenth Amendment's Equal Protection Clause. He reasoned that the school districts had used racial preferences not narrowly tailored to achieve a compelling interest.[57] In their dissents, Justice John Paul Stevens and Justice Stephen Breyer disagreed, reasoning that local, race-conscious plans must be allowed to survive strict scrutiny at the elementary, middle, and secondary levels to enforce equal protection. The dissenting justices saw eliminating racial isolation, achieving racial diversity, and increasing racial integration in schools as compelling interests—indeed educational goals, democratic goals, and necessary remedies for historical segregation.[58] Further, they opined that diversity and increased racial integration during the formative years of early education are essential for creating a more integrated society.[59] They concluded that the majority had essentially restored separate-but-equal educational facilities, citing *Brown* to do so.[60] From a democratic perspective, these dissenters' views are consistent with the aspirations the founders expressed in the Declaration of Independence and the values of the drafters of the Fourteenth Amendment. These views are morally mandated by the principle that everyone in a pluralistic society is entitled to equal justice under law.[61]

Protect Affirmative Action Plans in Higher Education

Affirmative action plans that pass constitutional muster are essential to defeating structural racism in higher education. In November 2020, in *Students for Fair Admissions, Inc. v. President and Fellows of Harvard College* (*SFFA v. Harvard*), the Honorable Sandra Lynch upheld the constitutionality of my alma mater's race-conscious admissions plan, reaffirming that "the Equal Protection Clause does not force universities to choose between a diverse student body and a reputation for academic excellence." This finding, and indeed whether the courts continue to recognize that the Equal Protection Clause and Title VI of the Civil Rights Act can be a potent weapon against the educational discrimination and disparities described here, will determine our success in dismantling structural racism. The evidence before the *SFFA v. Harvard* court showed that despite Harvard's considerable efforts to recruit underrepresented minority students, its applicant pool still does not mirror the demographics of the nation on many criteria, including race. The US Court of Appeals for the First Circuit found that as far back as the Civil War, Harvard had sought to bring students from different states together to improve public affairs and had "emphatically embrace[d] and reaffirm[ed] the University's long-held . . . view that student body diversity—including racial diversity—is essential to [Harvard's] pedagogical objectives and institutional mission." We too must value diversity in this way if our country is to make equally accessible to all families the educational opportunities that helped my family escape poverty. A strong and concerted effort to reverse inequality in education could reduce population health disparities for generations.

Restore Title IV Enforcement to Reverse School Resegregation

The goal to dismantle structural racism in education will be furthered by restoring the power of Title IV of the Civil Rights Act of 1964. This part of the law was designed to provide technical assistance and training to school districts as they desegregated. The program provided grant funding and advisory services, and it authorized the attorney general to institute civil actions against segregated public school systems.[62] However, federal funding was unavailable for de facto segregated school systems. Funding for student reassignment programs using race as a factor and busing methods was prohibited by Title IV.[63] Only de jure segregation could be remedied with Title IV funds and advising. In the wake of *Parents Involved*, we must broaden Title IV to place programs aimed at desegregating de facto segregated school systems within its reach.

Restore the Equal Educational Opportunities Act of 1974

In 1974, Congress passed the Equal Educational Opportunities Act (EEOA). This act prohibited states from denying equal educational opportunity to individuals by certain means, including deliberate racial segregation. The Justice Department was tasked with enforcing this bill, which was created partly in response to President Nixon's desire to transfer control over educational decisions from the judicial branch to the legislative branch.[64] While most debate surrounding the EEOA has been about English language learners, the act might also be amended to help combat discrimination based on race.[65] Such an amendment could allow for any necessary remedy for dismantling de jure or de facto segregation, including both interdistrict and intradistrict remedies. Instead of considering the gray area of future compliance, an amended EEOA could be deployed to address contemporary trends toward school resegregation. The reforms in education law proposed here will advance equal access to the quality of public education that could improve the chances of equal educational attainment for all.

There are many other areas in which civil rights laws intended to enforce the Equal Protection Clause's guarantees must be strengthened. Notably, Title VII, the law that prohibits racial discrimination in giving marginalized communities equal access to jobs, wages, and working conditions, will have broad population impacts that will advance just health if key areas are reformed. And as referenced earlier, the nation must reverse the weakening of the Voting Rights Act of 1968 to dismantling structural racism. Here, however, the recommendations have focused on two social determinants of health—education and housing— shown to have a substantial impact on health equity. In summary, the recommendations broadly address the legislative, administrative, and common law reforms to existing provisions that, together, are necessary to advance just health. However, merely reversing past departures from misguided interpretations of equal protection mechanisms will not guarantee just health. The massive deprivation that occurred as equal protection laws were misconstrued must be set right. Put simply, a new legal mechanism to address historical and contemporary deprivations must be enacted to grant just health for all.

Reparations

Reparations are required if this nation is to rectify the massive economic, social, and moral disruption to equal justice under law in America that structural racism has caused for four centuries. A wise Baptist preacher once explained that disruption this way: If a person steals my bicycle and keeps it, returning it some years later does not make me whole. We are not equal until the person also returns the wages and opportunities I lost. Over the years, I did not have my bike to ride to work and to school, and during that time, the person who stole my bike reaped unfair advantages by using my bike while I could not.[66] The prior section described reforms that are akin to returning a stolen bike—they restore equal protection of the laws. In contrast, this section proposes new reparations laws to compensate marginalized communities for their losses and for the fact that they have been unfairly disadvantaged compared with White communities, which have been and continue to be unfairly advantaged, by structural racism.

I recommend an approach that addresses three objectives. First, I join the other scholars and advocates who propose reparations in the form of direct and indirect payments to compensate for historical injury. Second, I propose institutional reparations to restore losses due to inequitable access to wealth-building resources such as land and home ownership, educational attainment, and job security—factors that are not only necessary for competing equally for economic opportunity in America but also fundamental to wealth accumulation for generational prosperity. Third, I propose structural reforms to rectify the systemic, inequitable access to the social determinants of health documented throughout this book. In support of these recommendations, I rely on a well-developed literature to adopt a broad definition of reparations and their purpose. Professor Alfred L. Brophy, one of the academy's leading reparations scholars, explains that "most serious reparations scholarship is premised in large part, though not exclusively, on the idea that by repairing past harm, our country can build something better for the future. Reparations are justified because past harm is causing current inequality." I introduce the term *structural reparations* to reflect the multigenerational, and multisystem nature of the losses to be addressed. Structural reparations are the solution to structural racism.

Structural Reparations

An accurate definition of reparations acknowledges the historical source of the societal compensatory obligation but also recognizes the continuing and current injuries that reparations must address. This temporal understanding is especially important to the backward- and forward-facing nature of the structural reparations recommended here. Although reparations for Black Americans are rightly conceived to address injuries due to and flowing from the American slave trade, the structural reparations recommended here also aim to restore the harms flowing from the model of structural racism set forth throughout this book. Thus, I propose reparations to redress the legalized dehumanization of Black people, a historical injury that predates the formal institutionalization of slavery and that has continued long after its abolition.

Similarly, the objective of structural reparations proposed here is to reverse the institutionalized subordination that legalized inequality imposed during Jim Crow, extending from the end of Reconstruction and continuing until the Civil Rights era. At that time, the US Congress, the Supreme Court, and the executive branch expressly reversed the language of US legislative and common law decisions that had supported White supremacy. As the empirical evidence presented throughout this book demonstrates, however, changing the letter of the law did not instantaneously change the practice of White supremacy. A fulsome concept of structural reparations must also account for the ongoing injury occasioned by refusal to enforce these civil rights laws and the equal protection mandate on which they are premised. Structural reparations should be proportional to the scale and scope of the systemic public health impacts of structural racism. In other words, to achieve just health, the program of structural reparations proposed here must (1) provide legal and moral redress for state-supported harm, (2) reshape the environments that have been marred by structural racism, and (3) be strong enough to address the full range of injuries attributable to structural racism. The next few paragraphs will describe these three attributes in detail.

First, structural reparations must operate as a legal and moral corrective for state-enabled harms. Their purpose is to reverse abuses of state under which governments directly violated the essential human equality of entire populations through its legal enactments and actors. Moreover, structural reparations must correct the indirect offenses of government through its abject failure to prohibit broad racial injustices that could not persist in the private sector apart from the sanction and sanctuary provided by law. In the case of structural reparations aimed at structural racism, the precise objective is to reverse America's legalized dehumanization and legalized inequality of Black people and other minorities. The International Center for Transitional Justice describes the objective well:

> Reparations serve to acknowledge the legal obligation of a state, or individual(s) or group, to repair the consequences of violations—either because it directly committed them or it failed to prevent them. They also express to victims and society more generally that the state is committed to addressing the root causes of past violations and ensuring they do not happen again.[67]

Second, in light of the broad ecological impacts of structural racism on public health, structural reparations must be designed to reshape the micro-, meso-, and macro-level environments that have been distorted by this form of racism. This recommendation does not take the artificially constrained view that reparations must match identifiable individuals or groups of wrongdoers with individuals or groups of victims to rectify past behaviors or events. No—the nature of structural racism does not operate in such a merely transactional manner. Instead, reparations should establish an overarching environment that directly contradicts the pervasive, relational hierarchy among racial groups that has been built through the use of laws that institutionalize the perverse norms of White supremacy. Therefore, structural reparations must extend to deconstruct the broad influence of those hierarchies on individuals, materials, social networks, and institutions to establish new norms built on the essential truth that all humankind is created equal.[68] Therefore, as Professor Brophy explains, rather than attempting a fit between payer and wrongdoer, structural reparations should have ecological objectives: "Most reparationists define reparations more broadly. They define reparations as programs designed to make life better, searching for a way, as Ralph Ellison wrote in his posthumously published book *Juneteenth*, for 'the future [to] deny the Past.'"[69]

Operationally, structural reparations reflect this view by encompassing both the legislative model of reparations, which involves government action to restore group-level rights, and the litigation model, which is based on ethical individualism.[70] The narrow litigation model alone cannot encompass the structural nature of racial damage that has affected victims of large-scale injustice.[71] The legislative model, however, extends to systemically rectifying the imbalance of resources, power, and opportunities that could advantage some and disadvantage others seeking to participate equally in the quest for the American Dream.

Finally, structural reparations must be sufficiently broad, deep, and robust enough to address the temporal and substantive reach of injuries attributable to structural racism. Financial compensation—or the payment money—is only one of many types of material reparations that can be provided to victims. Other types include restoring civil and political rights, erasing unfair criminal convictions, physical rehabilitation, and granting access to land, health care, or education. Sometimes, these measures are provided to victims' family members—often children—in recognition that providing them with a better future is an important way to overcome the enduring consequences of the violations.

Structural, rather than individual-level reparations are justified because structural racism not only produces systemic disadvantages but also simultaneously yields a consequential and systemic set of advantages to Americans who are not members of racial or ethnic minority groups. These advantages have been enabled, as previous chapters have demonstrated, either through affirmatively legalized dehumanization and inequality or by an absence of equal protection enforcement that set social norms for both state and private conduct. Each of the proposed three elements of reparations serves to compensate the affected people, restore their lost wealth, and equalize their access to the social determinants of health. Each objective is discussed below in turn.

Compensation

Structural reparations that compensate for historical injustices most commonly take the form of direct payment to victims. Examples of individual and group-level payments made as part of reparation programs abound throughout American history. For example, in 1702, a Massachusetts General Court declared the Salem witch trials unlawful and in 1711 restored the rights and good names of the accused while granting financial reparations to the families of the women executed.[72] After both the Revolutionary War and the Civil War, soldiers received compensation directly (such as pension payments) and indirectly (forgiveness of merchant debts) as compensation for losses they suffered during the war. Other forms of legislative reparations rooted deeply in English common law traditions were the "general mob liability acts," under which municipalities permitted lawsuits for monetary damages and levied taxes to compensate victims of riots.[73] In 1891, the US government paid $25,000 in reparations to the families of eleven Italian immigrants who had been lynched or shot by mobs after three of the victims had been acquitted of a police chief's murder in New Orleans.[74] In contrast, many efforts at reparations for past injustices done to African Americans have failed. These attempts include the Dyer Anti-Lynching Bill, proposed in 1919–1922 and intended to compensate the families of the slain victims of racial terror. The Dyer bill would have paid $10,000 to each family.[75]

Some reparations programs have compensated Indigenous tribes financially for land taken or have compensated them by returning sacred lands.[76] Reparations have been paid to Holocaust survivors and victims' families by the US and other governments.[77] And in 1988, Congress enacted the Civil Liberties Act of 1988 to authorize a payment of $20,000 for each living Japanese American who had been interned during World War II; the US government paid approximately $1.6 billion in reparations to more than 82,200 of these citizens under that law.[78] Reparations proposals that aim to compensate African Americans for losses due to the institution of slavery are the most commonly discussed and well developed in the literature. Professors William Darity Jr. and A. Kirsten Mullen, for example, have surveyed the various processes that could be used to make reparation payments; their plan is specific and detailed and appears in the final chapter of in their excellent book, *From Here to Equality*.[79]

Wealth Restoration

By 2016, White families in America had an average net worth of approximately $171,000—ten times greater than the average Black family's net worth of $17,150. Because wealth represents generational "getting ahead" resources for families, persistent racial inequality is guaranteed for generations as long as the racial gap in wealth, originally constructed and currently maintained by inequitable laws, remains deeply embedded in the United States.[80] Therefore, a comprehensive program to restore wealth lost to Black communities because of structural racism is a vital component of a structural reparations program whose goal is to ensure equal opportunity for all. The basis for such a program is the historical record that is replete with evidence of state-sponsored discrimination that has systemically excluded Black people from an equal opportunity to accumulate wealth. The earliest example is congressional mismanagement of the Freedman's Savings Bank, which shuttered in 1874 and left more than sixty-one thousand depositors—mostly newly emancipated African Americans—with losses of approximately $3 million, representing the majority of Black wealth that had accumulated in this country since emancipation.

As early as 1672, Quaker founder George Fox argued that freed slaves should be compensated by being provided "freedom dues" such as were commonly paid to White indentured servants who completed their terms of service. Those servants regularly received land, tools, and sometimes livestock to begin their new lives.[81] In contrast, Black people generally had no similar access to these basic factors of production necessary to build wealth in an agrarian society. In the most infamous exclusion of Black people for the right to compete equally for the nation's wealth, President Andrew Johnson rescinded General William T. Sherman's Special Field Order No. 15, commonly referred to as the "forty acres and a mule" order that would have granted to freed Black people the same access to wealth afforded to White former servants. Under this order, issued on January 16, 1865, General Sherman confiscated a strip of coastline from Charleston, South Carolina, to the St. John's River in Florida and redistributed this land to newly freed Black families in forty-acre apportionments.[82] Sherman's army provided for the settlement of around forty thousand Black residents under this policy, but President Johnson overturned Sherman's promise in the fall of 1865, after the Civil War ended and President Lincoln was assassinated. He returned most of the land in South Carolina, Georgia, and Florida to the White planters who had originally owned it. Sherman's order is seen as a promise from the US government to make restitution to Black Americans for the country's cruel history of slavery.[83] However, as Professors Darity and Mullen point out, the exclusion of African Americans from wealth accumulation did not end with slavery.

Federal social programs aimed at building middle-class wealth in the United States expressly excluded African Americans beginning in the 1930s. The Social Security Act of 1935 was structured in a way that excluded Black people by omitting agricultural and domestic workers, predominately Black occupational categories. In another example, while legal academics persuaded Congress to come to the aid of European immigrants who were victims of heinous racial violence during the 1920s, similar reparations have yet to be made for the domestic terrorism that decimated the wealth of prospering Black communities.[84] For example, there was massive property destruction and killing in the towns of Wilmington, North Carolina; Ocoee, Florida; Springfield, Illinois; and Tulsa, Oklahoma.[85]

During the 1930s, New Deal labor legislation excluded Black citizens from the benefit of wage protections by excluding domestic and workers, the occupations held by most African Americans during that era. The Servicemen's Readjustment Act of 1944, popularly known as the GI Bill, provided assistance and financial rewards for World War II veterans, but Black and White service members did not have equal access to the GI benefits when they returned home from war. Historians document that Black servicemen and servicewomen returning from World War II were unable to take full advantage of the GI benefits, especially in the South, where segregated educational and residential structures limited their options and discriminatory administration of the bill's benefits hampered their access to promised funds.[86] The bill's employment benefits were disparately administered by local agencies that were staffed almost exclusively by White people who blocked access to the bill's benefits for Black veterans.[87] As a result, while 3,229 veterans had received guaranteed home, business, and farm loans in Mississippi by 1947, only two of those loans were made to Black veterans.[88]

In *The Color of Law*, Rothstein reports extensively on the redlining practices the FHA employed to refuse to insure mortgages in or near Black neighborhoods. He also describes the federal government's practice of subsidizing development loans for developers building Whites-only subdivisions. The federal government expressly provided in its underwriting manual that "incompatible racial groups should not be permitted to live in the same communities." The importance of reversing these structural barriers to equal opportunity, says Thomas Shapiro of Brandeis University, is underscored by an understanding of the role of wealth in achieving equality in America:

> Wealth changes our conception of racial inequality, its nature and magnitude, origins and transmission, and whether it is increasing or narrowing. Importantly, an examination of wealth allows an analytic window into the contemporary relevance of the historical legacy of African-Americans; . . .

. . . Framing racial inequality from a wealth perspective raises the issue
of deeply embedded racial structure of the United States.[89]

Dr. Shapiro's explanation underscores the importance of reversing the
structural origins of wealth disparities to create a level playing field
that is race neutral. Thus, the form of reparations intended to achieve
equal opportunity must address the racial wealth gap that structural discrimination imposed on Black Americans in the form of opportunity
costs. The example Dr. Darity and Dr. Mullen point to as a model is
the German reparations program: "In addition to payments made to
individual victims and the relatives of victims, funds were given to the
state of Israel to aid its economic development and financial stability."[90]
Under its ongoing postwar reparations program, Germany has paid
more than $89 billion to compensate the nation of Israel and individual
Holocaust survivors and other victims' descendants.

Ironically, this wealth restoration approach toward reparations was
used to repay slaveholders for the loss of the Black human beings they
once purported to own. This approach made African Americans the objects rather than the recipients of reparations. For example, under an
1862 District of Columbia Emancipation Act, approximately one thousand loyal Union slaveholders in the nation's capital received reparations
for their loss of property when they lost ownership of approximately
three thousand enslaved Black people; each slaveholder received up to
$300 as "just compensation" in accordance with the Constitution's Fifth
Amendment.[91] Structural reparations would similarly account for the
loss of wealth-building property that would have been afforded to Black
people in the absence of legalized dehumanization and inequality.

Grant Equal Access to the Social Determinants of Health

Not all reparations efforts seek to pay compensation in retrospect; prospective reparations seek to disrupt future inequalities that would persist
but for intervention.[92] This final category of recommended reparations

would reverse the structural inequality that has disproportionately denied equal access to such social determinants as housing, food security, health care, and education and would extend the opportunity for equal access to these resources in the future. Recently, prospective institutional reform efforts have been included as part of reparations programs in isolated states or institutions to rectify egregious offenses. In 1994, for example, the Florida legislature passed a law that has provided contribution toward tuition for college education to 297 descendants of the 1923 Rosewood massacre, when White mobs burned a prospering Black town to the ground in Florida.[93] In another example, institutions of higher education—most notably, Georgetown and Brown Universities—and some religious institutions, such as the Catholic sisters of the Society of the Sacred Heart, have created reparations funds for descendants of enslaved people. Notably, these efforts have been scattered and primarily not aimed at structural reform.

This type of prospective compensation is premised on the disadvantage that descendants of past harms have suffered. But some argue that compensation is unnecessary since social programs such as the Great Society and affirmative action already represent sufficient reparations for historical injustices. James Forman, a civil rights pioneer who served briefly as foreign minister for the Black Panther Party, delivered an economic rationale for reparations in his 1969 Black Manifesto, which was a response to this concern.[94] The manifesto demanded $500 million in reparations because unpaid slave labor had helped establish the American economy and had created a wealth system that Black Americans had been largely excluded from even after slavery officially ended. Foreman further argued that White Christian churches and Jewish synagogues should recognize how Black resources, minds, bodies, and labor had been exploited for years and that these religious institutions should remedy past wrongs by paying for projects such as a Black university and a Southern land bank. In this way, Foreman's argument extends beyond the compensatory goals for reparations and argues for reparations that also serve retributive goals. Notwithstanding how comprehensive a reparations plan may be, the question of whether execution is feasible raises important questions.

Feasibility

America's view of reparations has matured, but the public remains divided on the issue. Nevertheless, structural reparations are well within our collective political, moral, and economic capacity. In 1989, Representative John Conyers introduced House Resolution 40, the Commission to Study Reparation Proposals for African Americans Act. Representative Conyers, who served as the congressman representing western Detroit from 1965 until 2017 (he died at age ninety just two years later, in October 2019), reintroduced HR 40 in every Congress from 1968 until the end of his time in office. His bill, if successful, would have acknowledged slavery as unjust and inhumane. It would have established a commission to study the racial and economic discrimination against freed Black people after slavery and the impact of such discrimination on Black Americans today. And finally, the bill would have instructed the commission to make recommendations to Congress about how to redress these harms. Representative Conyers thought his bill was unsuccessful during his lifetime because people want to leave the painful legacy of slavery in the past. However, he recognized that reparations are not a new concept to the US government and have great potential to remedy past wrongs and reduce the racial wealth gap that stems from slavery and the discriminatory policies that followed.[95]

As Ta-Nehisi Coates explained in a 2014 essay "The Case for Reparations," legalized discrimination extended long beyond the time that slavery ended. As this book has addressed, such systemic discrimination has affected the profits Black Americans can earn and their ability to access equal job, housing, education, and health-care opportunities. Consequently, a typical Black household has ten cents in wealth for every dollar that a typical White household has.[96] Reparations could be designed to remedy this quantifiable, cumulative effect, which has prevented Black Americans from equal opportunity for decades. The issue is again being raised in Congress. In 2020, in addition to introducing HR 40 in the House, the Senate put forward a companion bill, S. 1083, led by Senator Cory Booker. This is the first reparations bill to have been introduced in the post-Reconstruction US Senate, and it received cosponsorship from eighteen senators.[97]

During the Democratic primary campaigns for the 2020 election, reparations became a key topic of debate in the presidential race for the first time. While several candidates expressed openness to the idea of government reparations being paid to Black Americans as a form of restitution for slavery, few offered a formal reparations plan.[98] Reparations are not a popular solution to deeply rooted systemic racism in America. A July 2018 survey from the Data for Progress organization found that 26 percent of Americans supported a form of compensation or cash benefits for the descendants of those who were forcibly enslaved.[99] Similarly, a May 2016 Marist survey found that 26 percent of Americans believed the US government should pay reparations to "make up for the harm caused by slavery and other forms of racial discrimination."[100] However, the very fact that candidates began to discuss reparations in a mainstream fashion surprised Dr. Darity and other scholars studying reparations.[101] The moral consensus around reparations is changing. The fact that delivering reparations has become more difficult than it was during the "forty acres and a mule" days is a function of continued racism. But it does not absolve the national obligation or the historical justification for restitution. Delay has just compounded the injustice.

Reparations are logistically feasible. Many proposals, including guaranteed minimum income, could allow for restitution. Three possible examples for enacting reparations stem from work put forward by Dr. Darity (who is a scholar of economics, African and African American history, and public policy) and Dr. Thomas Craemer (a professor of public policy) and the US government's experience with reparations after Japanese American internment. Dr. Darity posits that direct payments to individual recipients should be a major component of efforts to eliminate the racial wealth gap. He suggests that to receive direct payments, an individual should meet two conditions: the person must be able to demonstrate that they have at least one ancestor who was enslaved in the United States, and the individual must demonstrate that they self-identified as Black, Negro, or African American for at least twelve years before the reparations program was enacted.[102]

Dr. Craemer describes his personal preference that reparations include a "substantial cash component."[103] He recognizes that cash payments were made to Japanese Americans who were interned and that the internment lasted only three years, whereas African American enslavement lasted hundreds of years, thus affecting a much larger portion of the American population. Moreover, Craemer emphasizes that reparations cannot be delayed. Using a "very conservative interest rate," he estimated in 2015 that reparations would equal one year's worth of the US gross domestic product.[104] African Americans were essentially made to give the United States an involuntary loan of labor to build the US economy, and waiting to repay this forced loan will only compound the interest due. The empirical record of structural inequality that Black Americans continue to experience provides evidence of the cost this population has incurred from forcible enslavement, legalized segregation, and years of inequitable access to the opportunity to be healthy.

The remedies proposed here to move our nation toward just health will require an implementation strategy to succeed. From the historical efforts after the enactment of the civil rights statutes, we know that merely placing laws on the books will not change behavior on the ground. Moreover, the legal community alone cannot persuade institutions to comply with new and reformed laws alone. The responsibility to make equality under the law a reality lies with many stakeholders. In particular, the concluding chapter invites those who best understand the urgent imperative of equalizing outcomes in population health to join in making just health a reality in America.

7

THE POWER OF MEDICAL-LEGAL PARTNERSHIPS

> To bring together, representatives of all the interests among hospitals, the public, the healing professions and government agencies, which are concerned with this [segregation] problem. To provide a complete, comprehensive picture of the situation throughout the country as it exists today. . . . To evolve in the atmosphere of common understanding and cooperation so created, recommendations and programs of remedial action which may be made known to the American people with the aim of securing widespread public support for their implementation.
>
> —*Journal of the National Medical Association*, "First Imhotep National Conference on Hospital Integration," 1957

Structural problems require structural solutions. Thus, by definition, structural solutions must cross sectors, settings, and stakeholder groups if they are to have lasting impact. This chapter builds on the success of the collaborative work that ended de jure segregation throughout the health-care industry and indeed affected the nation during the 1960s. It calls on health-care professionals and public health experts to join together with the communities they serve, and it urges civil rights lawyers to take decisive, collective action to defeat structural racism. Throughout this book, we have seen the public health urgency of dismantling structural racism and have examined the legal reforms that will accomplish this goal. The success of this work requires a broad coalition of us to call on our nation to live up to its humanist ideals by passing new and enforcing existing civil rights laws that will root out systemic discrimination in all the social determinants of health. This goal is within our reach, and within our lifetimes, if patients and providers again lead the way. History shows that the nation becomes considerably more willing to take the bold, necessary, *legal* steps to deconstruct structural racism when health-care providers, public health experts, and patients join the fight for racial equality. We have seen this powerful partnership work before.

Civil Rights Leadership from the Health Professions

It was the work of a group of health-care providers and ordinary members of the patient community—six physicians, three dentists, and two patients—that led Congress to enact Title VI of the Civil Rights Act of 1964. Their 1962 lawsuit, *Simkins v. Moses H. Cone Memorial Hospital*, was the culmination of advocacy for hospital desegregation that had been brewing for years. Civil rights lawyers from the National Association for the Advancement of Colored People (NAACP) and hospital advocates had worked with patients to bring class-action challenges to the separate and unequal clinical settings that provided inferior health care to Black Americans throughout the Jim Crow era. But their civil rights advocacy extended far beyond hospitals. George Simkins, a dentist and the named plaintiff in the landmark case, filed suits to desegregate golf courses, challenged discriminatory bank lending practices, and forced reform to the district voting system in his region to give voice to African American voters. Dr. Simkins's work compelled legal changes that not only set lawmaking in motion to desegregate 7,160 hospitals throughout the United States but also eliminated segregation in many other settings that constitute social determinants of health. But the collaboration between law, medicine, and community did not end with the passage of new laws. Enforcing those laws also required the power of this partnership.

The *Simkins* case inspired courts and legislatures to enact new civil rights legislation. However, health-care providers were initially no more willing than those who led massive resistance to school desegregation were to obey those laws. Instead, a nationwide coalition among health-care providers, public health professionals, hospitals, lawyers, and civil rights organizations launched a direct attack against reluctant providers to end rampant racial discrimination in health care. This coalition of advocates challenged discriminatory patient admissions practices, separate and unequal bed assignments, unfair credentialing and staff privileging policies, and inferior patient care. In other words, equal protection of the laws required much more than just the laws themselves. It required medical, legal, and community leaders working together to desegregate the health-care sector and arguably the entire nation.

Unlike the people who battled for equality in school and public transportation, and those whose efforts resulted in the Voting Rights Act of 1965, health-care providers saw few marches, encountered no ferocious dogs, or never felt the fury of fire hoses. Desegregation was a transaction compelled—albeit not altogether willingly—out of financial necessity. Indeed, the desegregation of health-care institutions that followed the Civil Rights Act of 1964 can be termed a quiet revolution. This chapter argues for a second quiet revolution—the reversal of structural racism that affects and infects public health in America—to be led by health-care providers uniting with lawmakers and policy makers to achieve just health.

The Quiet Revolution

Perhaps the most often-quoted admonition concerning health inequity is the 1966 statement attributed to the Rev. Martin Luther King Jr. In a speech at the second convention of the Medical Committee for Human Rights, he said, "Of all the forms of inequality, injustice in health care is the most shocking and inhumane."[1] Dr. King, therefore, spoke of medical rights as civil rights, and of civil rights as human rights. In light of this premise, medical and public health leaders are indispensable to the battle against structural racism. History bears this out. In his book *The*

Good Doctors, John Dittmer tells the story of health-care professionals engaged in the struggle for equality during the civil rights movement. While the full story is too lengthy for this book, examples of this successful model for civil rights engagement by the health community is instructive for today.

Before the 1960s, the United States saw the legacy of racial discrimination permeating all areas of health care and, of course, American life. Most medical and nursing schools refused to educate Black students. Nor would state and national medical societies admit Black doctors. Across the country, hospitals, clinics, dentist offices, and most White physicians would not care for Black Americans unless the practitioner did so in separate and unequal facilities.[2] Paul Cornely, a professor of preventive medicine at Howard University, recognized the adverse health impacts of this discrimination in studies he conducted in 1959. Consequently, Dr. Cornely worked through the American Public Health Administration to gain support from public health officers and hospital administrators in the quest for equal hospital access, regardless of race.

Around the same time, W. Montague Cobb, a physician and an anatomy professor at Howard University and the first African American to earn a PhD in anthropology, focused his scholarly attention on emphasizing social and historical factors rather than biological ones to explain the racial health disparities he observed. Moreover, he highlighted the impact that racism had on African American health, arguing that racism, not biological differences among races, accounted for disease and developmental disparities. A staunch opponent of White supremacist arguments advanced by medical eugenicists, Dr. Cobb worked to change the face of the medical community. He testified before Congress, served as president of the NAACP, and even served on White House committees to advocate for racial integration in the medical workforce.

By the late 1950s, Dr. Cobb's collaborative advocacy, bringing professionals from law and medicine together, began to bear fruit. Eleven of twenty-six Southern medical schools allowed Black students to receive a medical education, and nine of seventeen Southern state medical societies, including the medical society of the District of Columbia, offered membership to Black doctors. Diversifying the medical workforce was an essential first step. During the period, Dean Charles Hamilton Houston was shaping the Howard University Law School to become a training ground for a veritable army of Black civil rights lawyers who, like Howard graduates Thurgood Marshall, Conrad Pearson, and others, would change the face of the nation.

These attorneys joined the NAACP, the National Medical Association, and the National Urban League to form a coalition of lawyers, physicians, and community activists who launched a national agenda on racial integration. Three Black physicians—Dr. Cornely, Dr. Cobb, and Dr. Louis T. Wright, Harlem Hospital's chairman of surgery and chairman of the NAACP's board of directors—worked together to educate congressional leaders and the broader public on the damage that denial of hospital services to Black Americans had on community health nationwide. Dr. Cobb and Dr. Cornely organized the Imhotep National Conference on Hospital Integration, a series of conferences beginning in 1957 and designed to teach physicians about the health impacts of discriminatory hospital conditions. The stated purpose of these conferences, sponsored by the National Medical Association, the NAACP, and the Medico-Chirurgical Society of the District of Columbia was to educate representatives of law, health, government, and the public to inspire action toward change. This conference series was a part of the overall strategy to challenge hospital discrimination in the courts. As a result, groups of health professionals around the country became active legal advocates. For example, a group of physicians filed suit against fifty-six Chicago hospitals and five hospital organizations to argue that their racial discrimination violated the Sherman Antitrust Act. Another group joined US senators to introduce a bill to amend the law that financed the federal government's largest hospital construction program. The Hospital Survey and Construction Act of 1946, commonly called the Hill-Burton Act, required that hospital facilities of equal quality be built for minorities. At the Imhotep conferences, physicians learned that, despite the Hill-Burton Act's "separate-but-equal" clause, federal funds were disproportionately supporting superior hospital services for White Americans.

More than a decade later, President John F. Kennedy met with health and civil rights activists, and their advocacy culminated in the passage of the Civil Rights Act in the summer of 1964. But the coalition of advocacy did not stop there. Civil rights activists like Cobb, Cornely, and Wright maintained involvement in developing Title VI regulations, compliance review guidelines, and the implementation of major federal health programs. Such programs later included Medicare, which affected almost all US public hospitals. Indeed, once President Lyndon B. Johnson secured congressional passage of the Social Security Act that created the Medicare and Medicaid programs, more than seven thousand hospitals were subject to Title VI civil rights laws and regulations. Title VI, and its enabling regulations, provided the leverage to allow motivated health and government officials to broadly enforce civil rights laws in health care. Of essential importance, civil rights inspectors went door to door to hospitals after Title VI passed, to inspect, report on, and require compliance with civil rights laws. This on-the-ground legwork is an example of how changes in the civil rights laws encouraged changes in behavior by health-care providers and ultimately led to lasting changes in social norms surrounding health-care delivery throughout the nation.

Desegregation was always a good idea economically. Decades of medical segregation proved to be economically inefficient, creating an unnecessary duplication of services such as blood banks, cafeterias, and linens.[3] The cash boon for hospitals provided by such federally funded programs as the Hill-Burton Act and, eventually, Medicare was incentive enough for many hospitals to integrate. But even some willing hospitals needed further prodding. The desegregation effort was not without opposition. Some Southern hospitals needed an outright battle before integration would succeed. As one constituent complained to the then US senators for Georgia, "civil rights and Medicare should have nothing to do with each other."[4] Southerners largely felt that older citizens were being used as scapegoats by civil rights advocates to integrate American hospitals. President Johnson, born in Stonewall, Texas, and thus a Southerner himself, noted these concerns and walked a tightrope trying to enforce his Great Society ideals in the face of mounting Southern concerns. But ultimately, the president led an administration that partnered with health-care providers, civil rights activists, and ordinary citizens to fight for and win hospital desegregation.

When 70 percent of Southern hospitals remained segregated after the passage of Medicare in 1966, the Johnson administration made a game-changing decision in the battle for national hospital integration. The Department of Health, Education, and Welfare (HEW) established an administrative rule requiring hospitals to desegregate before they received payment for Medicare patients.[5] HEW created the Office of Civil Rights, an unprecedented action that elated civil rights activists. The first task facing this office was managing the desegregation of every US hospital that had failed to comply with the new Title VI legislation.[6]

Health-care providers advocating to end discrimination in health care moved toward their goal by gaining support from the judicial branch, professional organizations, Congress, and the public. Engaging in what was called a *triple-assault*, the combined efforts of the federal government, civil rights advocates, and health-care organizations, the providers launched attacks—both in and out of courts—against hospitals that did not desegregate.[7] Step by step, health-care providers, activists, politicians, and researchers, among others, worked together to push for reform. Hospital desegregation advanced health equity, but victories won on a legal basis alone were not enough.

Three Lessons in Fighting for Reforms

In addition to the overarching importance of a broad, multisector coalition in the fight for health equality, three other lessons from the Civil Rights era are worth highlighting. First, although legislatures can pass civil rights laws, and courts can enforce them in isolated cases, to gain widespread health-equity changes throughout the nation, members of the health professions must also participate in all phases of the work to dismantle structural inequality. From advocacy, to litigation, to drafting legislation and implementing that legislation on the ground—intimate involvement of health providers who recognize the adverse public health impacts of racial inequality is vital and indispensable. This collaboration is how sustainable change can occur.

Second, coalitions that affect sustainable changes must be built with the intimate involvement of members of the patient community who are affected by structural racism. True community engagement, therefore, is essential to the coordinated effort to dismantle structural racism and for achieving social justice reform in America. Community-engaged reform will shift the balance of power and leadership away from experts outside the communities affected by structural racism and toward those most intimately familiar with its harms. The partnership with communities will guarantee that the work done will tangibly benefit those historically marginalized and that the solutions will aim at real problems rather than theoretical ones. The knowledge of experts from affected communities must be valued, and community members must be compensated for the time they dedicate to advocacy, litigation, and legislation because their contributions are as indispensable and essential as the knowledge of professional, legal, medical, public health, and all other experts. The participation of all these parties is required to fashion and implement reform. Finally, full community collaboration will increase the chances that the reforms will work. All too often, the voices of marginalized populations are absent when solutions are developed. The legal and policy results have been incomplete. Participatory action research shows that reforms must be approached through partnerships with those who have been the most hurt by legalized dehumanization, inequality, and unequal protection of law. In the words of community activists, "Nothing about us, without us!"

The third lesson in fighting for reform is that the success of health-care desegregation depends on eliminating the traditional boundaries between medicine and public health. As the complexity and scope of health problems have grown, so too has the need for the surveillance, monitoring, and data-driven interventions that come from public health expertise when it is integrated with clinical expertise. Structural racism invades every social determinant of health. Therefore, to achieve health equity through the destruction of structural racism, we will need collaborations that combine medical and public health tools, like the 1994 Medicine and Public Health Initiative, if the reforms are to reach each sector that has a profound impact on health outcomes. The public health perspective will focus solutions on populations and communities rather than on individuals. Moreover, this perspective will thus engage the environments, cultures, histories, and ethical considerations that will determine the shape and effectiveness of legal reforms. Moreover, the "public" in *public health* points squarely at the state as the legal actor to solve the collective problems presented in this book. State action was an intrinsic part of the legalization of dehumanization and inequality; it is therefore indispensable to their reversal. The nation must summon the power and duty of state, local, and federal governments to protect, preserve, and promote health to create a society of just health. In the words of Professor Lawrence O. Gostin, public health law involves accessing

the legal powers and duties of the state, in collaboration with its partners (e.g., health care, business, the community, the media, and academe), to assure the conditions for people to be healthy (to identify, prevent, and ameliorate risks to health in the population) and the limitations on the power of the state to constrain the autonomy, privacy, liberty, proprietary, or other legally protected interests of individuals for the common good. The prime objective of public health law is to pursue the highest possible level of physical and mental health in the population, consistent with the values of social justice.[8]

The solutions called for in this book will require the power and duty of the state, informed by the knowledge and empathy of providers, who work in service of communities nationwide.

A Call for Collaboration

As a pervading theme of this book, racial discrimination is the common thread connecting every public health disparity described on these pages. Therefore, all the strategies set forth to address these disparities will require antiracism interventions to achieve health equity. The model proposed here is a cross-disciplinary collaboration aimed directly at eradicating the structural racism underlying health disparities. It is based on the view that the only way to accomplish truly substantial and sustainable legal reforms that will dismantle structural racism is for professionals and experts in health care, public health, and equal protection law to fight *together* for health equity.

Health providers who understand disease and anatomy, biochemistry, microbiology, nutrition, chemistry, pathology, and pharmacology cannot eradicate health disparities alone. Nor can public health specialists alone, despite having mastered health promotion, qualitative and quantitative research methods, prevention and advanced data sciences, and epidemiology. And neither will experts in all facets of constitutional law, antidiscrimination statutes, civil and criminal justice procedure, employment, housing, or business law succeed in reversing the health impacts of centuries of racial inequality alone. Plainly, the siloed approaches by a vast array of professionals who have attempted to achieve health equity across the nation have failed. This failure is not for lack of sincere effort or commitment. Instead, it stems from a lack of collaboration across disciplines and with patient communities. Therefore, I propose to revive the collaborative model that succeeded in the Civil Rights era. Now, as then, coalitions of public health professionals, medical providers, legal experts, and community members must work together in this all-important enterprise to dismantle the structural racism that is harming our communities, our economy, and our democracy.

Exemplary Health-Care Interventions: Necessary but Not Sufficient

Health-care providers have worked hard to create innovative interventions to address health disparities. Despite the importance of this work, however, it also has its limitations. Even the work that has emerged to integrate multiple sectors, blend financing sources, and waive reimbursement restrictions does not intervene at a structural level. Some interventions arguably intervene at a systemic level—connecting multiple sites of practice or patient populations to the problems each policy addresses. But the changes these efforts produce will continue to have limited impact as long as they must operate within the discriminatory institutions that prevail in our society. Moreover, just as I have argued that legal advocates alone cannot dismantle structural racism, nor can members of the health professions, working alone, adequately address structural problems that produce poor population health in America. A few examples of outstanding work in the health-care sector will help clarify these points.

Housing as Health-Care Intervention

Leading hospital systems have done impressive work to defeat the association between poor housing and poor health. Some address the substandard housing conditions that characterize homes in segregated neighborhoods. For example, the Healthy Homes Program at Children's Mercy of Kansas City, Missouri, partners with university-based health professionals and the federal government to assess homes for pollutants that can cause chronic health conditions. The program then provides education, advocacy, and referrals to address the factors that contribute to hospital visits. After Healthy Homes conducted more than 750 home assessments, the results suggest that participant asthma patients visit the emergency room less frequently, need less medication, and experience improved symptoms. In Cincinnati, the Avondale Home Improvement Program tackles housing conditions, for example, by providing interest-free home improvement loans in a neighborhood where 92 percent of the residents are African American. Other programs seek to link social determinants into supportive housing environments to reduce the health impacts of structural inequality. For example, since the early 1990s, the Affordable Housing Program at Bon Secours Health Systems has developed more than eight hundred affordable-housing units in Baltimore and has provided support services such as financial literacy education, early childcare, and case management for more than twelve hundred residents. The effort has produced some admirable outcomes, including reduced readmissions for congestive heart failure patients, an increased number of pregnancies carried to full term, and increased health insurance enrollment.[9]

Another impressive effort has been the focus on hospitals' development of affordable housing to remedy housing inequality.[10] United Healthcare is the largest for-profit US health insurance company, covering more than 70 million Americans nationwide.[11] After Medicaid data showed that Medicaid recipients who more effectively manage their health after receiving stable housing, United Healthcare invested $400 million in new, affordable housing. Affordable-housing projects created by United Healthcare aim to improve health and reduce some of the outstanding health-care costs many low-income individuals and people experiencing homelessness face. Steve Nelson, CEO of United Healthcare, explains: "Access to safe and affordable housing is one of the greatest obstacles to better health, making it a social determinant that affects people's well-being and quality of life."[12] Since launching its program in 2011, United Healthcare has covered eighty new affordable-housing communities across eighteen states, serving forty-five hundred families.

United Healthcare's $400 million investment in affordable housing aims to remove social barriers to better health. By scaling up local efforts on a national scale, the company hopes to improve the social conditions of target communities with the greatest needs, such as older adults, military veterans, people living with disabilities, and those struggling with homelessness. The financial burdens of unaffordable housing can prevent families from meeting other basic needs, including nutrition and health care. These burdens are particularly significant for low-income families, prompting them to have greater health-care needs in the long term and, consequently, greater health-care-related burdens financially. Essentially, United Healthcare theorizes that it is cheaper to provide affordable housing than it is to leave Medicaid recipients in the unstable circumstances that are causing them to constantly require more health-care services.

As a nationwide program, United Healthcare partnered with national and regional organizations to create affordable housing in areas such as Los Angeles; Austin, Texas; Minneapolis; Phoenix; New York City; and Ypsilanti, Michigan. To cover these major metropolitan areas, United Healthcare partnered with organizations such as Enterprise Community Partners, the Greater Minnesota Housing Fund, US Bank, Affordable Equity Partners, Chicanos Por La Causa, and several others. By accepting United Healthcare's investment, local organizations must provide on-site amenities such as health-care services, social and supportive counseling and monitoring, job training, academic support, adult education classes, childcare, computer labs, and playgrounds.

The investments and partnerships have had remarkable results. For example, United Healthcare's $11.7 million investment in Capital Studios in Austin was the first affordable-housing development built there in more than forty-five years. It provided more than 135 efficiency apartments. Like United Healthcare, Foundation Communities, the network that includes Capital Studios, subscribes to the idea of providing "barrier busters" to help those in need obtain affordable housing; it is based on the belief that at-risk clients will make fewer expensive visits to the emergency room if they have a safe place to live.[13] Another exceptional example of United Healthcare's partnership investments includes the company's $7.9 million joint venture with New Parkridge in Ypsilanti. The New Parkridge affordable-housing development includes 68 duplexes, townhouses, and apartments centered around a large community building featuring on-site support services that give residents greater access to health care, education, job training, and childcare.

United Healthcare's housing projects have enjoyed several notable successes. In one state, beneficiaries of United Healthcare's affordable housing reduced their emergency room visits by 60 percent, and total health-care costs for people enrolled in the programs dropped by 50 percent. Addressing social determinants of health thus appears more beneficial than does allowing Medicaid recipients struggling with homelessness to remain in their current situations. These advantages come from both a medical and an economic perspective, as well as a moral one.[14]

The remarkable success of United Healthcare's model is not an isolated incident. In Washington, D.C., for example, Unity Health Care and So Others May Eat (SOME) teamed up to open the Conway Center, a 320,000-square-foot low-income housing facility with a 3,900-square-foot on-site dental and medical center operated by Unity Health Care. SOME and Unity Health Care's partnership has led to 596 fewer Washingtonians self-reporting as homeless, and the Conway Center has had the same impact on health as many other housing-first models.[15]

Boston began similar efforts after the publication of the World Health Organization's report on the social determinants of health, PBS's airing of the documentary *Unnatural Causes*, and the explosion of other similar reports. The Boston Public Health Commission (BPHC) and the Boston Housing Authority (BHA) joined forces to create the Healthy Start in Housing Program (HSiH), recognizing the connection between affordable housing and infant mortality.[16] Planning for HSiH progressed quickly, largely because of the agencies' ability to draw from existing resources and avoid the need for new funding.[17] In 2011, BPHC and BHA signed a memorandum, bringing HSiH into full swing by prioritizing housing for pregnant women who were experiencing homelessness or home insecurity and who faced poor birth outcomes and other medical risks.

In this memorandum, BHA agreed to reserve seventy-five housing units for HSiH-eligible women. While the housing authority agreed to expedite the processing of the eligible applications, the health commission would oversee enrollment, guide women through the application process, and provide enhanced, long-term case management. BPHC staff were given intensive training in trauma-informed care to address the complex health and psychosocial needs of these eligible women. Aside from safe housing, HSiH also provided support groups, emergency food assistance, home visits, and assistance from other BPHC programs. Any woman who has been residing in Boston for three years, has an existing chronic condition, and is either pregnant or has a child under the age of five with a need for special care is eligible for HSiH.

BPHC staff worked with researchers from Boston University School of Public Health and School of Medicine to evaluate the pilot project. When the pilot was launched, among the 77 HSiH-eligible women in that original pool, 58 percent had preexisting medical conditions, 56 percent had mental health conditions that required attention, and 14 percent had previous adverse outcomes. Thirty percent fell into more than one of these categories. Standardized assessments conducted on the HSiH participants reflected that most participants exhibited symptoms of depression, and 41 percent had symptoms consistent with posttraumatic stress disorder.[18] After the pilot phase, HSiH touted several successes. Once the HSiH-eligible women had secure housing, some applied for future education, found employment, and addressed chronic health problems that they previously overlooked. Program participants' experience reduced their levels of stress and depression and improved their health overall. The BHA has also dedicated the seventy-five housing slots secured in the HSiH pilot phase strictly to housing-insecure pregnant women.

These outstanding partnerships between the health-care and housing sectors have had real impact; they are commendable and should be continued. Yet their scale and scope cannot, without structural support, sustainably transform the social and health outcomes they seek to influence. The programs that operate in multiple cities can still only reach a limited number of people—those who have insurance. Similarly, the projects that introduce affordable-housing alternatives can admirably change the financial reality faced by many families but cannot alter the concomitant educational, environmental, employment, or nutritional deficits these families continue to face. As I have shown, these important housing programs have changed upstream health outcomes such as hospital admissions, length of stay, and emergency room visits. But to change the health outcomes for entire populations—to close the infant-mortality and life-expectancy gaps, for example—our efforts must reach beyond housing affordability. Society must work on all the structural factors that influence people's health. Nevertheless, these efforts do add considerable value, and they form the basis for the structural interventions that are needed.

These interventions serve several important purposes and are required as part of any serious effort to reverse the health impacts of segregation seen across the country. First, the housing programs fashioned by health-care providers employ medical and clinical science in their methodological treatment of housing as a social determinant of health. Second, these programs reveal which housing interventions move—that is, improve—health outcomes. Third, the return on housing interventions in terms of reduced health-care costs and improved population health outcomes supports reversing segregation for those skeptical of the social justice reasons for this move.

These programs should be scaled up so that they reach across all marginalized sectors of the patient population throughout the nation. Moreover, they should reach beyond housing conditions to affect neighborhoods, food sources, and other social determinants of health. To reach these goals, the nation must reform the legal context in which these worthy efforts operate and must deploy the authority and power of governments to protect, preserve, and promote public health. This is the moral duty of the governments that have been instrumental in—indeed responsible for—the construction of structural racism.

Food Insecurity Interventions

Other neighborhood-level interventions operate in separate silos from the important housing-based interventions just described. One group of such programs addresses the negative health outcomes from the systemic deprivation known as food insecurity.[19] Different health-care-based programs and partnerships tackle varying goals related to preventing hunger. They support and encourage nutritional education and access to healthy foods to promote the overall health of a community's residents. For example, good nutrition is essential to improving and maintaining good health, and the partnership between Brockton (Massachusetts) Neighborhood Health Center (BNHC) and Vicente's Supermarket provides a model for aligning health-care services and support for healthy eating habits in one location.[20] A $22 million investment allowed the launch of the health center and adjacent grocery store, which received support from trusted Brockton community institutions. The partnership offers access to healthy food, health care, nutritional counseling, and nutritional education in one location, in an area where one in four residents is living in poverty, where diabetes and obesity rates surpass the state average, and where health-care services were limited. Local Initiatives Support Corporation, the nation's largest community development organization, facilitated complex financing for the partnership, which gains support from federal funding from the Treasury Department and Department of Health and Human Services and numerous foundations and for-profit corporations.[21] Together they stimulate private sector investments in businesses located in low-income areas.

Partnering with a statewide coalition, a local grocer, a college, and a hospital, the BNHC has sought to comprehensively fight hunger. Project Bread, a statewide program in Massachusetts, raises funds to help area organizations like BNHC meet food security needs of community residents.[22] To do so, BNHC refers patients to a social worker, who identifies their needs and connects them to community resources. Those with immediate hunger needs receive food vouchers, which can be used at Vicente's, and the supermarket provides store credit for healthy food choices. Project Bread funds further support community-supported agriculture subscriptions, which are used in the BNHC teaching kitchen and given away to those in need. BNHC also partners with Stonehill College. The college's campus farm sells produce to BNHC during the summer months. BNHC emphasizes working *with*, not *for*, community residents: community health workers trained in health promotion and case management are recruited from the patients' cultural communities and support those utilizing the clinic. For example, Ecuadorian immigrants in the area missed farming and contributing food to their family, so a social worker gained permission to use some of the supermarket's land as a garden plot. After weekly work in the garden, women gathered in the teaching kitchen for group therapy. Through recognizing community needs, BNHC thus offered physical health activities, mental health support, and opportunities to develop community bonds.

Some neighborhood intervention programs focus explicitly on children's wellness, recognizing that healthy food at an early age can reduce chronic conditions like high cholesterol, high blood pressure, and obesity. For example, the Children's Hospital of San Antonio connected with several organizations, including Baylor College of Medicine, the Culinary Institute of America, grocery chain H-E-B, Texas Children's Hospital, and the Goldsbury Foundation, to fund a nutritional health initiative supporting children's health through neighborhood education.[23] An in-hospital kitchen facility, created in partnership with the Culinary Institute of America, provides cooking classes for patients and the public. Patients and families have access to 2.4 acres of land, which can be used to learn about a healthy diet through teaching and healing gardens, encouraging toddler discovery surrounding a healthy diet's foundations. A program called Prescriptions for Produce, stemming from a partnership between the hospital and H-E-B, allows physicians to write patients prescriptions for fruits and vegetables, and these prescriptions are redeemable at certain H-E-B locations. Finally, the hospital cosponsored the Witte Museum's H-E-B Body Adventure exhibit, which emphasizes the demonstration kitchen and toddler discovery garden. These efforts promote conversation about health and wellness in the local community.

Food insecurity is a major health concern nationally, and throughout the United States, various efforts seek to reduce this problem. Eskenazi Health in Indianapolis has, among other endeavors, partnered with Meals on Wheels to support nutritional needs for older adults and has worked with partners such as Gleaners Community Food Bank, St. Luke's United Methodist Church, and Dow AgroSciences to create food pantries within walking distance for many residents.[24] EatSF in San Francisco provides food vouchers to encourage shoppers to regularly incorporate fruits and vegetables in their diets, helping to combat disease and health inequity.[25] Partnerships creating community gardens, food vouchers, nutritional education, food pantries, and other similar programs have seen great improvements in the nutritional health of participants. Among other benefits, these partnerships have been documented to reduce emergency room visits, decrease hospital readmission rates, and improve patient body mass indexes.[26]

As with housing interventions, the programmatic efforts to reduce food insecurity summarized here have shown admirable promise in the markets they serve. The evidence in this book, however, confirms that their impacts must become widespread to change the crisis of national health inequality we face. Making these interventions the norm is not beyond our capacity. The food interventions summarized here clearly demonstrate that equal access to healthy food can significantly improve people's health. The need, now, is to disseminate these efforts across the nation. Without question, this systemic change will require leadership and the involvement of health professionals who can give empirical evidence its of potential impact and the moral explanation of why equality is a right for all patients, all populations, all humankind.

Neighborhood Violence Interventions

Admirably, there are also a handful of medical-legal partnerships that reach beyond housing and food insecurity to focus on reducing neighborhood violence and the damage it inflicts on population health.[27] Project Ujima, a multidisciplinary violence prevention and treatment program established at the Children's Hospital of Wisconsin in Milwaukee, exemplifies such a partnership.[28] The traditional health-care system often fails to fully serve young victims of violence who survive injuries and have varying emotional, social, and physical needs.[29] With Project Ujima and other similar efforts, various stakeholders collaborate to support emergency department patients who are victims of violence. The Children's Hospital of Wisconsin, the Medical College of Wisconsin, the Children's Service Society of Wisconsin, and the Sojourner Family Peace Center collaborate with community stakeholders who, alongside hospital funding, financially support Project Ujima so that its extensive services are free to patients. Community partners include the district attorney's office, the Milwaukee Police Department, and Milwaukee County Behavioral Health.

Through Project Ujima, children aged seven to eighteen who are victims of violence are identified as patients in the emergency department. Case workers provide immediate support during these patients' hospital stay, and after the young person's acute injury has been treated, a community-based home visitation model begins. With this final step, a community liaison visits the child's home within two weeks of hospital discharge. The liaison person develops a service plan, helping all family members both reduce the risk that children return to risky environments and therefore increase the chances they will achieve family goals. To this end, the liaison strives to ensure that recovering children have access to medical, behavioral, health, legal, school, and social services.

The wisdom of programs such as this is to address violence prevention as a population health issue. Research has shown that by reducing violence among children, and reducing the violence that children are exposed to, hospitals can encourage children's healthy development through adulthood. Project Ujima demonstrates the power of health care and community partnership. When hospitals enter into partnership with the community, they offer the infrastructure, medical expertise, and technology to disrupt the cycle of violence harming children's health throughout their lifetime, while community organizations offer pathways to increase community trust in the providers. The partnership eases professionals' access to young people caught in a cycle of violence and helps disrupt this cycle and lower the readmission rate to hospitals as well as the likelihood that children will return to violent settings or activities. Project Ujima's outcomes confirm the program's effectiveness. By 2013, of those using Project Ujima's services, only 1 percent have returned to the emergency department for violence-related injuries. Before the project began in 1996, the Children's Hospital of Wisconsin's emergency department had a 12 percent readmission rate for such injuries. Scaling up programming targeted toward physical, emotional, and social needs of violently injured young people could encourage such positive results nationwide.

At present, there are few replicas of the Project Ujima program across the nation, despite the national public health crisis that violence represents in our nation. Yet the evidence that the project's methods are effective is convincing and worthy of replication across the United States. The spread of violence-reduction programs for young people at risk is not beyond our capacity. Indeed, considering the evidence on the severity of public health damage caused by unchecked community violence and the effectiveness of interventions such as Project Ujima, we as a nation can do no less than to enlarge the scale and scope of this transformative work across the country.

Education Interventions

School-based health interventions aim to ensure that all children have equal opportunities to lead a healthy lifestyle, despite educational inequality historically contributing to negative health outcomes.[30] For example, in California, Alameda County's Center for Healthy Schools and Communities recognizes that unaccompanied immigrant youth from Mexico and in Guatemala and other countries in Central America are statistically more likely to experience disparities in the social determinants of health outlined in this book.[31] Seeking to remedy such status-based inequity, which is rooted in discrimination, the Alameda County has used some of its federally qualified health centers to support and sponsor school-based health centers (SBHCs). After all, school attendance is compulsory—by sponsoring SBHCs, Alameda County addresses youth health disparities where students already are.

Alameda County's SBHCs have been remarkably successful in increasing students' access to health information, vaccinations, and treatments. After the influx of unaccompanied immigrant youth in the region, the county promised $2.5 million in funding, including the equivalent of Medicaid reimbursement, to youth who, regardless of their legal status, would otherwise not qualify for certain health screenings and treatment. The county uses this funding to offer students mental and behavioral health support, health education, and more, depending on individual needs. Various partnerships support these SBHCs. For example, the federally qualified health center in charge of one high school worked with a local nonprofit law center that provides case management and free legal aid to students. In addition to individual partnerships with federally qualified health centers, the county's overall Center for Healthy Schools and Communities has joined with the University of California San Francisco's Department of Family Health Care Nursing, which provides SBHCs with medical and technical assistance. Because of the implementation of these health centers throughout Alameda County, 94 percent of students at a high school that had been studied by a group of researchers reported that they felt they could go to their school's health center for information.[32] What's more, 89 percent believed it was easier to speak with SBHC staff than with other doctors and nurses, and 80 percent said they would not have sought out medical treatment if there were no health center at their school. Moreover, although 66 percent of students had primary care providers before the county started the SBHC program, only 16.7 percent were up-to-date on vaccinations. The SBHC in the study, however, provided students with all necessary vaccination and treatments.

The admirable efforts driven by health-care sector leaders produce measurable improvements insofar as they go. The argument here is not that these efforts are ineffective. To the contrary, they represent the investment of dedicated and caring providers. However, alone, interventions initiated by health providers to impact local or regional social conditions are not enough. When SBHCs improve the educational experience of students, they do so within school systems that are fundamentally inequitable. The students return to classrooms that are inferior, while the health-care programs do nothing to disrupt the structures that ultimately form the school-to-prison pipeline, which is disproportionately populated by Black and Latino students.

No more articulate or innovative leader in the fight against racial health inequity exists than Jay Bhatt, chief medical officer, president, and CEO of the American Hospital Association's Health Research and Education Trust. I quote Dr. Bhatt as an example of health-care leaders across the nation because of the extent of the positive influences he and the American Hospital Association have had in the fight for health equity. According to Dr. Bhatt, health-care organizations can advance health equity in three main ways. Health systems should leverage their leadership as economic engines to (1) deliver value-based care, (2) address patients' social needs, and (3) improve the social determinants of health.

This three-sided approach is a winning formula. But to achieve the transformation on a national scale will require, of course, a broad national effort. Not only must we transform the structural environments where health care is delivered, but we must also fix the environments where patients' full range of social needs manifest themselves and where all social determinants of health are organized and distributed. To accomplish this much larger goal, we must follow Dr. Bhatt's three-pronged approach, which has thus far been shown to be effective on a smaller scale. The vision is large, but it is attainable.

To achieve health equity, the United States must pursue equal justice. We can stop the causes of population health inequity suffered disproportionately by Black, Latino, and Indigenous people by reversing the structural institutions that have produced these inequities. Local efforts are important. After all, local organizations are best attuned to the needs of their communities. Only by working *with* communities can partnerships between health and legal professionals fully address the needs of a community's residents. But local efforts alone are not enough.

The federal government has a responsibility to the American people—a duty to uphold the Fourteenth Amendment and promote equality for *all*. We can hold our government accountable to this goal by resurrecting the coalition of legal and nonlegal voices calling for an end to racism. The history of the first Quiet Revolution of the Civil Rights era has shown that American health professional are essential to national reform and that change in the American health-care system precedes change throughout the rest of the social determinants of health.

This chapter demonstrates the already-strong commitment to health equality that exists among members of the health profession and the communities they serve. This book evinces the passionate commitment to equality that already exists among civil rights lawyers and lawmakers, and the communities that they serve. All these groups have invested heavily in efforts to reduce the persistent gap between health outcomes for White, Black, Latino, and Indigenous people in this country. These efforts run the gamut from implicit bias and cultural competence training to increasing health-care access, forming alliances such as medical-legal partnerships to remove legal barriers to care and reimbursement, improving data collection, instituting case management standards, developing health promotion strategies, increasing workforce diversity, and improving reimbursement for ancillary services. These efforts are important, but they are and will continue to be ineffective unless they are scaled up to aim squarely at eliminating the legal foundations of structural racism that is the fundamental cause of racial health disparities.

Together these stakeholders must turn their formidable collective attention toward legal reforms that could do the work of structural *anti*racism—the reversal of legislative, regulatory, and common law precedents that have legalized dehumanization, legalized inequality, and ensured unequal protection of laws. History shows the power of a multidisciplinary approach to dramatically influence lawmakers and to undertake a landmark legal reform plan that will effect lasting, structural change.

Today, an antiracism plan must include three elements. First, it must engage the community; we must solve structural racism in collaboration with the people who have lived closest to it—communities affected by the consequences of an inequitable society. Second, the plan must be directed toward implementing legal reforms by local, state, and federal governments. Because governments are the sources of the law that erected structural racism, government must therefore be held accountable for using its lawmaking and law-enforcement authority to dismantle structural racism and create a society characterized by just health. Third, health-care providers, health-care payers, and public health experts must coordinate their advocacy, exercising their power to influence governments and change laws. Finally, the plan must be based on public health practice—focusing on solutions that are preventive, population based, and grounded in the understanding that social, not medical, determinants of health produce health disparities. This is the formula that dismantled de jure segregation in America, and this is the plan that will succeed in dismantling structural racism so that all in this nation can enjoy the benefit and blessing of just health.

AFTERWORD

Then God said, "Let us make humanity in our image to resemble us so that they may take charge of the fish of the sea, the birds in the sky, the livestock, all the earth, and all the crawling things on earth."

God created humanity in God's own image,
in the divine image God created them,
male and female God created them.
—Genesis 1:26–27 (Common English Bible)

The point is, the standards and freedoms to which blacks should be raised should not be based upon what whites enjoy; rather the standards and freedoms should be based upon what humans should enjoy. There is a difference. This forces us to ask the question, are we treating all humans fairly and correctly, humans, regardless of skin color, who are created by God? Ultimately, our thinking should not be a white human or a black human but a God created human.
—Professor Keith Yearwood, 2020

There is much more to say about dismantling the structures of racism in America than I have laid out in this book. The work that follows this book, I hope, will take up the theory I have modeled and will pursue a better understanding of structural racism in employment, food policy, and political participation. I further hope that the role that I have argued our legal system must play in remedying structural racism will inspire stakeholders from across sectors and disciplines to engage in lawmaking. I would like the legacy of this book to be a newfound collaborative ownership of the lawmaking process. The process should include all the stakeholders, from grassroots communities to underpaid social workers and teachers, state and local civil servants, and health system and other C-suites—all those who are intimately involved with the work required for better outcomes in population health. This coalition would demand that our legal system cease institutionalizing inequality, dehumanization, and unequal protection of people who are racially identified as Black, Latino, and Indigenous. More importantly, all the members of this coalition would see themselves as indispensable to the legal process that will make that happen.

Finally, I am compelled to observe that structural inequality must be dismantled even more broadly than along the racial lines that have been the subject of this book. Structural inequalities that oppress people on the basis of gender, wealth, sexuality, and physical ability are abhorrent and destructive in ways that I wish I had the space to address in this book. But because I do not, I close with an admonition—actually a plea—that others will take up where I have left off. At the time of this writing, more than 4 million humans will have died from the COVID-19 pandemic, and more than 600,000 of them—the most of any nation on earth—will have died in the United States. I pray that we will heed the urgent lessons learned from this pandemic and use them to do all we can to rectify the terrible immorality of structural inequality. All of us must re-create our social order to equally value and protect the sacredness of every human life.

NOTES

Introduction

1 S. Galea, M. Tracy, K. J. Hoggatt, C. DiMaggio, and A. Karpati, "Estimated Deaths Attributable to Social Factors in the United States," *American Journal of Public Health*, 101, no. 8 (2011): 1456–1465.

2 J. M. Guralnik, "Assessing the Impact of Comorbidity in the Older Population,'" *Annals of Epidemiology*, 6, no. 5 (1996): 376–380.

3 T. F. Pettigrew, "Intergroup Contact Theory," *Annual Review of Psychology*, 49, no. 1 (1998): 65–85.

4 T. F. Pettigrew and L. R. Tropp, "A Meta-Analytic Test of Intergroup Contact Theory," *Journal of Personality and Social Psychology*, 90, no. 5 (2006): 751–783.

5 T. F. Pettigrew, L. R. Tropp, U. Wagner, and O. Christ, "Recent Advances in Intergroup Contact Theory," *International Journal of Intercultural Relations*, 35, no. 3 (2011): 271–280.

6 C. J. Murray, S. C. Kulkarni, C. Michaud, N. Tomijima, M. T. Bulzacchelli, T. J. Iandiorio, and M. Ezzati, "Eight Americas: Investigating Mortality Disparities Across Races, Counties, and Race-Counties in the United States," *PLoS Medicine*, 3, no. 9 (2006).

7 US Bureau of Labor Statistics, "Union Wages and Benefits: Local-Transit Operating Employees, July 1, 1979," US Department of Labor, Bureau of Labor Statistics, Bulletin 2074, August 1980, https://fraser.stlouisfed.org. In 1979, the year my father died, nonsupervisory local and interurban passenger transit workers earned an average hourly rate of between $7.86 and $8.33, or a maximum weekly salary of $333.20 (or $17,326.40 annually); see also US Bureau of Economic Analysis, "Wage and Salary Accruals: Domestic Private Industries: Banking (J4153C0A144NBEA)," FRED Economic Data, August 10, 2015, https://fred.stlouisfed.org. My father most likely doubled that salary by also working at the bank, since by 1979 nonsupervisory workers at depository institutions earned an average annual salary of $18,321.

8 US Bureau of the Census, "Money Income and Poverty Status of Families and Persons in the United States: 1979," report P60–125, October 1980, says that in 1979, the poverty threshold was $7,412 for a nonfarm family of four. See also Pew Research Center, Social and Demographic Trends, "The American Middle Class is Losing Ground, December 9, 2015, www.pewsocialtrends.org, which says that middle-income households earned a median income of $54,683 in 1970, and

upper-income households, $118,617. M. Escobari, "The Economy Is Growing and Leaving Low-Wage Workers Behind," Brookings Education Plus Development, December 19, 2019, www.brookings.edu.

9 F. C. Pampel, P. M. Krueger, and J. T. Denney, "Socioeconomic Disparities in Health Behaviors," *Annual Review of Sociology*, 36 (2010): 349–370.

10 A. Austin, *Native Americans and Jobs: The Challenge and the Promise* (Economic Policy Institute, 2013).

11 K. Fiscella and P. Franks, "Individual Income, Income Inequality, Health, and Mortality: What Are the Relationships?," *Health Services Research*, 35, no. 1, part 2 (2000): 307.

12 Richard V. Reeves, "Stop Pretending You're Not Rich," *New York Times*, June 10, 2017, www.nytimes.com.

13 K. E. Pickett and R. G. Wilkinson, "Income Inequality and Health: A Causal Review," *Social Science & Medicine*, 12 (2015): 316–326.

14 Norman Daniels, Bruce Kennedy, and Ichiro Kawachi, *Is Inequality Bad for Our Health?* (Boston: Beacon Press, 2000), 86.

15 "The History of the South Bronx, NY," accessed May 3, 2021, UrbanAreas.net, www.urbanareas.net.

16 Cindy A. Sousa, "Political Violence, Collective Functioning and Health: A Review of the Literature," *Medicine, Conflict and Survival*, 29, no. 3 (2013): 169–197.

17 G. S. Becker, "Crime and Punishment: An Economic Approach," in *The Economic Dimensions of Crime*, ed. Nigel G. Fielding, Alan Clarke, and Robert Witt, 13–68, esp. 25 (New York: Macmillan, 2000; this chapter originally published by University of Chicago Press, 1968).

18 M. Kelly, "Inequality and Crime," *Review of Economics and Statistics*, 82, no. 4 (2000): 530–539.

19 P. Fajnzylber, D. Lederman, and N. Loayza, "Inequality and Violent Crime," *Journal of Law and Economics*, 45, no. 1 (2002): 1–39.

20 Sherman A. James, "John Henryism and the Health of African-Americans," *Culture, Medicine and Psychiatry*, 18 (June 1994): 163–182.

21 M. M. Mello, "Obesity: Personal Choice or Public Health Issue?," *Nature Clinical Practice Endocrinology & Metabolism*, 4, no. 1 (2008): 2–3.

22 L. King, D. Hinterland, K. L. Dragan, C. R. Driver, T. G. Harris, R. C. Gwynn, N. Linos, O. Barbot, and M. T. Bassett, "Community Health Profiles 2015, Bronx Community District 9: Parkchester and Soundview," *NYC Health*, 21, no. 59 (2015): 1–16. www1.nyc.gov.

23 C. P. Jones, "Confronting Institutionalized Racism," *Phylon* 50, no. 1–2 (2003):7–22.

24 One triumph is that my dad bought one of those rental houses before he died. Thankfully, my brother still owns that home today. Well done, Daddy. Well done.

25 K. M. Molina and D. James, "Discrimination, Internalized Racism, and Depression: A Comparative Study of African American and Afro-Caribbean Adults in the US," *Group Process Intergroup Relations*, 19, no. 4 (2016): 439–461.

26 A. K. Bailey, S. E. Tolnay, E. M. Beck, and J. D. Laird, "Targeting Lynch Victims: Social Marginality or Status Transgressions?," *American Sociological Review*, 76, no. 3 (2011): 412–436; see also S. E. Tolnay and E. M. Beck, *A Festival of Violence: An Analysis of Southern Lynchings, 1882–1930* (Urbana: University of Illinois Press, 1995).

27 J. Bor, A. S. Venkataramani, D. R. Williams, and A. C. Tsai, "Police Killings and Their Spillover Effects on the Mental Health of Black Americans: A Population-Based, Quasi-Experimental Study," *Lancet*, 392, no. 10144 (2018): 302–310.

28 M. Alsan, and M. Wanamaker, "Tuskegee and the Health of Black Men," *Quarterly Journal of Economics*, 133, no. 1 (2018): 407–455.

29 Yin Paradies, Jehonathan Ben, Nida Denson, Amanuel Elias, Naomi Priest, Alex Pieterse, Arpana Gupta, Margaret Kelaher, and G. Gee, "Racism As a Determinant of Health: A Systematic Review and Meta-Analysis," *PloS One*, 10, no. 9 (2015).

30 Ilene Hyman, "Racism as a Determinant of Immigrant Health," policy brief, Strategic Initiatives and Innovations Directorate (SIID) of the Public Health Agency of Canada, 2009.

31 M. Alsan, and M. Wanamaker, "Tuskegee and the Health of Black Men," *Quarterly Journal of Economics*, 133, no. 1 (2018): 407–455.

32 Organisation for Economic Cooperation and Development (OECD), "Life Expectancy at Birth," 2021, *OECD iLibrary*, doi: 10.1787/27e0fc9d-en.

33 L. Ceriani and P. Verme, "The Origins of the Gini Index: Extracts from Variabilità e Mutabilità (1912) by Corrado Gini," *Journal of Economic Inequality*, 10, no. 3 (2012): 421–443.

1. Structural Racism

1 Eduardo Bonilla-Silva, "Rethinking Racism: Toward a Structural Interpretation," *American Sociological Review*, 62 (June 1996): 465–467 (emphasis added).

2 V. Wilson, and J. Williams, "Racial and Ethnic Income Gaps Persist Amid Uneven Growth in Household Incomes," Economic Policy Institute, 2019; US Census Bureau, "New Educational Attainment Data," March 30, 2020, www.census.gov; US Bureau of Labor Statistics, "Home Page," accessed February 19 2021, www.bls .gov; US Census Bureau, "Quarterly Residential Vacancies and Homeownership, Fourth Quarter," February 2, 2021, www.census.gov.

3 US Declaration of Independence, Paragraph 2 (US 1776).

4 "Life Expectancy at Birth by Race and Sex, 1930–2010," *Infoplease*, February 28, 2017, www.infoplease.com.

5 D. J. Witherspoon, S. Wooding, A. R. Rogers, E. E. Marchani, W. S. Watkins, M. A. Batzer, and L. B. Jorde, "Genetic Similarities Within and Between Human Populations," *Genetics*, 176, no. 1 (2007): 351–359, https://doi.org/10.1534/ genetics.106.067355.

6 US Department of Labor, W. Willard Wirtz, Secretary, *The Economic Situation of Negroes in the United States*, Bulletin S-3, Revised 1962, table 12.

7 Ibram X. Kendi, *How to Be an Antiracist* (New York: One World/Ballantine, 2019).

8   C. P. Jones, "Levels of Racism: A Theoretic Framework and a Gardener's Tale," *American Journal of Public Health*, 90, no. 8 (2019): 1212.

9   Z. D. Bailey, N. Krieger, M. Agénor, J. Graves, N. Linos, and M. T. Bassett, "Structural Racism and Health Inequities in the USA: Evidence and Interventions," *Lancet*, 389 (10077): 1453–1463; M. Groos, M. Wallace, R. Hardeman, and K. P. Theall, "Measuring Inequity: A Systematic Review of Methods Used to Quantify Structural Racism," *Journal of Health Disparities Research and Practice*, 11, no. 2 (2018): 13.

10 Gilbert C. Gee and Chandra L. Ford, "Structural Racism and Health Inequities: Old Issues, New Directions," *Du Bois Review*, 8, no. 1 (2011): 115–132; J. Feagin, and Z. Bennefield, "Systemic Racism and US Health Care," *Social Science and Medicine*, 103 (2014): 7–14; N. Krieger, "Does Racism Harm Health? Did Child Abuse Exist Before 1962? On Explicit Questions, Critical Science, and Current Controversies: An Ecosocial Perspective," *American Journal of Public Health*, 98, no. S1 (2008): S20–S25; see also D. R. Williams and S. A. Mohammed, "Racism and Health I: Pathways and Scientific Evidence," *American Behavioral Scientist*, 57, no. 8 (2013): 1152–1173.

11 J. C. Phelan and B. G. Link, "Is Racism a Fundamental Cause of Inequalities in Health?," *Annual Review of Sociology*, 41 (2015): 311–330; Gee and Ford, "Structural Racism and Health Inequities."

12 J. R. Feagin, *Racist America: Roots, Current Realities, and Future Reparations* (New York: Routledge, 2014).

13 J. R. Betancourt, A. R. Green, J. E. Carrillo, and I. I. Owusu Ananeh-Firempong, "Defining Cultural Competence: A Practical Framework for Addressing Racial/ Ethnic Disparities in Health and Health Care," *Public Health Reports*, 2016.

14 Centers for Disease Control and Prevention, "COVID-19 Cases in the U.S.," accessed December 31, 2020, www.cdc.gov.

15 APM Research Lab, "The Color of Coronavirus: COVID-19 Deaths by Race and Ethnicity in the U.S.," December 27, 2020, www.apmresearchlab.org.

16 White House, "Proclamation on the Suspension of Entry as Immigrants and Nonimmigrants of Persons Who Pose a Risk of Transmitting 2019 Novel Coronavirus and Other Appropriate Measures to Address This Risk," Presidential Proclamation 9984, January 31, 2020, www.whitehouse.gov.

17 Medical Xpress, "Iran Reports New Surge in Coronavirus Cases," February 29, 2020, https://medicalxpress.com; see also United States Institute of Peace, "Coronavirus Strikes Iran: Timeline," *Iran Primer*, April 21, 2020, https:// iranprimer.usip.org; White House, "Suspension of Entry As Immigrants and Nonimmigrants of Certain Additional Persons Who Pose a Risk of Transmitting 2019 Novel Coronavirus," Presidential Proclamation 9992, February 29, 2020, www.whitehouse.gov.

18 White House, "Suspension of Entry As Immigrants and Nonimmigrants of Certain Additional Persons Who Pose a Risk of Transmitting 2019 Novel

Coronavirus," Presidential Proclamation 9993, March 11, 2020, www.white house.gov.

19   White House, "Declaring a National Emergency Concerning the Novel Coronavirus Disease (COVID-19) Outbreak," Presidential Proclamation 9994, March 13, 2020, www.whitehouse.gov.

20   Khiara Bridges, quoted in Joe Penney, "Racism, Rather than Facts, Drove U.S. Coronavirus Travel Bans," *Intercept*, May 16, 2020, https://theintercept.com.

21   Carl Zimmer, "Most New York Coronavirus Cases Came from Europe, Genomes Show," *New York Times*, April 8, 2020, www.nyt.com.

22   Mount Sinai, "Mount Saini Study Finds First Cases of COVID-19 in New York City Are Primarily from European and US Sources," press release, April 9, 2020, www.mountsainai.org.

23   Pew Research Center, "More Americans Say They Are Regularly Wearing Masks in Stores and Other Businesses," August 27, 2020, www.pewresearch.org.

24   Rashawn Ray, "Why Are Blacks Dying at Higher Rates from COVID-19?," Brookings Institute, April 9, 2020, www.brookings.edu.

25   US Bureau of Labor Statistics, "Labor Force Characteristics by Race and Ethnicity, 2018," October 2019, www.bls.org.

26   US Bureau of Labor Statistics, "Labor Force Characteristics."

27   T. A. LaVeist and J. M. Wallace Jr., "Health Risk and Inequitable Distribution of Liquor Stores in African American Neighborhoods," *Social Science & Medicine*, 51, no. 4 (2000): 613–617; L. V. Moore and A. V. Diez Roux, "Associations of Neighborhood Characteristics with the Location and Type of Food Stores," *American Journal of Public Health*, 96, no. 2 (2006): 325–331; J. G. Lee, L. Henriksen, S. W. Rose, S. Moreland-Russell, and K. M. Ribisl, "A Systematic Review of Neighborhood Disparities in Point-of-Sale Tobacco Marketing," *American Journal of Public Health*, 105, no. 9 (2015): e8–e18. D. Hackbarth, B. Silvestri, and W. Cosper, "Tobacco and Alcohol Billboards in 50 Chicago Neighborhoods: Market Segmentation to Sell Dangerous Products to the Poor," *Journal of Public Health Policy*, 16 (1995): 213–230, https://doi.org/10.2307/3342593.

28   D. Acevedo-Garcia, T. L. Osypuk, N. McArdle, and D. R. Williams, "Toward a Policy-Relevant Analysis of Geographic and Racial/Ethnic Disparities in Child Health," *Health Affairs*, 27, no. 2 (2008): 321–333. N. I. Larson, M. T. Story, and M. C. Nelson, "Neighborhood Environments: Disparities in Access to Healthy Foods in the US," *American Journal of Preventive Medicine*, 36, no. 1 (2009): 74–81; E. Eisenhauer, "Poor Health: Supermarket Redlining and Urban Nutrition," *GeoJournal*, 53, no. 2 (2001): 125–133.

29   For the stresses of poverty, see A. Mani, S. Mullainathan, E. Shafir, and J. Zhao, "Poverty Impedes Cognitive Function," *Science*, 341, no. 6149 (2013): 976–980. For data on depression, anxiety, and anger, and hearts disease, see G. A. Panza, R. M. Puhl, B. A. Taylor, A. L. Zaleski, J. Livingston, and L. S. Pescatello, "Links Between Discrimination and Cardiovascular Health Among Socially Stigmatized

Groups: A Systematic Review," *PloS One*, 14, no. 6, " For connections between blood pressure and race, see M. Sims, A. V. Diez-Roux, A. Dudley, S. Gebreab, S. B. Wyatt, M. A. Bruce, S. A. James, J. C. Robinson, and H. A. Taylor, "Perceived Discrimination and Hypertension Among African Americans in the Jackson Heart Study," *American Journal of Public Health*, 102, no. S2 (2012): S258–S265.

30 Francesca Dominici, "Air Pollution Linked with Higher COVID-19 Death Rates," Harvard T. H. Chan School of Public Health, May 5, 2020, www.hsph.harvard .edu.

31 Vernice Miller-Travis, "The System Is Not Broken, It Was Built This Way," *Metropolitan Group Medium*, December 1, 2020, www.metgroup.medium.com.

32 D. B. Matthew, "Disastrous Disasters: Restoring Civil Rights Protections for Victims of the State in Natural Disasters," *Journal of Health and Biomedical Law*, 2 (2006): 213.

33 W. Neely, *The Great Okeechobee Hurricane of 1928* (iUniverse, 2014), 137.

34 Thomas Frank, "Flooding Disproportionately Harms Black Neighborhoods," *Scientific American*, June 2, 2020, www.scientificamerican.com.

35 Nayan Shah, *Contagious Divides: Epidemics and Race in San Francisco's Chinatown* (Berkeley: University of California Press, 2001), 1–2.

36 Shah, *Contagious Divides*, 12.

37 Shah, *Contagious Divides*, 7.

38 D. H. Chae, S. Clouston, M. L. Hatzenbuehler, M. R. Kramer, H. L. Cooper, S. M. Wilson, S. I. Stephens-Davidowitz, R. G. Gold, and B. G. Link, "Association Between an Internet-Based Measure of Area Racism and Black Mortality," *PloS One*, 10, no. 4 (2015): e0122963.

39 A. T. Geronimus, "The Weathering Hypothesis and the Health of African-American Women and Infants: Evidence and Speculations," *Ethnicity and Disease*, 2, no. 3 (1992): 207–221.

40 Chae et al., "Internet-Based Measure," 8.

41 D. H. Chae, S. Clouston, C. D. Martz, M. L. Hatzenbuehler, H. L. Cooper, R. Turpin, S. I. Stephens-Davidowitz, and M. R. Kramer, "Area Racism and Birth Outcomes Among Blacks in the United States," *Social Science & Medicine*, 199 (February 2018): 49–55.

42 A. Lukachko, M. L. Hatzenbuehler, and K. M. Keyes, "Structural Racism and Myocardial Infarction in the United States," *Social Science & Medicine*, 103 (2014): 42–50.

43 J. Orchard and J. Price, "County-Level Racial Prejudice and the Black-White Gap in Infant Health Outcomes," *Social Science & Medicine*, 181 (2017): 191–198.

44 Y. Lee, P. Muennig, I. Kawachi, and M. L. Hatzenbuehler, "Effects of Racial Prejudice on the Health of Communities: A Multilevel Survival Analysis," *American Journal of Public Health*, 105, no. 11 (2015): 2349–2355.

45 J. B. Leitner, E. Hehman, O. Ayduk, and R. Mendoza-Denton, "Blacks' Death Rate Due to Circulatory Diseases Is Positively Related to Whites' Explicit Racial Bias:

A Nationwide Investigation Using Project Implicit," *Psychological Science*, 27, no. 10 (2016): 1299–1311.

46 Project Implicit is a research group that has used internet-based questionnaires to collect the largest known repository of data on explicit and implicit racial bias.

47 Leitner et al., "Blacks' Death Rate Due to Circulatory Diseases."

48 B. P. Kennedy, I. Kawachi, K. Lochner, C. Jones, and D. Prothrow-Stith, "(Dis)Respect and Black Mortality," *Ethnicity & Disease*, 7, no. 3 (1997): 207–214.

49 S. McKetta, M. L. Hatzenbuehler, C. Pratt, L. Bates, B. G. Link, and K. M. Keyes, "Does Social Selection Explain the Association Between State-Level Racial Animus and Racial Disparities in Self-Rated Health in the United States?," *Annals of Epidemiology*, 27, no. 8 (2017): 485–492.

50 L. Villarosa, "Why America's Black Mothers and Babies Are in a Life-or-Death Crisis," *New York Times*, April 11, 2018, www.nyt.com.

51 S. Harper, R. F. MacLehose, and J. S. Kaufman, "Trends in the Black-White Life Expectancy Gap Among US States, 1990–2009," *Health Affairs*, 33, no. 8 (2014): 1375–1382.

52 Francis Collins, "Widening Gap in U.S. Life Expectancy," *NIH Director's Blog*, May 16, 2017, https://directorsblog.nih.gov.

53 Megan Henney, "Unemployment Surged to 14.7 Percent in April, Highest Since Great Depression, As Coronavirus Triggered 20.5 Million Job Losses," *Fox Business*, May 8, 2020, www.foxbusiness.com.

54 Camara Phyllis Jones, "Confronting Institutionalized Racism," *Phylon (1960-)* (2002): 7–22.

55 P. Braveman, "Health Disparities and Health Equity: Concepts and Measurement," *Annual Review of Public Health*, 27 (2006): 167–194.

56 N. Krieger, "Theories for Social Epidemiology in the 21st Century: An Ecosocial Perspective," *International Journal of Epidemiology*, 30, no. 4 (2001): 668–677.

2. Legalized Dehumanization

1 A. Waytz, and J. Schroeder, "Overlooking Others: Dehumanization by Commission and Omission," *TPM: Testing, Psychometrics, Methodology in Applied Psychology*, 21, no. 3 (2014).

2 Phillip A. Goff, Jennifer L. Eberhardt, Melissa J. Williams, and Matthew Christian Jackson, "Not Yet Human: Implicit Knowledge, Historical Dehumanization, and Contemporary Consequences," *Journal of Personality and Social Psychology*, 94, no. 2 (2008): 292–293; S. Sohrabji, "Halliburton Staff Called Muslim American Employees 'Terrorist' and 'Camel Jockey' at Workplace, Alleges EEOC Suit, India-West," *India West*, July 18, 2018, www.indiawest.com; and S. F. Aziz, "Sticks and Stones, the Words That Hurt: Entrenched Stereotypes Eight Years After 9/11," *New York City Law Review*, 13 (December 2009): 33; Jack G. Shaheen, "Reel Bad Arabs: How Hollywood Vilifies a People," *Annals of the American Academy of Political and Social Science*, 558 (July 2003):171–193, 177.

3 Nick Haslam and Steve Loughnan, "Dehumanization and Infrahumanization," *Annual Review of Psychology*, 65 (January 2014): 399, 402–403, describe animalistic versus mechanistic dehumanization.

4 N. Kteily, E. Bruneau, A. Waytz, and S. Cotterill, "The Ascent of Man: Theoretical and Empirical Evidence for Blatant Dehumanization," *Journal of Personality and Social Psychology*, 109, no. 5 (2015): 901.

5 Kteily et al., "Ascent of Man"; J. L. Alpert, "The Origin of Slavery in the United States: The Maryland Precedent," *American Journal of Legal History* 14, no. 3 (1970): 189–221, esp. 192.

6 W. M. Wiecek, "The Statutory Law of Slavery and Race in the Thirteen Mainland Colonies of British America," *William and Mary Quarterly*, 34, no. 2 (1977): 258–280.

7 A. J. Gross, *Double Character: Slavery and Mastery in the Antebellum Southern Courtroom* (Princeton, NJ: Princeton University Press, 2000). Emphasis added.

8 Thomas Jefferson, *Notes on the State of Virginia* (London: Stockdale, 1787) (Jefferson's personal copy of the 1787 edition is housed in the Albert and Shirley Small Special Collections Library, University of Virginia, Charlottesville, at page 145).

9 J. Krikler, "The Zong and the Lord Chief Justice," *History Workshop Journal*, 64, no. 1 (2007): 29–47.

10 Krikler, "Zong and the Lord Chief Justice," 37.

11 "Africans Thrown Overboard from a Slave Ship, Early 19th Cent.," *Slavery Images: A Visual Record of the African Slave Trade and Slave Life in the Early African Diaspora*, accessed January 1, 2021, www.slaveryimages.org.

12 G. W. Allport, K. Clark, and T. Pettigrew, *The Nature of Prejudice* (Cambridge, MA: Addison-Wesley, 1954).

13 N. S. Kteily and E. Bruneau, "Darker Demons of Our Nature: The Need to (Re)Focus Attention on Blatant Forms of Dehumanization," *Current Directions in Psychological Science*, 26, no. 6 (2017): 487–494.

14 Charles Patterson, *Eternal Treblinka: Our Treatment of Animals and the Holocaust* (New York: Lantern Books, 2002), 28; J. Steizinger, "The Significance of Dehumanization: Nazi Ideology and Its Psychological Consequences," *Politics, Religion & Ideology*, 19, no. 2 (2018): 139–157; J. Lang, "Questioning Dehumanization: Intersubjective Dimensions of Violence in the Nazi Concentration and Death Camps," *Holocaust and Genocide Studies*, 24, no. 2 (2010): 225–246.

15 Kennedy Ndahiro, "Dehumanisation: How Tutsis Were Reduced to Cockroaches, Snakes to Be Killed," *New York Times*, March 13, 2014, www.nyt.com; C. Taylor, "The Cultural Face of Terror in the Rwandan Genocide of 1994," in *Annihilating Difference: The Anthropology of Genocide*, ed. Alexander Laban Hinton, 137–178 (University of California Press, 2002); K. R. White, "Scourge of Racism: Genocide in Rwanda," *Journal of Black Studies*, 39, no. 3 (2009): 471–481.

16 Nick Turse, *Kill Anything That Moves: The Real American War in Vietnam* (New York: Metropolitan Books/Henry Holt and Co., 2013), 28.

17 See Kteily et al., "Ascent of Man."

18 See "Jefferson's Attitudes Toward Slavery," Monticello, accessed June 26, 2021, www.monticello.org.

19 "Jefferson's Attitudes Toward Slavery," 145.

20 *Wintz v. Morrison*, 17 Tex. 372, 381 (1856).

21 *Wintz v. Morrison*, 401–402; Kteily and Bruneau, "Darker Demons," 489–490n84.

22 Kteily and Bruneau, "Darker Demons," 490n84.

23 Kteily et al., "Ascent of Man," 904n25.

24 N. Kteily and E. Bruneau, "Backlash: The Politics and Real-World Consequences of Minority Group Dehumanization," *Personality and Social Psychology Bulletin*, 43, no. 1 (2017): 87–104, doi:10.1177/0146167216675334.

25 J. L. Alpert, "The Origin of Slavery in the United States: The Maryland Precedent," *American Journal of Legal History*, 14, no. 3 (1970): 189–221.

26 Leviticus 25:39–50 (King James Version).

27 "An Act for the encourageing the importation of negros and slaves into this province," 2 Md. Archives 272, April 1671, Archives of Maryland Online, Proceedings and Acts of the General Assembly, April 1666–June 1676, https://msa .maryland.gov.

28 P. A. Goff, J. L. Eberhardt, M. J. Williams, and M. C. Jackson, "Not Yet Human: Implicit Knowledge, Historical Dehumanization, and Contemporary Consequences," *Journal of Personality and Social Psychology*, 94, no. 2 (2008): 292.

29 S. Demoulin, B. P. Cortes, T. G. Viki, A. P. Rodriguez, R. T. Rodriguez, M. P. Paladino, and J. P. Leyens, "The Role of in-Group Identification in Infra-Humanization," *International Journal of Psychology*, 44, no. 1 (2009): 4–11. See also G. W. Allport (intro. by K. Clark and foreword by T. Pettigrew), *The Nature of Prejudice*, 25th anniv. ed. (Reading, MA: Addison-Wesley 1979), 31, 41–43.

30 Alpert, "Maryland Precedent," 195.

31 *Encyclopedia Britannica*, s.v. "slave code," updated May 18, 2020, www.britannica .com.

32 "An act for keepeing a register of birthes marriages and burialls in each respective county," Assembly Proceedings, October–November 1678, *Maryland State Archives*, vol. 7, 76, http://aomol.msa.maryland.gov.

33 Peter Holtz and Wolfgang Wagner, "Essentialism and Attribution of Monstrosity in Racist Discourse: Right-Wing Internet Postings About Africans and Jews," *Journal of Community and Applied Social Psychology*, 19 (2009): 411, 420, 423.

34 William Waller Hening, *Statutes at Large; Being a Collection of All the Laws of Virginia* (Richmond, VA, 1809–23), vol. 11, 170, 260, 266, 270, www.swathmore.edu.

35 A. Fede, *Homicide Justified: The Legality of Killing Slaves in the United States and the Atlantic World*, vol. 2 (Athens: University of Georgia Press, 2017).

36 Fede, *Homicide Justified*.

37 Marc Santora, "St. Mary's Hospital in Brooklyn to Close After Years of Losses," *New York Times*, June 4, 2005, www.nyt.com.

38 D. Satcher, G. E. Fryer Jr, J. McCann, A. Troutman, S. H. Woolf, and G. Rust, "What If We Were Equal? A Comparison of the Black-White Mortality Gap in 1960 and 2000," *Health Affairs*, 24, no. 2 (2005): 459–464.

39 United Nations, "Goal 6: Ensure Access to Water and Sanitation for All," UN Sustainable Development Goals, accessed February 19 2021, www.un.org.

40 P. H. Gleick, "The Human Right to Water," *Water Policy*, 1, no. 5 (1998): 487–503.

41 C. L. Moe and R. D. Rheingans, "Global Challenges in Water, Sanitation and Health," *Journal of Water and Health*, 4, no. S1 (2006): 41–57.

42 Mitch Smith, Julie Bosman, and Monica Davey, "Flint's Water Crisis Started 5 Years Ago. It's Not Over," *New York Times*, April 25, 2019, www.nyt.com; see also Erica L. Green, "Flint's Children Suffer in Class After Years of Drinking the Lead-Poisoned Water," *New York Times*, November 6, 2019, www.nyt.com.

43 Michigan Legislature, Public Act 436 of 2012, www.legislature.mi.gov, authorized removal of a democratically elected official to install an emergency manager in order to "safeguard and assure the financial accountability of local units of governments and school districts." The act also allowed "a deceleration of a financial emergency within a local unit of government, to prescribe remedial measures to address a financial emergency within a local unit of government" without any consideration of the health or human safety of people being governed.

44 Michigan Legislature, Public Act 436 of 2012, 9.

45 David A. Dana and Deborah Tuerkheimer, "After Flint: Environmental Justice As Equal Protection," *Northwestern University Law Review*, 111 (2017): 93, 95.

46 M. B. Pell and Joshua Schneyer, "Thousands of U.S. Areas Afflicted with Lead Poisoning Beyond Flint's," *Scientific American*, December 19, 2016, www.scientificamerican.com.

47 D. B. Matthew, "On Charlottesville," *Virginia Law Review*, 105 (2019): 269.

48 Coty Montag, *Water/Color: A Study of Race and the Water Affordability Crisis in America's Cities* (New York: Thurgood Marshall Institute at the NAACP Legal Defense and Educational Fund, 2019), 9.

49 Werner Troesken, "The Limits of Jim Crow: Race and the Provision of Water and Sewerage Services in American Cities, 1880–192," *Journal of Economic History*, 62, no. 3 (2002): 734–772, esp. 743–747.

50 Troesken, "Limits of Jim Crow."

51 Claire Suddath, "Making Water a Matter of Race," *Time*, July 14, 2008, http://content.time.com.

52 461 F.2d 1172.

53 See, for example, M. A. Hall, "The Scope and Limits of Public Health Law," *Perspectives in Biology and Medicine*, 46, no. 3 (2003): S199–S209.

54 G. B. Murrow and R. Murrow, "A Hypothetical Neurological Association Between Dehumanization and Human Rights Abuses," *Journal of Law and the Biosciences*, 2, no. 2 (2015): 336–364.

55 Herbert C. Kelman, "Violence Without Moral Restraint: Reflections on the Dehumanization of Victims and Victimizers," *Journal of Social Issues*, 29, no. 4 (1973): 25–61, esp. 51.

56 *Rice v. Sioux City Memorial Park Cemetery*, 102 F. Supp. 658, 669 (1952).

57 H. G. Kelman, "Violence Without Moral Restraint: Reflections on the Dehumanization of Victims and Victimizers," *Journal of Social Issues*, 29, no. 4 (1973): 25–61, esp. 51.

58 A. Onwuachi-Willig, "Reconceptualizing the Harms of Discrimination: How Brown V. Board of Education Helped to Further White Supremacy," *Virginia Law Review*, 105 (2019): 343.

3. Legalized Inequality

1 P. Braveman, "A New Definition of Health Equity to Guide Future Efforts and Measure Progress," *Health Affairs Blog*, June 22, 2017, www.healthaffairs.org.

2 S. Sullivan, "Inheriting Racist Disparities in Health: Epigenetics and the Transgenerational Effects of White Racism," *Critical Philosophy of Race*, 1, no. 2 (2013): 190–218.

3 Sara M. Moorman and Jeffrey E. Stokes, "Solidarity in the Grandparent–Adult Grandchild Relationship and Trajectories of Depressive Symptoms," *Gerontologist*, 56, no. 3 (June 2016): 408–420, https://doi.org/10.1093/geront/gnu056.

4 M. Van Dyke, S. Greer, E. Odom, Linda Schieb, Adam Vaughan, Michael Kramer, and Michele Casper, "Heart Disease Death Rates Among Blacks and Whites Aged ≥35 Years: United States, 1968–2015," *Morbidity and Mortality Weekly Report, Surveillance Summaries*, 67, no. SS-5 (2018):1–11, http://dx.doi.org/10.15585/mmwr .ss6705a1.

5 This was also the year that heroin and other opioid drug overdose death rates began to skyrocket as the tragic opioid crisis began claiming lives among White people faster than any other racial group in America.

6 George M. Fredrickson, *White Supremacy: A Comparative Study in American and South African History* (New York: Oxford University Press, 1982), 162; Francis Lee Ansley, "White Supremacy (and What We Should Do About It,)" in *Critical White Studies: Looking Behind the Mirror*, ed. Richard Delgado and Jean Stefancic, 592–595 (Philadelphia: Temple University Press, 1997).

7 See "Proceedings and debates of the house of representatives of the United States at the Second Session of the Second Congress, Begun at the City of Philadelphia, November 5, 1792," Annals of Congress, 2nd Congress, 2nd Session, November 5, 1792 to March 2, 1793, pp. 1414–1415, www.ushistory.org.

8 Samuel May Jr., *The Fugitive Slave Law and Its Victims* (No. 15) (New York: American Anti-Slavery Society, 1861).

9   John Locke, cited in A. Broers, "John Locke on Equality, Toleration, and the
    Atheist Exception," *Inquiries Journal/Student Pulse*, 1, no. 12 (2009): www
    .inquiriesjournal.com.

10 Thomas Paine, *Common Sense* (1776), available at Independence Hall Association,
    www.ushistory.org.

11 Paine, *Common Sense*.

12 Samuel Johnson, *A Dictionary of the English language: in which the words are
    deduced* [. . .], (London: J. Knapton, 1755), 713–714.

13 T. Marshall, "Reflections on the Bicentennial of the United States Constitution,"
    Harvard Law Review, 101 (1987): 1, 2.

14 12 United States Statutes at Large, 36th Congress, 2nd Session, 1861, p. 251.

15 Abraham Lincoln, First Inaugural Address, March 4, 1861, https://avalon.law.yale
    .edu.

16 Ohio, Kentucky, Rhode Island, Illinois, West Virginia, and Maryland, which
    rescinded its ratification in 2014.

17 Mississippi became the last state to ratify this amendment in 2013.

18 M. Goodwin, "The Thirteenth Amendment: Modern Slavery, Capitalism, and
    Mass Incarceration," *Cornell Law Review*, 104 (2018): 899.

19 Ruth Delaney, Ram Subramanian, Alison Shames, and Nicholas Turner,
    "American History, Race, and Prison," Vera Project, 2021, www.vera.org.

20 Alex Lichtenstein, *Twice the Work of Free Labor: The Political Economy of Convict
    Labor in the New South* (New York: Verso, 1996), 41–42.

21 Cong. Globe, 39th Cong., 1st Sess. 1122 (Mar. 1, 1866) (Rogers statement), 1117
    (Rep. James Wilson Statement). See also Cong. Globe, 39th Cong., 1st Sess. 1291
    (Mar. 9, 1866) (Bingham's statement about no right to vote or hold public office),
    (Wilson's statement); Cong. Globe, 39th Cong., 1st Sess. 1366–67 (Mar. 13, 1866)
    (Wilson's statement and act's passage). See also Michael W. McConnell, "The
    Originalist Case for *Brown v. Board of Education*," *Harvard Journal of Law and
    Public Policy*, 19 (1996): 960.

22 See Cong. Globe, 39th Cong., 1st Sess. 474 (Jan. 29 1866); and McConnell,
    "Originalist Case for *Brown v. Board of Education*," 958.

23 A. H. Kelly, "The Fourteenth Amendment Reconsidered: The Segregation
    Question," *Michigan Law Review*, 54, no. 8 (1956): 1049–1086.

24 J. R. McKivigan, ed., *Abolitionism and American Politics and Government*, vol. 3
    (Philadelphia: Taylor and Francis, 1999), 392.

25 Cong. Globe, 39th Cong., 1st Sess. 2459 (1866) (introducing H.R. Res. 127, which
    became the Fourteenth Amendment).

26 J. A. Delle and M. A. Levine, "Equality of Man Before His Creator," in *The Limits
    of Tyranny: Archaeological Perspectives on the Struggle Against New World Slavery*,
    ed. James A. Delle, 121 (Knoxville: University of Tennessee Press, 2015) (emphasis
    added). See also C. G. Woodson, "Thaddeus Stevens," *Negro History Bulletin*,
    13, no. 3 (1949): 51.

27 Cong. Globe, 39th Cong., 1st Sess. 2498 (1866) (Rep. Broomall statement).

28 US Const. amend. XIV, § 1.

29 Charles Postel, *Equality: An American Dilemma 1866–1896* (New York: Farrar, Straus and Giroux, 2019), 8–9. As Postel also notes, "Equality, of course, had been a potent idea in American affairs since the country's founding."

30 McConnell, "Originalist Case for *Brown v. Board of Education*," 457, 461. See also Michael Klarman, "An Interpretive History of Modern Equal Protection," *Michigan Law Review*, 19 (1991): 213, 220, 228–229.

31 US Const. amend. XV (Tennessee became the last state to ratify this amendment in 1997).

32 See Oxford Reference, "Overview: Reconstruction Acts, Quick Reference (1867–68)," Oxford University Press, accessed June 26, 2021, www.oxford reference.com.

33 E. Foner, *The Second Founding: How the Civil War and Reconstruction Remade the Constitution* (New York: W. W. Norton & Co., 2019), 56.

34 E. Swinney, "Enforcing the Fifteenth Amendment, 1870–1877, *Journal of Southern History*, 28, no. 2 (1962): 202–218.

35 "Civil Rights Act of 1870," Stat. 140, (1870), Federal Judicial Center, www.fjc.gov, accessed April 24, 2021; Swinney, "Enforcing the Fifteenth Amendment."

36 Sess. II. Ch. 99 41st Congress 433. (Also called the "Second Force Act"), www .senate.gov.

37 See Cong. Globe, 42nd Cong., 1st Sess. 68–71, 317 (1871) (Rep. Shellabarger statements); see also 16 Stat. 140 (1870). 18 U.S.C. § 241 (1964) (Congress's first attempt to provide protection against violence through the Enforcement Act of 1870); see also Avins, 333–334.

38 See Cong. Globe, 42nd Cong., 1st Sess. 85–86 (1871) (Rep. John Bingham statements).

39 "The Constitutional Amendment! Geary Is for Negro Suffrage," wood engraving (Philadelphia, 1866), available at Library of Congress, www.loc.gov.

40 Cong. Globe, 41st Cong., 2d Sess. 3434 (May 13, 1870) (Sen. Charles Sumner statement); see also Cong. Globe, 42d Cong., 2d Sess. 244 (1872) (read on Dec. 20, 1871) (Sen. Charles Sumner bill proposal); see also McConnell, "Originalist Case for *Brown v. Board of Education*," 987–988.

41 Cong. Globe, 42d Cong., 2d Sess. 241–42 (1872) (discourse between liberal Republican Sen. Charles Sumner and moderate Republican Sen. Joshua Hill on Dec. 20, 1871 regarding separate-but-equal facilitating racial inequality through the rule of law; racial equality, here expressed as integration, is not a legal and political right, but a social right also. Social rights is equitable access, treatment, and benefit everywhere.); see also McConnell, "Originalist Case for *Brown v. Board of Education*," 988–989.

42 US Senate, "The Caning of Senator Charles Sumner, May 22, 1856," US Senate Art and History, www.senate.gov.

43 See 2 Cong. Rec. 555 (Jan. 10, 1874), 428 (Jan. 6, 1874); Cong. Globe, 42d Cong., 2d Sess. 4321 (June 7, 1872) (statement of Sen. Brooks). See also, for example, 3 Cong. Rec. 949 (Feb. 3, 1875) (statement of Rep. Finck); 2 Cong. Rec. 411 (Jan. 6, 1874) (statement of Rep. Blount); Cong. Globe, 42d Cong., 2d Sess. 3251 (May 9, 1872) (statement of Sen. Blair), 819 (Feb. 5, 1872) (statement of Sen. Norwood), app. 9 (Jan. 30, 1872) (statement of Sen. Saulsbury), 242 (1872) (statement of Sen. Hill on Dec. 20, 1871). See also McConnell, "Originalist Case for *Brown v. Board of Education*," 1014–1015.

44 L. Schweninger, "Black-Owned Businesses in the South, 1790–1880," *Business History Review*, 63 (spring 1989): 22–60.

45 Currier and Ives, "The First Colored Senator and Representatives in the 41st and 42nd Congress of the United States," lithograph, 1872, Library of Congress Prints and Photographs Division Washington, DC, www.loc.gov.

46 See, for example, B. M. Campney, "'Light Is Bursting upon the World!': White Supremacy and Racist Violence Against Blacks in Reconstruction Kansas," *Western Historical Quarterly*, 41, no. 2 (2010): 171–194.

47 C. Clinton, "Bloody Terrain: Freedwomen, Sexuality and Violence During Reconstruction," *Georgia Historical Quarterly*, 76, no. 2 (1992): 313–332.

48 A. O. Sherif, "The Primacy of the Law and the Constitution–Their Consistency and Compliance with International Law: The Egyptian Experience," *Yearbook of Islamic and Middle Eastern Law Online*, 10, no. 1 (2003): 3–19.

49 A. V. Dicey, *Introduction to the Study of the Law of the Constitution*, 8th ed. (New York: Macmillan, 1915; repr., Indianapolis: Liberty Classics, 1982), 120.

50 M. J. Radin, "Reconsidering the Rule of Law," *BUL Review*, 69 (1989): 781, 784.

51 *The Civil Rights Cases*, 109 U.S. 3 (1883).

52 *The Civil Rights Cases*, 109 U.S. 3, 11–12 (1883). That holding, reaffirmed in *United States v. Morrison*, 529 U.S. 598 (2000), remains "good" law today.

53 *The Civil Rights Cases*, 109 U.S. 3, 11–12 (1883), 49 (Justice Harlan dissenting) (internal quotation marks omitted).

54 *Plessy v. Ferguson*, 163 U.S. 537, 559 (1896) (Harlan, J., dissenting).

55 *Plessey*, 163 U.S., 544.

56 R. L. Rice, "Residential Segregation by Law, 1910–1917," *Journal of Southern History*, 34, no. 2 (1968): 179–199.

57 See *Harper v. Virginia State Board of Elections*, 395 U.S. 621 (1969) (Holding state poll tax violates Equal Protection Clause).

58 H. Wilson, "The Role of Carter Glass in the Disfranchisement of the Virginia Negro," *Historian*, 32, no. 1 (1969): 69–82.

59 Pauli Murray ed., *States' Laws on Race and Color, and Appendices Containing International Documents, Federal Laws and Regulations, Local Ordinances and Charts* (Cincinnati: Women's Division of Christian Service, Board of Missions and Church Extension, Methodist Church, 1950).

60 Charlottesville, Va., Ordinances ch. 15, § 5 (1894) ("White Persons Only").

61 *Dred Scott v. Sandford*, 60 U.S. 393, 410 (1857).

62 Kenneth O'Reilly, "The Jim Crow Policies of Woodrow Wilson," *Journal of Blacks in Higher Education*, 17 (1997): 117. See also Michael Dennis, "Looking Backward: Woodrow Wilson, the New South, and the Question of Race," *American Nineteenth Century History*, 3 (spring 2002): 77, 82, discussing Wilson's view that Black voting was politically illegitimate, restoration of Southern White control by "real citizens" was desirable, and Reconstruction was a "tragic era" characterized by "the dominance of an ignorant and *inferior* race was justly dreaded." See also Bernard Baruch, *War Industries Board, American Industry at War: A Rep. of the War Industries Board* (March 1921), who also quotes Wilson as saying that Reconstruction was a period when "the dominance of an ignorant and inferior race was justly dreaded). See also John S. Ezell, "Woodrow Wilson As Southerner, 1856–1885: A Review Essay," *Civil War History*, 15, no. 2 (June 1969): 160–167, 162n9, which cites Arthur S. Link, ed., *The Papers of Woodrow Wilson*, 480, 484, 477; II, 19 (Princeton, NJ: Princeton University Press 1966–1968).

63 *Tyson v. Simpson and others*, 3 N.C. 147, 147 (1801).

64 *Richardson v. State*, 148 Tex. Crim. 536, 257 S.W.2d 308, 308–309 (1953) (Texas Court reversed rape conviction where prosecutor made this argument).

65 See, for example, *State v. Treadaway*, 42 So 500 (1910) (Louisiana court enforcing the states' anti-cohabitation statute by reviewing the meaning of the words "negro" and "colored" under sister state laws.)

66 P. A. Lombardo, "Medicine, Eugenics, and the Supreme Court: from Coercive Sterilization to Reproductive Freedom," *Journal of Contemporary Health Law and Policy*, 13, no. 1 (1996): 6.

67 S. Kuhl, *The Nazi Connection: Eugenics, American Racism, and German National Socialism* (New York: Oxford University Press, 2002).

68 Kuhl, *Nazi Connection*, 1–4.

69 T. A. Ochieng'Nyongó, *The Amalgamation Waltz: Race, Performance, and the Ruses of Memory* (Minneapolis: University of Minnesota Press, 2009).

70 For "vicious pseudoscientific activity," see Kuhl, *Nazi Connection*, 80 (quoting Professor Franz Boas, Columbia University, New York City). See, for example, F. E. Vizcarrondo "Human Enhancement: The New Eugenics," *Linacre Quarterly*, 81, no. 3 (2014): 239–243, https://doi.org/10.1179/2050854914Y.0000000021.

71 *Brown v. Board of Education*, 347 U.S. 483 (1954) (held racial segregation in public education violates the Equal Protection Clause of the Fourteenth Amendment); *Hernandez v. Texas*, 347 U.S. 475 (1951) (held excluding Mexicans to seat all-White jury to try Mexican American defendant violated Fourteenth Amendment's Equal Protection Clause)

72 *Garner v. Louisiana*, 368 U.S. 157 (1961) (state cannot criminalize peaceful sit-in protest to oppose segregation at lunch counters under Fourteenth Amendment

Due Process Clause); *McLaughlin v. Florida*, 379 U.S. 184 (1964) (held Florida statute banning unmarried interracial couples violated Equal Protection Clause); *Loving v. Virginia*, 388 U.S. 1 (1967) (held Virginia anti-miscegenation law violated the Equal Protection Clause).

73 42 U.S.C. § 1971 et seq., Pub. L. 88–352, 78 Stat. 241 (July 2, 1964).

74 52 U.S.C. §10101.

75 42 U.S.C. 3601 et seq.

76 The state of Mississippi ratified the Thirteenth Amendment of the US Constitution, outlawing slavery, in 2013, 150 years after the Emancipation Proclamation and 148 years after the amendment became a part of the Constitution. See Amber McKynzie, "Mississippi Becomes Final State to Abolish Slavery," *Black Enterprise*, February 20, 2013, www.blackenterprise.com.

77 H.R. 35 (116th Congress, 2019–2020, www.congress.gov.

78 W. H. Frey, "Black-White Segregation Edges Downward Since 2000, Census Shows," Brookings Institution, 2018.

79 See, for example, *McCleskey v. Kemp*, 481 U.S. 279 (1987) (involving a Black man convicted of murdering a Georgia police officer; the court rejected evidence that Black defendants who kill White victims are 4.3 times more likely than White defendants are to receive the death penalty in Georgia's race-conscious criminal justice system).

80 *Hawkins v. Town of Shaw, Mississippi*, 461 F.2d 1171, 1172 (1972).

81 *Norwalk CORE v. Norwalk Redevelopment Agency*, 395 F.2d 920 (1968).

82 *Kennedy Park Homes Ass'n. v. City of Lackawanna, NY*, 436 F.2d 108 (1970)

83 D. D. Reidpath and P. Allotey, "Infant Mortality Rate As an Indicator of Population Health," *Journal of Epidemiology and Community Health*, 57, no. 5 (2003): 344–346.

84 See B. Bastian, B. Tejada Vera, E. Arias, et al., "Mortality Trends in the United States, 1900–2017," Centers for Disease Control and Prevention, National Center for Health Statistics, 2019, www.cdc.gov. See also B. Bastian, A. Lipphardt, J. M. Keralis, L. Lu, and Y. Chong, "Mortality Trends in the United States, 1900–2018," Centers for Disease Control and Prevention, National Center for Health Statistics, Data Visualization Gallery, August 25, 2020, www.cdc.gov.

85 See, for example, T. A. LaVeist, "Segregation, Poverty, and Empowerment: Health Consequences for African Americans," *Milbank Quarterly*, 71, no. 1 (1993): 41–64, esp. 54.

4. Unjust Housing and Neighborhoods

1 D. S. Massey, "Still the Linchpin: Segregation and Stratification in the USA," *Race and Social Problems*, 12, no. 1 (2020): 1–12.

2 N. A. Denton and D. S. Massey, "Residential Segregation of Blacks, Hispanics, and Asians by Socioeconomic Status and Generation," *Social Science Quarterly*, 69, no. 4 (1988): 797.

3   K. White, J. S. Haas, and D. R. Williams, "Elucidating the Role of Place in Health Care Disparities: The Example of Racial/Ethnic Residential Segregation," *Health Services Research*, 47, no. 3, part 2 (2012): 1278–1299.

4   D. R. Williams and C. Collins, "Racial Residential Segregation: A Fundamental Cause of Racial Disparities in Health," *Public Health Reports*, 116, no. 5 (2001): 404–416.

5   J. Gibbons and T. C. Yang, "Self-Rated Health and Residential Segregation: How Does Race/Ethnicity Matter?," *Journal of Urban Health*, 91, no. 4 (2014): 648–660.

6   T. LaVeist, K. Pollack, R. Thorpe Jr., R. Fesahazion, and D. Gaskin, "Place, Not Race: Disparities Dissipate in Southwest Baltimore When Blacks and Whites Live Under Similar Conditions," *Health Affairs*, 30, no. 10 (2011): 1880–1887.

7   This is not to say that living among Black people is dehumanizing per se. Nothing could be further from the truth. As described in chapter 3, African Americans like my mother may not internalize dehumanization at all just because they live among Black and not White neighbors. But as also discussed, the resource deprivation due to structural racism that accomplishes structural or group dehumanization still has a deadly effect on their lives and the lives of the population as a whole.

8   See, for example, Jing Fang, Shantha Madhavan, William Bosworth, and Michael H. Alderman, "Residential Segregation and Mortality in New York City," *Social Science & Medicine*, 47, no. 4 (1998): 469–474.

9   James N. Weinstein, Amy Geller, Yamrot Negussie, and Aline Baciu, *Communities in Action: Pathways to Health Equity* (Washington, DC: National Academies Press, 2017), 111.

10 Ernie Hood, "Dwelling Disparities: How Poor Housing Leads to Poor Health," *Environmental Health Perspectives*, 113, no. 5 (3005): A310–A317.

11 D. E. Jacobs, "Environmental Health Disparities in Housing," *American Journal of Public Health*, 101, no. S1 (2011): S115–S122. See also National Center for Healthy Housing, "Audiences We Serve," accessed May 4, 2021, https://nchh.org.

12 M. R. Kramer and C. R. Hogue, "Is Segregation Bad for Your Health?," *Epidemiologic Reviews*, 31, no. 1 (2009): 178–194.

13 J. Krieger and D. L. Higgins, "Housing and Health: Time Again for Public Health Action," *American Journal of Public Health*, 92, no. 5 (2002): 758–768; J. Raymond, W. Wheeler, and M. J. Brown, "Inadequate and Unhealthy Housing, 2007 and 2009," *Centers for Disease Control and Prevention Morbidity and Mortality Weekly Report*, 60 (2011): 21–27, www.cdc.gov.

14 Kramer and Hogue, "Is Segregation Bad for Your Health?"

15 Rachel Meltzer and Alex Schwartz, "Housing Affordability and Health: Evidence from New York City," *Housing Policy Debate*, 60 (2015): 80–82.

16 Diane Alexander and Janet Currie, "Is It Who You Are or Where You Live? Residential Segregation and Racial Gaps in Childhood Asthma," *Health Economics*, 55 (2017): 186–187.

17 Megan Sandel and Matthew Desmond, "Investing in Housing for Health Improves Both Mission and Margin," *Journal of the American Medical Association*, 318 (2017): 2291.

18 See Matthew Desmond and Monica Bell, "Housing, Poverty, and the Law, *Annual Review of Law & Social Sciences*, 11 (2015): 15–20, which links "poor housing conditions to a wide array of health problems, from asthma, lead poisoning, and respiratory complications to developmental delays, heart disease, and neurological disorders."

19 Samiya Bashir, "Home Is Where the Harm Is: Inadequate Housing as a Public Health Crisis," *American Journal of Public Health*, 92 (2002), 733.

20 M. Smith, T. Delves, R. Lansdown, B. Clayton, and P. Graham, "The Effects of Lead Exposure on Urban Children: The Institute of Child Health/Southampton Study," *Developmental Medicine and Child Neurology*, 47 (1983): 1–54. See also W. G. Sciarillo, G. Alexander, and K. P. Farrell, "Lead Exposure and Child Behavior," *American Journal of Public Health*, 82, no. 10 (1992): 1356–1360; R. L. Canfield, T. A. Jusko, and K. Kordas, "Environmental Lead Exposure and Children's Cognitive Function," *Rivista italiana di pediatria* (Italian journal of pediatrics), 31, no. 6 (2005): 293, which concludes that there is no safe level of lead exposure for children.

21 Krieger and Higgins, "Housing and Health," 758n3.

22 Krieger and Higgins, "Housing and Health," 758n3.

23 Housing Assistance Council, *Taking Stock: Rural People, Poverty and Housing in the 21st Century* (Washington, DC: Housing Assistance Council, 2012), www.ruralhome.org.

24 Stanford Center on Poverty and Inequality, "State of the Union Millennial Dilemma Report," special issue, *Pathways*, 2019, https://inequality.stanford.edu.

25 Patrick Sisson, "New Study Finds Rent Burden Higher in Segregated Neighborhoods," *Curbed*, May 24, 2018, www.curbed.com; "Is Renting Bad for Your Health?," Milken Institute School of Public Health, George Washington University, January 25, 2019, https://publichealthonline.gwu.edu; Richard Rothstein, *The Color of Law: A Forgotten History of How Our Government Segregated America* (New York: Liveright, 2017).

26 Rothstein, *Color of Law*. See also Vincent Roscigno et al., "The Complexities and Processes of Racial Housing Discrimination," *Social Problems*, 56 (2009): 49–69.

27 Tim Henderson, "Can Cities Desegregate? Some Show How It's Done," Pew Research, October 2015, www.pewtrusts.org.

28 Survey evidence confirms that US residential segregation is not preferred, but that on average, African Americans and Latino are willing to live in integrated neighborhoods, whereas White people are not. See Dolores Acevedo-Garcia, "Residential Segregation and the Epidemiology of Infectious Diseases," *Social Science & Medicine*, 51 (2000):1143–1161, esp. 1145.

29 C. J. DuBose-Simons, "Movin' On Up: African Americans in the South Bronx in the 1940s," *New York History*, 95, no. 4 (2014): 543–557.

30 Williams and Collins, "Racial Residential Segregation."

31 Williams and Collins, "Racial Residential Segregation," 516.

32 Thomas A. LaVeist, "Segregation, Poverty, and Empowerment: Health Consequences for African Americans," *Milbank Quarterly*, 71 (1993): 41–64, esp. 41, 42–43.

33 Alfred Yankauer, "The Relationship of Fetal and Infant Mortality to Residential Segregation: An Inquiry Into Social Epidemiology," *American Sociological Review*, 15, no. 5 (1950): 644–648, explains that Black and White infant mortality rates are higher in segregated New York neighborhoods.

34 LaVeist, "Segregation, Poverty, and Empowerment."

35 See also M. C. Lu and R. Halfon, "Racial and Ethnic Disparities in Birth Outcomes: A Life-Course Perspective," *Maternal and Child Health Journal*, 7 (2003): 13–30, https://doi.org/10.1023/A:1022537516969.

36 Sue C. Grady, "Racial Disparities in Low Birthweight and the Contribution of Residential Segregation: A Multilevel Analysis," *Social Science & Medicine*, 63 (2006): 3013, 3014, 3026.

37 D. S. Massey and N. A. Denton, "Hypersegregation in U.S. Metropolitan Areas: Black and Hispanic Segregation Along Dimensions," *Demography*, 26 (1989): 373–391.

38 Grady, "Racial Disparities in Low Birthweight," 3026.

39 Kramer and Hogue, "Is Segregation Bad for Your Health?"

40 Acevedo-Garcia, "Residential Segregation," 1143–1144.

41 Dolores Acevedo-Garcia, "Zip Code-Level Risk Factors for Tuberculosis: Neighborhood Environment and Residential Segregation in New Jersey, 1985–1992," *American Journal of Public Health*, 91, no. 5 (2001): 734.

42 Carol S. Aneshensel and Clea A. Sucoff, "The Neighborhood Context of Adolescent Mental Health," *Journal of Health and Social Behavior*, 37, no. 4 (1997): 293, 305.

43 A. V. D. Roux, S. S. Merkin, D. Arnett, L. Chambless, M. Massing, F. J. Nieto, P. Sorlie, M. Szklo, H. A. Tyroler, R. L. Watson, "Neighborhood of Residence and Incidence of Coronary Heart Disease," *New England Journal of Medicine*, 345, no. 2 (2001): 99–106.

44 See, in general, Rothstein, *The Color of Law*, which outlines the system of racially explicit federal laws, regulations, and government practices that were consistently employed throughout the twentieth century to enforce residential racial segregation.

45 See Vincent J. Roscigno Diana L. Karfin, and Griff Tester, "The Complexities and Processes of Racial Housing Discrimination," *Social Problems*, 56, no. 1 (2009): 49–69.

46 Eduardo Bonilla-Silva, *White Supremacy and Racism in the Post-Civil Rights Era* (Boulder, CO: Lynne Rienner, 2001); see also Daniel J. Hopkins and Samantha Washington, "The Rise of Trump, the Fall of Prejudice? Tracking White Americans' Racial Attitudes 2008–2018 via a Panel Survey," *Public Opinion Quarterly*, 84, no. 1 (2019): 119–140.

47 Leonardo Bursztyn, Georgy Egorov, and Stefano Fiorin, "From Extreme to Mainstream: The Erosion of Social Norms," *American Economic Review*, 110, no. 11 (2020): 3522–3548.

48 See, for example, Roscigno et al., "Racial Housing Discrimination"; Anne-Marie G. Harris, Geraldine R. Henderson, and Jerome D. Williams, "Courting Customers: Assessing Consumer Racial Profiling and Other Marketplace Discrimination," *Journal of Public Policy & Marketing*, 24, no. 1 (2005); and Samantha Friedman, "Commentary: Housing Discrimination Research in the 21st Century," *Cityscape: A Journal of Policy Development and Research*, 17, no. 3 (2015):143–150.

49 Sun Jung Oh and John Yinger, "What Have We Learned from Paired Testing in Housing Markets?," *Cityscape: A Journal of Policy Development and Research*, 17, no. 3 (2015): 15.

50 Julia Angwin and Terry Parris Jr., "Facebook Lets Advertisers Exclude Users by Race," *ProPublica*, October 28, 2016, www.propublica.org.

51 Tara Bahrampour, "Large Cities Still Segregated Even As Nation Becoming More Diverse," *Washington Post*, December 6, 2018, www.washingtonpost.com.

52 John Iceland, "Residential Segregation: Transatlantic Analysis," Migration Policy Institute, September 2014, www.migrationpolicy.org.

53 E. Gonzalez, *The Bronx* (New York: Columbia University Press, 2007).

54 George Lipsitz, "The Racialization of Space and the Spatialization of Race Theorizing the Hidden Architecture of Landscape,'" *Landscape Journal*, 26, no. 1 (2007): 10–23.

55 Bruce Mitchell and Juan Franco, "HOLC 'Redlining' Maps: The Persistent Structure of Segregation and Economic Inequality," National Community Reinvestment Coalition, March 20, 2018, https://ncrc.org/holc/.

56 Olivia Limone and Nadia Sanchez, "Mapping Food Deserts (and Swamps) in Manhattan and the Bronx," *Medium*, December 16 2019, https://medium.com.

57 "mariomario080," "South Bronx Story Map of the Environmental Crisis," web mapping application, December 18, 2010, www.arcgis.com. But compare "Race and Ethnicity in South Bronx, New York, New York City (Neighborhood)," Statistical Atlas, accessed May 4, 2021, https://statisticalatlas.com.

58 Williams and Collins, "Racial Residential Segregation."

59 M. R. Lee, "Concentrated Poverty, Race, and Homicide," *Sociological Quarterly*, 41, no. 2 (2000): 189–206; R. J. Sampson, "Urban Black Violence: The Effect of Male Joblessness and Family Disruption," *American Journal of Sociology*, 93, no. 2 (1987): 348–382; J. Fagan and R. B. Freeman, "Crime and Work," *Crime and Justice*, 25 (1999): 225–290; "South Bronx, New York, NY Employment," AreaVibes, accessed May 4, 2021, www.areavibes.com.

60 City of New York, *Food Metrics Report, 2015* (New York: City of New York, 2015), www.nyc.gov/foodpolicy.

61 National Academies, *The Public Health Effects of Food Deserts: Workshop Summary* (Washington, DC: National Academies Press, 2009), www.ncbi.nlm .nih.gov.

62 M. L. Alaniz, "Alcohol Availability and Targeted Advertising in Racial/Ethnic Minority Communities," *Alcohol Health and Research World*, 22, no. 4 (1998): 286; J. G. Lee, D. L. Sun, N. M. Schleicher, K. M. Ribisl, D. A. Luke, and L. Henriksen, "Inequalities in Tobacco Outlet Density by Race, Ethnicity and Socioeconomic Status, 2012, USA: Results from the ASPiRE Study," *Journal of Epidemiology and Community Health*, 71, no. 5 (2017): 487–492.

63 S. C. Lucan, A. R. Maroko, O. C. Sanon, and C. B. Schechter, "Unhealthful Food-and-Beverage Advertising in Subway Stations: Targeted Marketing, Vulnerable Groups, Dietary Intake, and Poor Health," *Journal of Urban Health*, 94, no. 2 (2017): 220–232.

64 "Medically Underserved Areas/Populations," Health Resources & Services Administration, accessed April 30, 2021, https://data.hrsa.gov. See also Taylor Tepper and Jacob Hodes, "The Doctor Drain," Craig Newmark Graduate School of Journalism, City University of New York, May 10, 2012, https://doctordrain .journalism.cuny.edu.

65 K. White, J. S. Haas, and D. R. Williams, "Elucidating the Role of Place in Health Care Disparities: The Example of Racial/Ethnic Residential Segregation," *Health Services Research*, 47, no. 3, part 2 (2012): 1278–1299.

66 J. H. Davis, C. Ruddock, and J. Billings, "Racial and Ethnic Disparities in Health: A View from the South Bronx," *Journal of Health Care for the Poor and Underserved*, 17, no. 1 (2006): 116–127; Sue A. Kaplan et al. "Stirring Up the Mud: Using a Community-Based Participatory Approach to Address Health Disparities Through a Faith-Based Initiative," *Journal of Health Care for the Poor and Underserved*, 20, no. 4 (2009): 1111–1123, doi: 10.1353/hpu.0.0221.

67 In 2018, New York City Council passed a law capping the amount of garbage handled in the South Bronx transfer stations to reduce the burden on residential communities in this part of the city. See William Neuman, "New York's Push to End Inequality Extends to Garbage," *New York Times*, August 16, 2018, www.nytimes.com.

68 Zvia Segal Naphtalia, Carlos E. Restrepo, Rae Zimmerman, and Robert F. Wagner, "Maps Expand Asthma Hazards Awareness: GIS Helps Policy Makers See Where Childhood Asthma, Schools, and Pollution Sources Collide," *HealthyGIS* (ESRI) (January 1, 2008): 4–5, www.esri.com.

69 Paul Mohai, Paula M. Lantz, Jeffrey Morenoff, James S. House, and Richard P. Mero, "Racial and Socioeconomic Disparities in Residential Proximity to Polluting Industrial Facilities: Evidence from the Americans' Changing Lives Study," *American Journal of Public Health*, 99 (2009): S649. See also Robert D. Bullard, *Dumping in Dixie: Race, Class, and Environmental Quality*, 3rd ed. (New York: Routledge, 2000).

70 Robert Bullard, "New Report Tracks Environmental Justice Movement Over Five Decades," *Dr. Robert D. Bullard, Father of Environmental Justice* (blog), February 9, 2014, https://drrobertbullard.com.

71 Paul Mohai, Byoung-Suk Kweon, Sangyun Lee, and Kerry Ard, "Air Pollution Around Schools Is Linked to Poorer Student Health and Academic Performance," *Health Affairs*, 30, no. 5 (2011): 852, 858.

72 Institute for Civil Infrastructure Systems, Robert F. Wagner Graduate School of Public Service, New York University, "South Bronx Environmental Health and Policy Study: Asthma and Air Pollution in the South Bronx," 2004, www.icisnyu.org.

73 K. Warman, E. J. Silver, and P. R. Wood, "Modifiable Risk Factors for Asthma Morbidity in Bronx Versus Other Inner-City Children," *Journal of Asthma*, 46, no. 10 (2009): 995–1000.

74 Cecilia Butini, "Asthma by the Numbers," *Medium*, January 20, 2018, https://medium.com.

75 Mike Maciag, "Residential Segregation Data for U.S. Metro Areas," Governing, January 10, 2019, www.governing.com.

76 Based on data reported from the US Census Bureau's 2010–2014 American Community Survey, as reported by William Frey, "Census Shows Modest Declines in Black-White Segregation," Brookings Institution, December 8, 2015, www.brookings.edu.

77 Monica C. Bell, "Anti-Segregation Policing," 95 *New York University Law Review*, 95 (June 2020): 650. Professor Monica Bell points out, for example, that using the measure to report that segregation is declining in the United States masks the fact that racial experiences due to segregation may not have changed. See also P. E. Carrillo and J. L. Rothbaum, "Counterfactual Spatial Distributions," *Journal of Regional Science*, 56, no. 5 (2016): 868–894, which says that much of the increase in integration can be explained by changes in individual characteristics such as income, education, and age.

78 Williams and Collins, "Racial Residential Segregation."

79 Williams and Collins, "Racial Residential Segregation," 116.

80 S. Esmeir, "On Making Dehumanization Possible," *PMLA*, 121, no. 5 (2006): 1544–1551.

81 J. F. Dovidio, S. L. Gaertner, and K. Kawakami, "Intergroup Contact: The Past, Present, and the Future," *Group Processes & Intergroup Relations*, 6, no. 1 (2003): 5–21.

82 S. L. Gaertner, J. F. Dovidio, M. C. Rust, J. A. Nier, B. S. Banker, C. M. Ward, G. R. Mottola, and M. Houlette, "Reducing Intergroup Bias: Elements of Intergroup Cooperation," *Journal of Personality and Social Psychology*, 76, no. 3 (1999): 388.

83 S. C. Wright, A. Aron, T. McLaughlin-Volpe, and S. A. Ropp, "The Extended Contact Effect: Knowledge of Cross-Group Friendships and Prejudice.," *Journal of Personality and Social Psychology*, 73, no. 1 (1997): 73.

84 D. M. Wilner, R. P. Walkley, and S. W. Cook, "Residential Proximity and Intergroup Relations in Public Housing Projects," *Journal of Social Issues*, 8, no. 1 (1952): 45–69.

85 Daniel M. Wilner, Rosabelle Price Walkley, and Stuart W. Cook, *Human Relations in Interracial Housing* (Minneapolis: University of Minnesota Press, 1995).

86 Dovidio et al., "Past, Present, and the Future," 609.

87 W. E. Pickren, "Psychologists, Race, and Housing in Postwar America," *Journal of Social Issues*, 67, no. 1 (2011): 27–41.

88 Jo Phelan and Bruce G. Link, "Is Racism a Fundamental Cause of Inequalities in Health?," *Annual Review of Sociology*, 41 (2015): 311–330.

5. Unjust Education

1 *Swann v. Charlottes-Mecklenburg Board of Education*, 402 U.S. 1 (1971).

2 Catherine E. Ross and Chia-ling Wu, "The Links between Education and Health," *American Sociological Review* (1995): 719–745.

3 Ross and Wu, "Links between Education and Health," 721.

4 Robert A. Hahn and Benedict I. Truman, "Education Improves Public Health and Promotes Health Equity," *International Journal of Health Services*, 45, no. 4 (2015): 657–678.

5 Hahn and Truman, "Education Improves Public Health," 664.

6 *Brown v. Board of Education*, 347 U.S. 483 (1954).

7 Emily B. Zimmerman, Steven H. Woolf, and Amber Haley, "Understanding the Relationship Between Education and Health," Agency for Healthcare Research and Quality, Rockville, MD, 2015; see also Emily Zimmerman and Steven H. Woolf, "Understanding the Relationship Between Education and Health," Institute of Medicine of the National Academies, National Academy of Sciences, June 5, 2014, https://nam.edu, 2.

8 Zimmerman, Woolf, and Haley "Education and Health," 1.

9 F. C. Pampel, P. M. Krueger, and J. T. Denney, "Socioeconomic Disparities in Health Behaviors," *Annual Review of Sociology*, 36 (2010): 349–370.

10 Jennifer K. Montez, Robert A. Hummer, and Mark D. Hayward, "Educational Attainment and Adult Mortality in the United States: A Systematic Analysis of Functional Form," *Demography*, 49, no. 1 (2012): 315–336.

11 Montez et al., "Educational Attainment and Adult Mortality," 331.

12 Zimmerman, Woolf, and Haley, "Education and Health"; see also Robert M. Kaplan, Michael L. Spittel, and Daryn H. David, eds. *Population Health: Behavioral and Social Science Insights* (Rockville, MD: Agency for Healthcare Research and Quality, 2015).

13 *Brown v. Board of Education*, 347 U.S. 483 (1954).

14 J. S. Coleman, "Equality of Educational Opportunity," *Integrated Education*, 6, no. 5 (1968): 19–28.

15 G. J. Whitehurst, R. V. Reeves, and E. Rodrigue, "Segregation, Race, and Charter Schools: What Do We Know?," Center on Children and Families at Brookings, October 2016; G. J. Whitehurst, "New Evidence on School Choice and Racially Segregated Schools," *Evidence Speaks Reports*, 2, no. 33 (2017).

16 Kaiser Family Foundation, "Poverty by Race/Ethnicity," 2018, www.kff.

17 Whitehurst, "School Choice and Racially Segregated Schools," 8.

18 Natasha Warioo and Nadirah Farah Foley, "How Elite Schools Stay So White," *New York Times*, July 24, 2018, www.nyt.com.

19 Eliza Shapiro, "Only 7 Black Students Got Into Stuyvesant, N.Y.'S Most Selective High School, Out of 895 Spots," *New York Times*, March 18, 2019, www.nyt.com; Ginia Bellafante, "Stop Fixating on One Elite High School, Stuyvesant; There Are Bigger Problems," *New York Times*, March 21, 2019, www.nytimes.com.

20 E. A. Hanushek and S. G. Rivkin, *School Quality and the Black-White Achievement Gap*, No. w12651, National Bureau of Economic Research, 2006.

21 E. Garcia and E. Weiss, "Education Inequalities at the School Starting Gate: Gaps, Trends, and Strategies to Address Them," Economic Policy Institute, September 27, 2017.

22 Some erroneously read the Coleman Report to conclude that family background such as parental education, number of siblings, and parental reading are more powerful predictors of a child's educational achievement than school resources. (See, for example, D. E. Bartz, "Revisiting James Coleman's Epic Study Entitled Equality of Educational Opportunity," *National Forum of Educational Administration & Supervision Journal*, 34, no. 4 [2016].) This is a gross mischaracterization of Coleman's analysis and conclusions, both of which were focused overwhelmingly on the relationship between segregation in public schools and other characteristics of those schools and student achievement.

23 C. T. Clotfelter, H. F. Ladd, and J. L. Vigdor, "Teacher Mobility, School Segregation, and Pay-Based Policies to Level the Playing Field," *Education Finance and Policy*, 6, no. 3 (2011): 399–438.

24 US Department of Education, Office for Civil Rights, "Civil Rights Data Collection: Data Snapshot (College and Career Readiness)," Issue Brief 3, March 21, 2014, https://cdn.uncf.org.

25 Rhonda Tsoi-A-Fatt Bryant, "College Preparation for African American Students: Gaps in the High School Educational Experience," CLASP Policy Solutions, United Negro College Fund, February 2015, https://cdn.uncf.org.

26 Hanushek and Rivkin, *Black-White Achievement Gap*. See also E. A. Hanushek and S. G. Rivkin, "Harming the Best: How Schools Affect the Black-White Achievement Gap," *Journal of Policy Analysis and Management*, 28, no. 3 (2009): 366–393.

27 E. A. Hanushek, J. F. Kain, and S. G. Rivkin, "New Evidence About Brown V. Board of Education: The Complex Effects of School Racial Composition on Achievement," *Journal of Labor Economics*, 27, no. 3 (2009): 349–383.

28 Erica L. Green and Annie Waldman, "'You Are Still Black': Charlottesville's Racial Divide Hinders Students," *New York Times*, October 16, 2018, www.nytimes.com.

29 Hanushek and Rivkin, *Black-White Achievement Gap*, 27.

30 Daniel J. Losen, "Silent Segregation in Our Nation's Schools," *Harvard Civil Rights-Civil Liberties Law Review*, 34 (1999): 517.

31 Losen, "Silent Segregation," 520–521.

32 T. Loveless, *The Tracking Wars: State Reform Meets School Policy* (Washington, DC: Brookings Institution Press, 2011).

33 See Roslyn Arlin Mickelson, "Subverting Swann: First- and Second-Generation Segregation in the Charlotte-Mecklenburg Schools," *American Educational Research Journal*, 38, no. 2 (2001).

34 D. Conger, "Within-School Segregation in an Urban School District," *Educational Evaluation and Policy Analysis*, 27, no. 3 (2005): 225–244, https://journals.sagepub.com.

35 Conger, "Within-School Segregation," 238.

36 Charles T. Clotfelter, Steven W. Hemelt, Helen F. Ladd, and Mavzuna Turaeva, "School Segregation in the Era of Immigration and School Choice: North Carolina, 1998–2016," working paper 198-0618-1, National Center for Analysis of Longitudinal Data in Education Research, 2018; C. T. Clotfelter, H. F. Ladd, C. R. Clifton, and M. Turaeva, "School Segregation at the Classroom Level in a Southern 'New Destination' State," working paper 230-0220, National Center for Analysis of Longitudinal Data in Education Research, 2020.

37 Sarah D. Sparks, "Hidden Segregation Within Schools Is Tracked in New Study," *Education Week*, February 25, 2020, www.edweek.org.

38 US Department of Education, "US Department of Education Announces Resolution of South Orange-Maplewood, N.J., School District Civil Rights Investigation," October 28, 2014, www.ed.gov.

39 Erica L. Green and Annie Waldman, "You Are Still Black: Charlottesville's Racial Divide Hinders Students," *New York Times*, October 16, 2018, www.nyt.com.

40 US Government Accountability Office, "K–12 Education: Discipline Disparities for Black Students, Boys, and Students with Disabilities," March 2018, 12, www.gao.gov. Though the differences were not as large, Alaska Natives and American Indian students are similarly overrepresented in school suspensions compared with White students. However, because the vast extent to which Black girls and Black boys are overrepresented and are the only racial group overrepresented in every form of discipline on which data are collected, this chapter focuses on them.

41 A. B. Cyphert, "Addressing Racial Disparities in Preschool Suspension and Expulsion Rates," *Tennessee Law Review*, 82, no. 4 (2015): 893–936.

42 P. A. Goff, M. C. Jackson, B. A. L. Di Leone, C. M. Culotta, and N. A. DiTomasso, "The Essence of Innocence: Consequences of Dehumanizing Black Children," *Journal of Personality and Social Psychology*, 106, no. 4 (2014): 526; Carl Suddler, *Presumed Criminal: Black Youth and the Justice System in Postwar New York* (New York: New York University Press, 2019); see also K. Welch, "Black Criminal Stereotypes and Racial Profiling," *Journal of Contemporary Criminal Justice*, 23, no. 3 (2007): 276–288.

43 Cyphert, "Preschool Suspension and Expulsion," 896.

44 Travis Riddle and Stacey Sinclair, "Racial Disparities in School-Based Disciplinary Actions Are Associated with County-Level Rates of Racial Bias," *Proceedings of the National Academy of Sciences*, 116, no. 17 (2019): 8255–8260.

45 Riddle and Sinclair, "School-Based Disciplinary Actions."

46 M. Lang, "Seeing in Color: How Are Teachers Perceiving Our Diverse Autistic Students?," *Ought: The Journal of Autistic Culture*, 1, no. 1 (2019): 11.

47 Johanna Lacoe and Matthew P. Steinberg, "Do Suspensions Affect Student Outcomes?," *Educational Evaluation and Policy Analysis*, 41, no. 1 (2019): 34–62.

48 Lang, "Seeing in Color."

49 N. Hwang, "Suspensions and Achievement: Varying Links by Type, Frequency, and Subgroup," *Educational Researcher*, 47, no. 6 (2018): 363–374.

50 Lacoe and Steinberg, "Do Suspensions Affect Student Outcomes?," 44.

51 E. M. Chu and D. D. Ready, "Exclusion and Urban Public High Schools: Short- and Long-Term Consequences of School Suspensions," *American Journal of Education*, 124, no. 4 (2018): 479–509.

52 L. M. DeRidder, "How Suspension and Expulsion Contribute to Dropping Out," *Education Digest*, 56, no. 6 (1991): 44.

53 Emily Brooks, review of *Presumed Criminal: Black Youth and the Justice System in Postwar New York*, by Carl Suddler, Gotham Center for New York City History, March 12, 2020, www.gothamcenter.org.

54 S. Jay Olshansky, Toni Antonucci, Lisa Berkman, Robert H. Binstock, Axel Boersch-Supan, John T. Cacioppo, Bruce A. Carnes, Laura L. Carstensen, Linda P. Fried, Dana P. Goldman, James Jackson, Martin Kohli, John Rother, Yuhui Zheng, and John Rowe, "Differences in Life Expectancy Due to Race and Educational Differences Are Widening, and Many May Not Catch Up," *Health Affairs*, 31, no. 8 (2012): 1803–1813.

55 Johanna Wald and Daniel J. Losen, "Defining and Redirecting a School-to-Prison Pipeline," *New Directions for Youth Development* 99 (2003): 9–15.

56 Wald and Losen, "School-to-Prison Pipeline."

57 Michelle Alexander, *The New Jim Crow: Mass Incarceration in the Age of Colorblindness* (New York: New Press, 2012); Angela J. Davis, ed., *Policing the Black Man: Arrest, Prosecution, and Imprisonment* (New York: Vintage, 2017); Angela J. Davis, "Race, Cops, and Traffic Stops," *University of Miami Law Review*, 51 (1996): 425; P. Butler, "Stop and Frisk and Torture-Lite: Police Terror of Minority Communities," *Ohio State Journal of Criminal Law*, 12 (2014): 57; R. A. Fairfax Jr., "The Grand Jury's Role in the Prosecution of Unjustified Police Killings-Challenges and Solutions," *Harvard Civil Rights-Civil Liberties Law Review*, 52 (2017): 397.

58 R. Chetty, N. Hendren, M. R. Jones, and S. R. Porter, "Race and Economic Opportunity in the United States: An Intergenerational Perspective," *Quarterly Journal of Economics*, 135, no. 2 (2020): 711–783.

59 See David S. Abrams. Marianne Bertrand, and Sendhil Mullainathan, "Do Judges Vary in Their Treatment of Race?," 41 *Journal of Legal Studies*, 41 (2012): 347, 350; Dylan Matthews, "The Black/White Marijuana Arrest Gap, in Nine Charts," *Washington Post*, June 4, 2013, www.washingtonpost.com; B. L. Kutateladze, N. R. Andiloro, B. D. Johnson, and C. C. Spohn, "Cumulative Disadvantage: Examining Racial and Ethnic Disparity in Prosecution and Sentencing," *Criminology*, 52, no. 3 (2014): 514–551. See Ursula Noye, "Blackstrikes: A Study of the Racially Disparate Use of Peremptory Challenges by the Caddo Parish District Attorney's Office," Reprieve Australia, August 2015, https://doksi.net (https://perma.cc/JLB2-JMLZ); D. B. Mustard, "Racial, Ethnic, and Gender Disparities in Sentencing: Evidence from the US Federal Courts," *Journal of Law and Economics*, 44, no. 1 (2001): 285–314. See also Joe Palazzolo, "Racial Gap in Men's Sentencing," *Wall Street Journal*, February 14, 2013, www.wsj.edu.

60 B. Pettit and B. Western, "Mass Imprisonment and the Life Course: Race and Class Inequality in US Incarceration," *American Sociological Review*, 69, no. 2 (2004): 151–169.

61 Andrew Gelman, Jeffrey Fagan, and Alex Kiss, "An Analysis of the New York City Police Department's 'Stop-and-Frisk' Policy in the Context of Claims of Racial Bias," *Journal of the American Statistical Association*, 102, no. 479 (2007): 813–823.

62 Jamie Fellner, "Punishment and Prejudice: Racial Disparities in the War on Drugs," *Human Rights Watch*, 12, no. 2 (May 2000), www.hrw.org.

63 C. Wildeman and E. A. Wang, "Mass Incarceration, Public Health, and Widening Inequality in the USA," *Lancet*, 389, no. 10077 (2017): 1464–1474.

64 M. L. Hatzenbuehler, K. Keyes, A. Hamilton, M. Uddin, and S. Galea, "the Collateral Damage of Mass Incarceration: Risk of Psychiatric Morbidity Among Nonincarcerated Residents of High-Incarceration Neighborhoods," *American Journal of Public Health*, 105, no. 1 (2015): 138–143; C. Wildeman and C. Muller, "Mass Imprisonment and Inequality in Health and Family Life," *Annual Review of Law and Social Science*, 8, (2012): 11–30.

65 The Marshal Project, "A State-by-State Look at Coronavirus in Prisons," updated April 30, 2021, www.themarshallproject.org; Ernest M. Drucker, *A Plague of Prisons: The Epidemiology of Mass Incarceration in America* (New York: New Press, 2013); see also Sandro Galea, "Incarceration and the Health of Populations," Boston University School of Public Health, March 22, 2015, www.bu.edu.

66 N. E. Adler and K. Newman, "Socioeconomic Disparities in Health: Pathways and Policies," *Health Affairs*, 21, no. 2 (2002): 60–76.

67 R. Catalano, H. T. Hansen, and T. Hartig, "The Ecological Effect of Unemployment on the Incidence of Very Low Birthweight in Norway and Sweden," *Journal of Health and Social Behavior*, (1999): 422–428.

68 R. Chetty, J. N. Friedman, N. Hilger, E. Saez, D. W. Schanzenbach, and D. Yagan, "How Does Your Kindergarten Classroom Affect Your Earnings? Evidence from Project STAR," *Quarterly Journal of Economics*, 126, no. 4 (2011)): 1593–1660.

69 Chetty et al., "Kindergarten Classroom,"1656.

70 R. Chetty, M. Stepner, S. Abraham, S. Lin, B. Scuderi, N. Turner, A. Bergeron, and D. Cutler, "The Association Between Income and Life Expectancy in the United States, 2001–2014," *Journal of the American Medical Association*, 315, no. 16 (2016): 1750–1766.

71 Chetty et al. "Race and Economic Opportunity."

6. A Call to National Action

1 Steven A. Schroeder, "We Can Do Better: Improving the Health of the American People," *New England Journal of Medicine*, 357 (2007): 1221, 1225.

2 A. R. Tarlov, "Public Policy Frameworks for Improving Population Health," *Annals of the New York Academy of Sciences*, 896, no. 1 (1999): 281–293.

3 Tarlov, "Public Policy Frameworks."

4 See, for example, S. Overton, *Stealing Democracy: The New Politics of Voter Suppression* (New York: Norton, 2006).

5 *Buchanan v. Warley*, 245 U.S. 60 (1917).

6 *Shelley v. Kraemer*, 334 U.S. 1 (1948).

7 Richard Rothstein, 2019, July. "We Can End Racial Segregation in America," *Jacobin Magazine*, July 22, 2019, www.jacobinmag.com.

8 W. H. Frey, "Census Shows Modest Declines in Black-White Segregation," Brookings Institution, 2015, www.brookings.edu.

9 M. R. Kramer and C. R. Hogue, "Is Segregation Bad for Your Health?," *Epidemiologic Reviews*, 31, no. 1 (2009): 178–194, 188.

10 42 U.S.C. § 3604 (2012).

11 42 U.S.C. § 3604(a).

12 Robert G. Schwemm, *Housing Discrimination Law and Litigation* (St. Paul, MN: Thomson Reuters, 2010– ; July 2019 update), section 12B:4. See, for example, *Meyer v. Holley*, 537 U.S. 280, 283 (2003) (finding that the Fair Housing Act imposed vicarious liability on corporation for unlawful acts of its employees). See also, for example, *City of Chicago v. Matchmaker Real Estate Sales Ctr., Inc.*, 982 F.2d 1086, 1099 (7th Cir. 1992) (finding the realty corporation and its sales agents liable for compensatory damages when the agent consistently steered White testers toward White areas and Black testers toward Black areas, and denied information to Black testers readily given to similarly situated White testers).

13 Walter F. Mondale, "The Civil Rights Law We Ignored," *New York Times*, April 10, 2018, www.nytimes.com.

14 Mondale, "Civil Rights Law We Ignored."

15 M. Adams, "The Unfulfilled Promise of the Fair Housing Act," *New Yorker*, April 11, 2018, www.newyorker.com.

16 Adams, "Unfulfilled Promise"; New York Times Editorial Board, "Housing Apartheid, American Style," *New York Times*, May 16, 2015, www.nyt.com.

17 42 U.S.C. § 3604 (2012).

18 42 U.S.C. § 3604 (2012).

19 42 U.S.C. § 3604 (2012).

20 Morgan Williams and Stacy Seicshnaydre, "The Legacy and the Promise of Disparate Impact," in *The Fight for Fair Housing: Causes, Consequences, and Future Implications of the 1968 Federal Fair Housing Act*, ed. G. D. Squires, 170–187 (New York: Routledge, 2017).

21 Williams and Seicshnaydre, "Legacy and the Promise," citing J. Nesbit, "Study of Census Data Finds a Segregated America, Especially for Blacks, *U.S. News and World Report*, July 24, 2012); GAO, Progress made, but opportunities exist to improve HUDs oversight of FHA lenders, retrieved from www.gao.gov/products /GAO-05-13.

22 Martha M. Galvez, Solomon Greene, Katherine Thomas, and Claudia D. Solari, "What HUD's Proposed Rule Gets Wrong About Fair Housing," Urban Institute, March 16, 2020, www.urban.org; see also "Kaine, Colleagues Introduce Legislation to Strengthen Fair Housing Programs," US Senator Tim Kaine web page, December 4, 2020, www.kaine.senate.gov.

23 *Texas Department of Housing and Community Affairs v. Inclusive Communities Project, Inc.*, 576 U.S. 519 (2015). For the HUD discriminatory-effects standard, see Williams and Seicshnaydre, "Disparate Impact." See also Robert G. Schwemm, "Fair Housing Litigation After Inclusive Communities: What's New and What's Not," *Columbia Law Review*, 115 (2015): sidebar 106, www.columbialawreview.org.

24 Williams and Seicshnaydre, "Promise of Disparate Impact," quoting 24 CFR §100.500.

25 *Inclusive*, 576 U.S. 519, 539.

26 576 U.S. 519, 2522.

27 576 U.S. 519, *540*.

28 576 U.S. 519, 537.

29 576 U.S. 519, 542.

30 576 U.S. 519, 543.

31 576 U.S. 519, 541, 544.

32 Williams and Seicshnaydre, "Disparate Impact," 183, citing *Mhany Mgmt., Inc. v. County of Nassau*, 819 F.3d 581, 2016 WL 1128424 (2d. Cir. March 23, 2016).

33 Williams and Seicshnaydre, "Disparate Impact," 184.

34 Williams and Seicshnaydre, "Legacy and the Promise," citing K. McClure, A. F. Schwartz, and L. B. Taghavia, "Housing Choice Voucher Location Patterns a Decade Later," *Housing Policy Debate*, 25 (2015): 215, 233; M. W. Metzger, "The Reconcentration of Poverty: Patterns of Housing Voucher Use, 2000 to 2008," *Housing Policy Debate*, 24 (2014): 544.

35 Williams and Seicshnaydre, "Legacy and the Promise,"185, citing *Ojo v. Farmers Grp., Inc.*, 600 F.3d 1205, 1207 (9th Cir. 2010); L. Rice and D. Swesnik, "Discriminatory Effects of Credit Scoring on Communities of Color," National Fair Housing Alliance, 2012, 3, http://nationalfairhousing.org.

36 Williams and Seicshnaydre, "Legacy and the Promise," 185.

37 See, for example, L. Lees, T. Slater, and E. Wyly, *Gentrification* (New York: Routledge, 2013).

38 D. K. Levy, J. Comey, and S. Padilla. *Keeping the Neighborhood Affordable: A Handbook of Housing Strategies for Gentrifying Areas* (Washington, DC: Urban Institute, 2006).

39 "The E.P.A.'s Civil Rights Problem," *New York Times*, July 7, 2016, www.nytimes.com.

40 US Commission on Civil Rights, *Environmental Justice: Examining the Environmental Protection Agency's Compliance and Enforcement of Title VI and Executive Order 12,898* (Washington, DC: US Commission on Civil Rights, 2016), 50, www.usccr.gov.

41 Lilian S. Dorka (director of External Civil Rights Compliance Office, Office of General Counsel, EPA), letter to Heidi Grether (director of Michigan Department of Environmental Quality), in reference to EPA file no. 01R-94-R5, January 19, 2017, www.epa.gov.

42 D. B. Matthew, "Health Care, Title VI, and Racism's New Normal," *Georgetown Journal Law and Modern Critical Race Perspectives*, 6, no. 3 (2014).

43 *Guardians Ass'n. v. Civil Service Com'n. of City of New York*, 463 U.S. 582, 589 (1983), citing *Lau v. Nichols*, 414 U.S. 563 (1974).

44 *Alexander v. Sandoval*, 532 U.S. 275 (2001).

45 *Regents of the University of California v. Bakke*, 438 U.S. 265 (1978).

46 *Guardians Association v. Civil Service Commission*, 463 U.S. 582 (1983)

47 *Alexander v. Choate*, 469 U.S. 287 (1985).

48 *Guardians Association v. Civil Service Commission*, 505 U.S. 717, 743 (1992).

49 *Grutter v. Bollinger*, 539 U.S. 306, 345 (2003) (Ginsburg, J., concurring).

50 D. B. Matthew, "A New Normal," in *Just Medicine: A Cure for Racial Inequality in American Health Care* (New York: New York University Press, 2018); see Note, "After Sandoval: Judicial Challenges and Administrative Possibilities in Title VI Enforcement," *Harvard Law Review*, 116 (April 2003): 1774. Justice Scalia went further, strongly hinting that Section 602 of Title VI might not support disparate-impact claims alleging unintentional discrimination, though he declined to decide the question in *Sandoval*.

51 D. B. Matthew, "Health Care, Title VI, and Racism's New Normal," *Georgetown Journal of Law and Modern Critical Race Perspectives*, 6, no. 3 (2014).

52 *Swann v. Charlotte-Mecklenburg Board of Education*, 40 U.S. 1 (1971).

53 *Milliken v. Bradley*, 418 U.S. 717 (1974); *Alexander v. Choate*, 469 U.S. 287 (1985), 812–20.

54 *Board of Education of Oklahoma City Public Schools v. Dowell*, 498 U.S. 237; *Alexander v. Choate*, 469 U.S. 287 (1985), 820–25.

55 *Dowell*, 498 U.S., 238.

56 K. J. Robinson, "Resurrecting the Promise of Brown: Understanding and Remedying How the Supreme Court Reconstitutionalized Segregated Schools,"

North Carolina Law Review, 88 (2010): 787, 837–839, http://scholarship.law.unc. edu; Kimberly A. Pacelli, "*Fisher v. University of Texas at Austin*: Navigating the Narrows Between *Grutter* and *Parents Involved*," *Maine Law Review*, 63 (2011): 569, https://digitalcommons.mainelaw.maine.edu.

57 551 U.S. 701, 703; see also M. Adams, "Stifling the Potential of Grutter v. Bollinger: Parents Involved in Community Schools v. Seattle School District No. 1," *Boston University Law Review*, 88 (2008): 937, 977–978, https://larc.cardozo.yu.edu.

58 *Parents Involved in Community Schools v. Seattle School District No 1*, 551 U.S. 701, 838–844 (Justice Breyer dissenting).

59 *Parents Involved*, 551 U.S. 701, 838–844 (Justice Breyer dissenting).

60 551 U.S. 701, 799 (Justice Stevens dissenting).

61 551 U.S. 701.

62 R. D. Moss, "Participation and Department of Justice School Desegregation Consent Decrees," *Yale Law Journal*, 95 (1986): 1811, 1824, https://digitalcommons. law.yale.edu.

63 E. Frankenberg and K. Taylor, "De Facto Segregation: Tracing a Legal Basis for Contemporary Inequality," *Journal of Law & Education*, 47 (2018): 189, 194.

64 J. R. Berenyi, "'Appropriate Action,' Inappropriately Defined: Amending the Equal Educational Opportunities Act of 1974," *Washington and Lee Law Review*, 65 (2008): 639, 645.

65 See Berenyi, J.R., "'Appropriate action," inappropriately defined: Amending the Equal Educational Opportunities Act of 1974, 65 *Wash & Lee Law Review*, 639 (2008).

66 This idea was presented by the Reverend Lehman D. Bates II, pastor of Ebenezer Baptist Church in Charlottesville, Virginia.

67 "Reparations," International Center for Transitional Justice, accessed August 1, 2020, www.ictj.org.

68 B. Cislaghi and L. Heise, "Theory and Practice of Social Norms Interventions: Eight Common Pitfalls," *Globalization and Health*, 14, no. 1 (2018): 1–10.

69 Alfred L. Brophy, "Reconsidering Reparations," *Indiana Law Journal*, 81 (2006): 811, 823.

70 Eric Posner and Adrian Vermeule, "Reparations for Slavery and Other Historical Injustices," *Columbia Law Review*, 103 (2003): 689.

71 Reparations opponents argue that no form of compensation can account for the too-distant injustice of slavery and that, therefore, Black self-reliance is preferable (see, e.g., Gregory Kane, "Why the Reparations Movement Should Fail," *University of Maryland Law Journal of Race, Religion, Gender and Class*, 3 [2003]: 189).

72 Jess Blumberg, "A Brief History of the Salem Witch Trials," *Smithsonian Magazine*, October 23, 2007, www.smithsonian.com.

73 "Liability of the Municipality for Mob Violence," *Fordham Law Review*, 6 (1937): 270, https://ir.lawnet.fordham.edu.

74 NewsOne Staff, "Sounds About White: Government Paid Reparations for Italian Americans Who Were Lynched," NewsOne, March 31, 2019, https://newsone.com,

notes that "more than 4,700 people—mostly African-American—were lynched between the years 1882 and 1968." See also Owen Daugherty, "New Orleans Mayor to Apologize to Italian-Americans for 1891 Lynching," *Hill*, April 1, 2019, https://thehill.com; Janet McConnaughey, "Mayor to Apologize for 1891 Lynching of 11 Italian Americans," *Apple News*, March 30, 2019, www.applenews.com.

75 A.W. Herzog, "The Dyer Anti-Lynching Bill," editorial, *Medico-Legal Journal*, 40, no. 1 (January–February 1923).

76 Alaska Native Claims Settlement Act, 43 U.S.C. § 1601–1629 (2000); Native American Graves Protection and Repatriation Act, 25 U.S.C. § 3005 (2000).

77 See, for example, Burt Neuborne, "Holocaust Reparations Litigation: Lessons for the Slavery Reparations Movement, *N.Y.U Annual Survey of American Law*, 58 (2001–2003): 615; Stuart E. Eizenstat, "What Holocaust Restitution Taught Me About Slavery Reparations," *Politico Magazine*, October 27, 2019, www.politico.com; and Irwin Cotler, "The Holocaust 'Thefticide' and Restitution: A Legal Perspective," in *The Plunder of Jewish Property During the Holocaust: Confronting European History*, ed. Avi Beker, 66–82 (New York: Palgrave Macmillan, 2001).

78 Leslie T. Hatamiya, *Righting a Wrong: Japanese Americans and the Passage of the Civil Liberties Act of 1988* (Stanford, CA: Stanford University Press, 1994).

79 William A. Darity Jr. and A. Kirsten Mullen, *From Here to Equality: Reparations for Black Americans in the Twenty-First Century* (Chapel Hill: University of North Carolina Press, 2020).

80 Thomas M. Shapiro, "Race, Homeownership and Wealth," *Washington University Journal of Law & Policy*, 20 (2006): 53.

81 Manisha Sinha, "The Long History of American Slavery Reparations," *Wall Street Journal*, September 20, 2019, www.wsj.com.

82 Barton Myers, "Sherman's Field Order No. 15," *New Georgia Encyclopedia*, September 29, 2020, www.georgiaencyclopedia.org.

83 Myers, "Sherman's Field Order No. 15."

84 C. H. Watson, "Need of Federal Legislation in Respect to Mob Violence in Cases of Lynching of Aliens," *Yale Law Journal*, 25, no. 7 (1916): 561–581; J. W. Garner, "Responsibility of States for Injuries Suffered by Foreigners Within Their Territories on Account of Mob Violence, Riots and Insurrection," in *Proceedings of the American Society of International Law at Its Annual Meeting (1921–1969)*, 21: 49–81 (Washington, DC: American Society of International Law, 1921–1969).

85 The 1898 Wilmington massacre, led by white congressmen, burned a Black newspaper office and other parts of the town (see Adrianne LaFrance and Vann Newkirk, "The Lost History of an American Coup D'Etat," *Atlantic*, August 12, 2017, www.theatlantic.com). For the Ku Klux Klan lynching, burning, and killing in a massacre prompted by a Black man's attempt to vote in the 1920 presidential election, see Carlee Hoffmann and Claire Strom, "A Perfect Storm: The Ocoee Riot of 1920," *Florida Historical Quarterly*, 93, no. 1 (2014): 25–43. In 1908, a race

riot occurred when white mobs accused two Black men of raping two white women in a five-week period. They responded by avenging the "pretty" and "attractive" women (see James L. Crouthamel, "The Springfield Race Riot of 1908," *Journal of Negro History*, 45, no. 3 (July 1960): 164–181). The year 1921 saw the Greenwood Massacre in Tulsa, where white mobs, including city officials, killed an estimated three hundred Black people and destroyed more than twelve hundred Black-owned homes and businesses, as well as schools, a hospital, a public library, and churches (see Dreisen Heath, "The Case for Reparations in Tulsa," *Human Rights Watch*, May 20, 2020, www.hrw.org).

86 Hilary Herbold, "Never a Level Playing Field: Blacks and the GI Bill," *Journal of Blacks in Higher Education*, 6 (winter 1994): 104–108.

87 D. H. Onkst, "First a Negro . . . Incidentally a Veteran": Black World War Two Veterans and the GI Bill of Rights in the Deep South, 1944–1948," *Journal of Social History* (1998): 517–543.

88 Onkst, "First a Negro"; Darity and Mullen, *From Here to Equality*.

89 Shapiro, "Race, Homeownership and Wealth," 58.

90 Shapiro, "Race, Homeownership and Wealth"; Darity and Mullen, *From Here to Equality*, n32.

91 Damani Davis, "Slavery and Emancipation in the Nation's Capital," *Genealogy Notes*, 42, no. 1 (spring 2010), www.archives.gov. Even today, some may maintain the absurd view that the end of slavery represented a monetary loss to enslavers (see, e.g., Sinha, "American Slavery Reparations"). The destruction of slavery during and after the Civil War resulted in the largest confiscation of private property by the state in US history, with the freeing of nearly four million slaves valued at around $3 billion at the time.

92 Some reparations theorists seek a fulsome program of restorative and distributional justice. See, for example, William Bradford "Beyond Reparations: An American Indian Theory of Justice," *Ohio State Law Journal*, 66 (2005): 1, which proposes a seven-stage process of acknowledgement, apology, peacemaking, commemoration, compensation, land restoration, legal reformation, and reconciliation.

93 Robert Samuels, "After Reparations," *Washington Post*, April 3, 2020, www.washingtonpost.com.

94 D. Martin, "James Forman Dies at 76: Was Pioneer in Civil Rights," *New York Times*, January 12, 2005, www.nyt.com; "Black Manifesto," in "The Church Awakens: African Americans and the Struggle for Justice," Archives of the Episcopal Church, accessed July 26, 2020, https://episcopalarchives.org.

95 John Conyers, "Representative John Conyers and the Commission to Study Reparation Proposals for African Americans Act," *Africology: Journal of Pan African Studies*, 9, no. 5 (2016): 112–114, www.jpanafrican.org.

96 P. Cohen, "What Reparations for Slavery Might Look Like in 2019," *New York Times*, May 23, 2019, www.nytimes.com.

97 S. 1083–116th Cong. (2019–2020); see also "Booker Reparations Bill Reaches 12 Senate Cosponsors," Senator Cory Booker web page, June 14, 2019, www.booker .senate.gov.

98 P. Lockhart, "The 2020 Democratic Primary Debate Over Reparations," *Vox*, March 11, 2019, www.vox.com; P. Bacon Jr., "What Americans Think About Reparations and Other Race-Related Questions," *FiveThirtyEight*, February 26, 2019, www.fivethirtyeight.com.

99 "Polling the Left Agenda," Data for Progress, accessed April 26, 2021, www .dataforprogress.org.

100 "Nature of the Sample: Exclusive *Point Taken*—Marist Poll of 1,221 National Adults," May 2016, http://maristpoll.marist.edu; Bacon, "Reparations and Other Race-Related Questions."

101 E. Goldberg, "How Reparations for Slavery Became a 2020 Campaign Issue," *New York Times*, June 18, 2020, www.nyt.com.

102 N. King, "'From Here to Equality' Author Makes a Case, and a Plan, for Reparations," *NPR*, June 17, 2020, www.npr.org.

103 Maya Moore, "A Professor's Case for African-American Reparations," *CT Mirror*, August 23, 2019, https://ctmirror.org.

104 Moore, "African-American Reparations."

7. A Second "Quiet Revolution"

1 "King Berates Medical Care Given Negroes," *Oshkosh (Wisc.) Daily Northwestern*, March 26. 1966.

2 P. P. Reynolds, "The Federal Government's Use of Title VI and Medicare to Racially Integrate Hospitals in the United States, 1963 Through 1967," *American Journal of Public Health*, 87, no. 11 (1997): 1850–1858, doi:10.2105/ajph.87.11.1850.

3 Reynolds, "Title VI and Medicare."

4 D. B. Smith, *The Power to Heal: Civil Rights, Medicare, and the Struggle to Transform America's Health Care System* (Nashville, TN: Vanderbilt University Press, 2016), 142.

5 Stewart Auyash and Y. W. Clarke, "The Epic Conquest of Medicare and Hospital Desegregation," *American Journal of Public Health*, 109, no. 6 (2019): 828–829, http://dx.doi.org/10.2105/AJPH.2019.305100.

6 Auyash and Clarke, "Medicare and Hospital Desegregation."

7 "Three-Pronged Assault Planned for Hospitals," *Call and Post (Cleveland)*, April 16, 1966.

8 Lawrence O. Gostin, "A Theory and Definition of Public Health Law," *Journal of Health Care Law and Policy*, 10 (2007): 1–12.

9 "Bon Secours Hospital Case Study," ChangeLab Solutions, May 31, 2018, 7, https:// changelabsolutions.org.

10 For example, "The Conway Center: Tax Credits At the Center of Health, Housing, and Economic Mobility," Local Initiatives Support Corporation, accessed

December 28, 2019, www.lisc.org; M. Cohn, "Bon Secours Joins Effort to Build, Sustain Affordable Housing Projects," *Baltimore Sun*, 2019, February 21, 2019, www.baltimoresun.com; "Care Transitions Program Reduces Readmissions in Humboldt County," Align Forces for Quality, accessed May 31, 2019, http://forces4quality.org; Michelle Kondo, "A Comparative Case Study of Changes in Crime Surrounding a Home Renovation/Rebuild Program of the Nationwide Children's Hospital in Columbus, OH," *Injury Prevention*, 26 (2020): A4; M. Sandel, E. Faugno, A. Mingo, J. Cannon, K. Byrd, D. A. Garcia, S. Collier, E. McClure, and R. B. Jarrett, "Neighborhood-Level Interventions to Improve Childhood Opportunity and Lift Children Out of Poverty," *Academic Pediatrics*, 16, no. 3 (2016): S128–S135, doi:10.1016/j.acap.2016.01.013.

11 Cathy Schoen and Sara R. Collins, "The Big Five Health Insurers' Membership and Revenue Trends: Implications for Public Policy," *Health Affairs Journal*, December 4, 2017, www.healthaffairs.org.

12 United Healthcare, "UnitedHealthcare's Investments in Affordable Housing to Help People Achieve Better Health Surpass $400 Million," press release, March 26, 2019, https://newsroom.uhc.com.

13 Edgar Walters, "To Reduce Health Costs, Insurer Spends on Housing for Homeless," *Texas Tribune*, September 21, 2015, www.texastribune.org.

14 A. Pacurar, "UnitedHealthcare Bets $17M on Affordable Housing," *Multi-Housing News*, August 5, 2016, www.multihousingnews.com.

15 "New Community Health Center Improves Care in Northeastern Washington D.C.," WSP, accessed December 29, 2020, from www.wsp.com.

16 World Health Organization, Commission on Social Determinants of Health, "Closing the Gap in a Generation: Health Equity through Action on the Social Determinants of Health," final report, August 27, 2008, Geneva, Switzerland; PBS, *Unnatural Causes: Is Inequality Making Us Sick?*, four-part television series, 2008, www.pbs.org.

17 E. Feinberg, B. Trejo, B. Sullivan, and Z. Suarez, "Healthy Start in Housing: A Case Study of a Public Health and Housing Partnership to Improve Birth Outcomes," *Cityscape*, 16, no. 1 (2014): 141–164, www.jstor.org.

18 D. Allen, E. Feinberg, and H. Mitchell, "Bringing Life Course Home: A Pilot to Reduce Pregnancy Risk Through Housing Access and Family Support," *Maternal and Child Health Journal*, 18, no. 2 (2014): 405–412, https://doi.org/10.1007/s10995 -013-1327-5.

19 For example, "Food Pantry Feeds One Million," Boston Medical, accessed April 26, 2021, https://development.bmc.org; Randy Oostra, "Starving for a Solution: Hunger as a Health Issue," ProMedica, accessed April 26, 2021, www.promedica.org.

20 "Brockton Neighborhood Health Center and Vicente's Tropical Grocery Celebrate Opening of Joint Venture," *Cision, PR Newswire*, September 3, 2015, www .prnewswire.com.

21 The Healthy Futures Fund of LISC, Morgan Stanley, the Kresge Foundation, Massachusetts Housing Investment Corporation, JPMorgan Chase, the Reinvestment Fund, Boston Community Capital, and New Markets Tax Credits.

22 National Association of Community Health Centers, "Community Health Centers as Food Oasis Partners: Addressing Food Insecurity for Patients and Communities," July 2017, www.nachc.org.

23 Mark Gilger, "Program Aims to Link Nutrition, Child Wellness," *My San Antonio*, June 13, 2014, www.mysanantonio.com.

24 American Hospital Association, "Food Insecurity and the Role of Hospitals," Social Determinants of Health Series, Health Research & Educational Trust, Chicago, June 2017, www.hpoe.org.

25 EatSF, "EatSF in San Francisco: Vouchers 4 Veggies—EatSF Stretches the Healthy Food Budget for Low-Income Families," accessed December 26, 2020, https://eatsfvoucher.org; see also the "About Us" page on this website.

26 American Hospital Association, "Food Insecurity and the Role of Hospitals"; M. Cavanagh, J. Jurkowski, C. Bozlak, J. Hastings, and A. Klein, "Veggie Rx: An Outcome Evaluation of a Healthy Food Incentive Programme," *Public Health Nutrition*, 20, no. 14 (2016): 2636–2641, doi:10.1017/s1368980016002081.

27 T. L. James, S. Bibi, B. K. Langlois, E. Dugan, and P. M. Mitchell, "Boston Violence Intervention Advocacy Program: A Qualitative Study of Client Experiences and Perceived Effect. *Academic Emergency Medicine*, 21, no. 7 (2014): 742–751. doi:10.1111/acem.12409.

28 American Hospital Association, "Hospital Approaches to Interrupt the Cycle of Violence." March 2015, www.aha.org.

29 T. J. Corbin, J. A. Rich, S. L. Bloom, D. Delgado, L. J. Rich, and A. S. Wilson, "Developing a Trauma-Informed, Emergency Department–Based Intervention for Victims of Urban Violence," *Journal of Trauma & Dissociation*, 12, no. 5 (2011): 510–525, doi:10.1080/15299732.2011.593260; M. A. Zimmerman, S. E. Stewart, S. Morrel-Samuels, S. Franzen, and T. M. Reischl, "Youth Empowerment Solutions for Peaceful Communities: Combining Theory and Practice in a Community-Level Violence Prevention Curriculum," *Health Promotion Practice*, 12, no. 3 (2010): 425–439, doi:10.1177/1524839909357316.

30 For example, K. A. Parke, C. L. Meireles, and C. Sickora, "a Nurse-Led Model of Care to Address Social and Behavioral Determinants of Health at a School-Based Health Center," *Journal of School Health*, 89, no. 5 (2019): 423–426, doi:10.1111/josh.12748.

31 Naomi A. Schapiro, J. Raul Gutierrez, Amy Blackshaw, and Jyu-Lin Chen, "Addressing the Health and Mental Health Needs of Unaccompanied Immigrant Youth Through an Innovative School-Based Health Center Model: Successes and Challenges," *Children and Youth Services Review*, 92 (September 1, 2018): 133–142, doi:10.1016/j.childyouth.2018.04.016; "Alameda County School Health Services," Alameda County, CA, accessed May 4, 2021,www.acgov.org/health/indigent/

school.htm; Alameda Family Services, School Based Health Center, accessed May 4, 2021, www.alamedafs.org.

32 Samira Soleimanpour, Sara P. Geierstanger, Shelly Kaller, Virginia McCarter, and Claire D. Brindis, "The Role of School Health Centers in Health Care Access and Client Outcomes," *American Journal of Public Health*, 100 (2010): 1597–1603, https://ajph.aphapublications.org.

INDEX

Page numbers in *italics* indicate Figures.

ABOUT THE AUTHOR

DAYNA BOWEN MATTHEW, JD, PhD, is Dean and Harold H. Greene Professor of Law at the George Washington University Law School. Dr. Matthew, a leader in public health and civil rights law, has also held many public policy roles. These include serving as senior adviser to the Office of Civil Rights for the US Environmental Protection Agency and as a member of the health policy team for US Senator Debbie Stabenow of Michigan.